Journal of Roman Pottery Studies

VOLUME 20

Edited by

ENIKO HUDAK

Published by

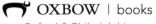 OXBOW | books
Oxford & Philadelphia

for
The Study Group for Roman Pottery

Published in the United Kingdom in 2024 by
OXBOW BOOKS
The Old Music Hall, 106–108 Cowley Road, Oxford, OX4 1JE

and in the United States by
OXBOW BOOKS
1950 Lawrence Road, Havertown, PA 19083

© Oxbow Books and the individual authors 2024

ISSN: 0958-3491
Paperback Edition: ISBN 979-8-88857-034-0
Digital Edition: ISBN 979-8-88857-035-7 (epub)

A CIP record for this book is available from the British Library

Printed in the United Kingdom by Short Run Press

Typeset in India by Lapiz Digital Services, Chennai.

For a complete list of Oxbow titles, please contact:

UNITED KINGDOM
Oxbow Books
Telephone (0)1226 734350
Email: oxbow@oxbowbooks.com
www.oxbowbooks.com

UNITED STATES OF AMERICA
Oxbow Books
Telephone (610) 853-9131, Fax (610) 853-9146
Email: queries@casemateacademic.com
www.casemateacademic.com/oxbow

Oxbow Books is part of the Casemate Group

Front cover: Selection of 'Nene Valley colour-coated ware' from the Hykeham Road kiln, Bracebridge, Lincoln (see Paper 9 this volume)
Title page: 50th Anniversary SGRP logo designed by Mark Hoyle
Back cover: Top: Experimental Roman kiln firing by Beryl Hines at the Nottingham SGRP conference 2010; Bottom: Ceramic grave goods, fragmented after deposition, in cremation 1855 from the early Roman cemetery at Strood Hall, Essex.
© Oxford Archaeology and Wessex Archaeology.

Contents

Editorial Board of the *Journal of Roman Pottery Studies*

Contributors to this Journal

MARTIN AUER
University of Innsbruck
Institute of Archaeology
Austria
Martin.Auer@uibk.ac.at

EDWARD BIDDULPH
Oxford Archaeology
edward.biddulph@oxfordarchaeology.com

BARBARA BORGERS
University of Vienna
Institute of Classical Archaeology
Austria
Paris-Lodron University of Salzburg
Department of Environment and Biodiversity
Research fields of Geology and Physical Geography
Austria
barbara.borgers@univie.ac.at

DUNCAN H. BROWN
Historic England

SOPHIE CHAVARRIA
Université Grenoble Alps
France
sophie.chavarria@univ-grenoble-alpes.fr

ALEXANDRA CROOM
Tyne & Wear Archives & Museums
alex.croom@twmuseums.org.uk

FRANZISKA DÖVENER
Franziska.Dovener@inra.etat.lu

HUGH G. FISKE
Ian Rowlandson Archaeological Consultancy
hugh.fiske@gmail.com

JAMES GERRARD
School of History
Classics and Archaeology
Newcastle University
james.gerrard@newcastle.ac.uk

WILLIAM GRIFFITHS
Tyne & Wear Archives & Museums
bill.griffiths@twmuseums.org.uk

KAYT HAWKINS
Archaeology South-East
kayt.hawkins@ucl.ac.uk

LANAH HEWSON
Museum of London Archaeology – Northampton
lhewson@mola.org.uk

ENIKO HUDAK
School of History, Classics and Archaeology
Newcastle University
e.hudak2@newcastle.ac.uk

CAROLINE M. JACKSON
Department of Archaeology
University of Sheffield
c.m.jackson@sheffield.ac.uk

IAN M. ROWLANDSON
Ian Rowlandson Archaeological Consultancy
ian_row@yahoo.co.uk

FIONA SEELEY
fiseeley@tiscali.co.uk

JANE TIMBY
janertimby@gmail.com

STEVEN WILLIS
Department of Classics and Archaeology
University of Kent
s.willis@kent.ac.uk

CHRISTOPHER YOUNG
youngoakthorpe@btinternet.com

Event flyer for the 50th anniversary conference of the Study Group for Roman Pottery held online at Newcastle University in 2021

Editorial

It is a cliché to say that a fresh start is nerve-racking but also exciting. It is probably another one that by stepping into the role of Editor of a long-standing and eminent publication such as the *Journal of Roman Pottery Studies*, a position held by so many brilliant specialists amongst us, one has some big shoes to fill. Clichés are defined as trite phrases that tire both the writer and the reader, but the job as the new Editor for me feels just like they say: nerve-racking, exciting, and combined with the desire to do both past editors and the Journal justice. I would like to start my first Editorial by thanking the Study Group for Roman Pottery (SGRP) for placing their trust in me and also acknowledging my predecessor, Steve Willis, for all his guidance and help with getting me started.

The first volume of the Journal was published in 1986 and was edited by Rob Perrin and John Samuels. As Perrin notes in the introduction to the volume (Perrin 1986), its publication stemmed from a call from the growing membership of the SGRP to publish conference proceedings and was born to provide an alternative print medium for the changing nature of pottery reports and archaeological publications of the time. I hope you agree when I say that over the following Journal volumes, it has not only stayed true to these initial aims but went above and beyond to promote and celebrate Roman pottery research both in Britain and in Europe. The Journal is now the home of nearly four decades of Roman pottery research development (with Volumes 1–12 available on the SGRP website) both by our established and early career researchers and, since 2020, as an ERIH PLUS status academic journal. Volume 20 is dedicated to celebrating all *Journal of Roman Pottery Studies* achievements and contents since its very first volume: national and international Roman pottery research from our experienced and new researchers, our partners in other archaeological disciplines, and five decades of SGRP history and conferences.

The last few years have seen significant changes to SGRP conferences. Our last 'traditional' annual meeting was in July 2019 at Atherstone, organised by Jane Evans and Jane Faiers, complete with excellent research papers, pottery viewing, excursions, fantastic dinners, and a very warm welcome from the Mayor of Atherstone and the Atherstone Civic Society. At the AGM, we were all looking forward to our next meeting in 2020 at Leicester, and that was where James Gerrard and I offered Newcastle University as the venue for the 2021 meeting, being the 50th Anniversary Conference.

Then the pandemic changed everything. The Leicester conference had to be postponed to 2022, and the 50th Anniversary Conference (2021) was moved to a digital platform provided by Newcastle University (see flyer on opposite page). Our conference routine was disrupted, but the appetite for Roman pottery research and the desire to see our pottery family (even if only digitally) made space for these changes: the anniversary conference (with its own social media tag, #SGRP50) attracted a huge audience from far and wide across the globe, with attendees from the US to Japan and Brazil to Sweden. Instead of gathering around tables of pottery, we had digital breakout rooms, and instead of an anniversary dinner, we had an introduction to fish sauces by Sally Grainger and a Roman banquet photo competition.

The first digitalisation of our annual meeting created new opportunities to engage even more people who are interested in Roman pottery studies. As we found our way out of the pandemic and engaged with the new realities of everyday life, the opportunity was there to have the best of both worlds: safe, in-person meetings simultaneously broadcast to our audience at home. Organised by Nick Cooper at the University of Leicester, our first hybrid conference was an absolute success with near equal numbers of delegates attending in person as online. We had our tables of pottery back and we were able to share them online. It is hoped that this will be the new normal, a new tradition of SGRP annual meetings.

The constant in this changing atmosphere of conferences was the quality of our research. The papers in this volume are from these three conferences and from our international members, reflecting the perseverance and ingenuity of Roman pottery research through globally challenging times. The volume starts with a paper from our last traditional conference at Atherstone on the glass working at Mancetter-Hartshill. It is followed by papers from the SGRP50 conference, drawn from its themed sessions on the past, present, and future of the SGRP; research by our early career members; collaborative projects with other archaeological disciplines (including archiving); and recent Roman pottery research. There is an international contribution on techniques of grey ware production in Noricum dedicated to Roberta Tomber; and lastly an article from our first hybrid conference at Leicester on riverside pottery production at Lincoln. The volume could not be complete without book reviews of the 2021 publication of the excavations in the north-east quarter of the historic centre of Leicester, and 2022 *magnum opus* of Malcolm Lyne on Late Roman BB1. I would like to take the opportunity here to thank all authors for their magnificent contributions, the anonymous peer reviewers, the Editorial Board for their time and comments, Mark Hoyle for his help with illustrations and the design of the 50th anniversary SGRP logo, Franziska Dövener for the German and Sophie Chavarria for the French translations of the abstracts.

2021 and 2022 were certainly exciting years of transformation and change for the conferences, and also the SGRP committee. After four years in the post, Rob Perrin stepped down from his position as the President of the SGRP. This was Rob's second term in office (1996–1999, 2018–2022), and he is the only SGRP president to have held the office twice. We thank Rob for his continued commitment to our pottery family (having held many other committee positions including newsletter editor and journal editor in the past), especially during the challenging events of the last few years. We elected our new president at the Leicester AGM in 2022, Dr Alice Lyons. Andrew Peachey, our diligent newsletter editor of a decade's worth of pottery news, also stepped down, and Megan Tirpak was elected in his place. Please join me in offering the warmest of welcomes to our new President, Alice, and all new committee members, who together hope to continue and enhance the great work of the SGRP: promoting the love and research of Roman ceramics and assisting the training of the new generations of pottery specialists.

These years, however, also marked great losses within our Roman pottery family. We said our final goodbyes to several of our members, defining researchers in their fields, our friends, and mentors: Maggi Darling, Roberta Tomber, Geoff Dannell, and Paul Bidwell. All of them were subject leaders in their fields with key publications of their research that has helped and will help generations of specialists. Roberta, Maggi, and Paul all served as Presidents of the SGRP, while Geoff was one of the foremost advocates of Samian and pottery research, promoting new technologies and training. I am not alone in saying that it is never easy to hear the sad news, but personally, I found Paul Bidwell's passing especially hard. Paul was one of the first people I met on my specialist journey. I will always fondly remember sitting in his office, with the (then) brand new volumes of *Names on Terra Sigillata*, struggling to find the potters, and his generosity and patience with me. *Sit Tibi Terra Levis*. We are incredibly grateful for all their work, their friendship, and their presence. I would also like to thank the writers of the obituaries for Roberta, Maggi, and Paul (Geoff's to follow in due course) in this volume, and those sending the accompanying photos found in our members' archives.

To conclude my first Editorial, I would like to add some good news. Congratulations to Kay Hartley, who has been awarded an honorary doctorate by Newcastle University for her lifetime's work and achievements! Parts of Kay's extensive mortarium stamp archive have now been published on the Archaeology Data Service (https://doi.org/10.5284/1090785) thanks to the hard work of Kay, Ruth Leary, and Yvonne Boutwood. Our compliments are extended to Nick Cooper, currently SGRP committee member and member of the *Journal of Roman Pottery Studies* editorial board, who is retiring from his position at the University of Leicester and ULAS after 38 years of service. Lastly, congratulations to James Gerrard, who has become Professor of Roman Archaeology at Newcastle University, adding yet another professor to our Roman pottery group!

Welcome to the 20th volume of the *Journal of Roman Pottery Studies*. Here's to more excellent Roman pottery research, another 50 years of the SGRP, and (at least) another 20 Journal volumes in the future.

Eniko Hudak
Newcastle University
June 2023

Bibliographical note: Perrin, R. (1986) 'Introduction', *Journal of Roman Pottery Studies* 1, 4–5.

Obituaries

Margaret Jane Darling MPhil FSA MIFA (1939–2021)

Maggi Darling at the CLAU. Photo supplied by Ian M. Rowlandson.

Margaret (Maggi) Jane Darling was born in Bletchley, Buckinghamshire on 13 April 1939, and died in Lincolnshire in December 2021 after a short illness. Maggi was a founding member of the SGRP and a protégée of the late Graham Webster. Her research in Roman pottery saw the publication of a number of key Roman forts including Wroxeter and the late Roman fortress at Caister-on-Sea.

At Lincoln she advanced the use of computers for digitally recording pottery and analysis of large assemblages from complicated urban deposits.

Maggi was schooled in Bedfordshire before her father was posted to India, which inspired a life-long interest in the country's culture and food. Whilst in India she worked for the Canadian Immigration Service. In 1961 she returned to England and set up her Farm Management Consultancy business, which she continued alongside her archaeological interests until taking full time archaeological work in 1973.

Maggi's first introduction to field archaeology was in 1965 on a prehistoric site on Dartmoor and the following year at the Gloucester Market Hall site in 1966. From 1967 she worked with Graham Webster at Wroxeter as part of his University of Birmingham Excavation techniques courses and at Barnsley Park. In 1970 Maggi passed her University of London Diploma in Archaeology focusing on European Prehistory. She continued her work at Barnsley Park as supervisor in 1971 and in 1972–3 worked at the Lake Farm, Wimbourne excavations.

In 1973 Maggi took on a full-time post as a Roman pottery researcher at the Trust for Lincoln Archaeology where, as part of her role she was first thrown into supervising excavations at St Mark's, Lincoln and the Heighington tile kiln. During this time, she completed the publication of key late Roman assemblages from The Park, Lincoln and submitted her successful MPhil theses to the University of Nottingham, a study of the pottery from the legionary fortress at Wroxeter, publishing some of the results in the BAR volume *Roman Pottery Studies in Britain and Beyond*. In this period Maggi also worked on publications of assemblages from Wroxeter, Kingsholm and Inchtuthil.

In 1977 Maggi was seconded to the Norwich Castle Museum to prepare a publication of the excavation of the late Charles Green on the Roman costal defensive site at Caister-on-Sea (1993) and during this time worked with Tony Gregory to catalogue all of the coins, pottery and finds in the museum collections. In 1986 she returned to the City of Lincoln Archaeological Unit (CLAU) to work on pottery from excavations at Lincoln, the Fenland Research Committee, and other units. Whilst at Lincoln she developed Paul Tyers' UNIX programme *Plotdate* to assess the residual content of pottery groups to inform decisions on the analysis of finds groups at Lincoln (Darling 1994a; Darling and Precious 2014). After leaving CLAU in 1996, Maggi established herself as an independent pottery researcher and continued working on pottery from the East Midlands, East Anglia and Yorkshire producing nearly 300 developer funded reports.

It was at this time that I first met Maggi. She shared an office with Barbara Precious at 25 West Parade, Lincoln. The big bay window in their office overlooked the site of The Park excavations where a section of the *colonia* wall remains exposed beneath the council buildings. At the time they were working on numerous projects from Lincolnshire and the West Heslerton assemblage. I have fond memories of me joining Maggi after a day working on site, looking at pottery, drinking coffee, and smoking cigarettes (in the days before we both quit). Often the evening pottery work was accompanied by a soundtrack of 'Camel Spotting', a mix of north African music, or one of her classical music CD's. It was a fantastic introduction to recording pottery. Maggi and Barbara always lent me plenty of reading material from their library and were generous with their time to point me in the right direction.

A founding member of the Study Group for Roman Pottery, Maggi also served as the group's president from 1996–1999. She organised the Lincoln conference in 1993 and acted as the convener of the guidelines document published in 1994 (rev 2004). Her spirited contributions to SGRP conferences and continental meetings hosted by *SFECAG* and the *Rei Cretariae Romanae Favtorvm* will long be remembered. She was honoured by the SGRP with the John Gillam award in 2015 for her work with Barbara Precious on the corpus of Roman pottery from Lincoln (2014). She was also elected a Fellow of the Society of Antiquaries of London in 1995.

The breadth and depth of her work reveal that Maggi was a perfectionist with an exceptional dedication to detail. One aspect of looking over her paperwork has been to see her archive of correspondence stretching back to the 1960s, often in triplicate. There are countless letters from other researchers that she consulted on points of detail for her publications or helping specialists from other regions with identifying 'problem sherds'. Latterly emails took over from the typed letter and I have a collection of my own exchanges with Maggi about Lincolnshire pottery and facepots.

Professional standards were a topic close to Maggi's heart and she was an early member of the Institute of Field Archaeologists serving on the council as Careers Officer from 1989–92 and as Secretary of the Career Development and Training Sub-Committee. She undertook a training scheme processing the pottery from the Market Rasen kilns and published on the benefits of workplace learning schemes for training Roman pottery researchers

(Brisbane and Darling 1994). I was fortunate to be taught and mentored by her from 2006–9.

Maggi's interests included Opera and travel. Maggi enjoyed taking holidays with Lauren Gale, Brian Gilmour and Martin Henig, notably to India.

Lauren recalls:

Maggi was a devoted godmother to Ed in his early months. He wasn't an easy baby and wouldn't settle or sleep. My maternity leave was almost over (12 weeks). In the ninth week (it must have been late November) we found a cheap package holiday to Malta and spent a long weekend there. In those days refurbishing British Leyland buses was a cottage industry, you could ride all over the island in these multi-coloured buses, which seemed to calm Ed down. Nights were difficult and Maggi stayed up with me helping to amuse the baby. Fortunately he wasn't heavy. We managed to take in a surprising amount of archaeology too. I should add that boarding the flight, I learned it was Maggi's first, she was terrified both of flying and uncertain whether she'd survive without cigarettes all that time! She was splendid.

Martin recalls first encountering Maggi:

My first memory of Maggi was when she sent me illustrations of a mould for making a phallus, a letter in which she told me quite clearly and she said she had difficulty in extracting her finger after ascertaining its shape. I enjoyed her quiet humour.

Much of Maggi's approach to pottery research can be found in her 1989 paper 'Nice Fabric, Pity about the Form'. She always stressed the importance of researching and recording pottery to inform the main report and overall narrative of the site – quoting Sir Mortimer Wheeler, 'The archaeologist is digging up, not things, but people.'[1] In this respect Maggi's studies of the military in the conquest period, Saxon shore forts, Roman ovens, ritual vessels and water organs sought to transcend the sherds themselves and reveal new insights into past lives.

Ian M. Rowlandson

Publications of Maggi Darling

1975. Roman Pottery, in M. Darling (ed.) Lincoln Archaeological Trust 1974–1975, *Annual Report of the Lincoln Archaeological Trust 3*, Lincoln Archaeological Trust, Lincoln, 26–7.

1976a. The pottery from the legionary fortress at Wroxeter and associated military sites, unpublished M.Phil. Thesis, University of Nottingham.

1976b. Roman Pottery, in M. Darling (ed.) *Lincoln Archaeological Trust 1975–1976, Annual Report of the Lincoln Archaeological Trust 4*, Lincoln Archaeological Trust, Lincoln, 29–30.

1977a. A Group of late Roman pottery from Lincoln, *The Archaeology of Lincoln*, 16/1.

1977b. Pottery from early military sites in western Britain, in J. Dore and K. Greene (eds) *Roman Pottery Studies in Britain and Beyond*, British Archaeological Reports S30, 57–100.

1977c. Romano-British chimney-pots and finials, *The Antiquaries Journal* 57, 315–16.

1977d. A phallic mould from Heighington, near Lincoln. *The Antiquaries Journal* 57, 336–8.

1977e. Roman Pottery, in M. Darling (ed.) *Lincoln Archaeological Trust 1976–1977, Annual Report of the Lincoln Archaeological Trust* 5, Lincoln Archaeological Trust, Lincoln, 12–14.

1980a. Summary of pottery dating evidence, in M.J. Jones (ed.) *The Defences of the Upper Roman Enclosure*, The Archaeology of Lincoln 7–1, CBA, London, 12–13.

1980b. Current work on Roman Pottery, in M. Darling (ed.) *Lincoln Archaeological Trust 1979–1980, Annual Report of the Lincoln Archaeological Trust* 8, Lincoln Archaeological Trust, Lincoln, 30–31.

1981a. A Roman face-pot from St Mark's, in Nurser, E. (ed) *Lincoln Archaeological Trust 1980–81, Annual Report of the Lincoln Archaeological Trust* 9, Lincoln Archaeological Trust, Lincoln, 27–8.

1981b. Early red-slipped ware from Lincoln, in A.C. Anderson and A.S. Anderson (eds) *Roman Pottery Research in Britain and North-west Europe. Papers presented to Graham Webster*, BAR International Series 123, 397–416.

1984. Roman Pottery from the Upper Defences, *Archaeology of Lincoln*, 16/2.

1985a. The Other Roman Pottery', in Pitts, L.F. and Joseph, J.K.S. *Inchtuthil: The Roman Legionary Fortress*, Britannia Monograph 6, London, 323–338.

1985b. Roman Pottery, in H.R. Hurst, *Kingsholm: Excavations at Kingsholm Close and other sites with a discussion of the archaeology of the area, Gloucester*, 67–93.

1986. A review of Perrin, J.R. Roman Pottery from the Colonia: Skeldergate and Bishophill, The Archaeology of York 16/2, in *Britannia* 17, 467–8.

1987. The Caistor-by-Norwich 'massacre' reconsidered, *Britannia* 18, 263–72.

1988. The pottery, in M.J. Darling and M.J. Jones, Early Settlement in Lincoln, *Britannia* 19, 9–37.

1989a. A figured colour-coated beaker from excavations of the East Gate at Lincoln, by Petch, D.F. in 1959–62, *Journal of Roman Pottery Studies* 2, 29–32.

1989b. Nice fabric, pity about the form…, *Journal of Roman Pottery Studies* 2, 98–101.

1989c. A review article on Andrews, G. The Coarse wares, in Hinchliffe, J. and Green, C.S. *Excavations at Brancaster 1974 and 1977*, East Anglian Archaeology 23, 1985, and Johnson, S. *Burgh Castle, Excavations by Charles Green 1958–61*, East Anglian Archaeology 20, 1983, in *Journal of Roman Pottery Studies* 2, 102–105.

1990. The blacksmiths of St Mark's and their god, in M.J. Jones (ed.) *Lincoln Archaeology 1989–90, Annual Report of the City of Lincoln Archaeological Unit* 2, 21–3, City Lincoln Archaeological Unit, Lincoln.

1991. A review of West, S. *West Stow: The Prehistoric and Romano-British Occupations*, East Anglian Archaeology 48, 1990, in *Journal of Roman Pottery Studies* 4, 1991, 81–2.

1994a. Roman Pottery: some benefits of computerisation, in Jones, Michael, J. (ed) *Lincoln Archaeology 1993–4, Annual Report of the City of Lincoln Archaeology Unit* 6, 21–3, City Lincoln Archaeology Unit, Lincoln.

1994b. The South Carlton Roman Pottery Project, in Jones, Michael, J. (ed) *Lincoln Archaeology 1993–4, Annual Report of the City of Lincoln Archaeology Unit* 6, 35–6, City Lincoln Archaeology Unit, Lincoln.

1994c. A review of Manning, W.H. (ed.), *Report on the Excavations at Usk 1965–1976: The Roman Pottery*, 1993, in *Britannia* 25, 331–2.

1994d. *Guidelines for the Archiving of Roman Pottery*, The Study Group for Roman Pottery.

1998a. Samian from the City of Lincoln: A question of status, in J. Bird (ed,) *Form and fabric: Studies in Rome's material past in honour of B R Hartley*, 169–77.

1998b. A review of May, J. Dragonby Report on excavations at an Iron Age and Romano-British Settlement in North Lincolnshire, Oxbow Monograph 61, Oxford, 1996, *Britannia* 29, 486–488.

1999. Roman Pottery, in C. Colyer, B.J.J. Gilmour and M.J. Jones, *The Defences of the Lower City. Excavations at The Park and West Parade 1970–2*, CBA Research Report 114, 52–135.

2000. The Period 1 pottery, in P. Ellis (ed), *The Roman Baths and Macellum at Wroxeter, a report on excavations by Graham Webster, 1955–85*, EH Archaeological Rep 9, London, 258–63.

2001a. Roman pottery (Middleton, Norfolk), in T. Lane and E.L. Morris (eds), *A Millennium of Saltmaking: Prehistoric and Romano-British salt production in the Fenland*, Lincolnshire Archaeology. English Heritage Reports 4, 202–17.

2001b. Summary of Roman pottery from sites in Wigford, in K. Steane, M.J. Darling, J. Mann, A. Vince and J. Young, *The Archaeology of Wigford and the Brayford Pool*, Lincoln Archaeological Studies 2, Oxbow Books, Oxford, 319–23.

2002a. Pottery, in G. Webster, *The Legionary fortress at Wroxeter, Excavations by Graham Webster, 1955–85*, EH Archaeological Report 19, London, 137–223.

2002b. Graham Webster: Small Finds and Pottery, *ARA The Bulletin of The Association for Roman Archaeology* 12 (March 2002), 13.

2004a. Report on the pottery, in C. Palmer-Brown and W. Munford, Roman-British life in north Nottinghamshire: Fresh evidence from Raymoth Lane, Worksop, *Transactions of the Thoroton Society*, 108, 37–51.

2004b. Guidelines for the Archiving of Roman Pottery (1994), updated in *Journal of Roman Pottery Studies* 11, 67–74.

2004c. A review of Manning, W.H. (ed.), *Report on the Excavations at Usk 1965–1976: The Roman Pottery*, 1993, in *Journal of Roman Pottery Studies* 11, 121–4.

2004d. Graham Alexander Webster, OBE, MA, PhD, DLitt, FSA, Hon MIFA, 1913–2001, *Journal of Roman Pottery Studies* 11, 125–8.

2005. Brough-on-Humber fine wares production, *Journal of Roman Pottery Studies* 12, 83–96.

2006. Summary of Roman pottery from sites in the Upper City, in K. Steane (ed.), *The Archaeology of The Upper City and Adjacent Suburbs*, Lincoln Archaeological Studies No.3, Oxbow Books, Oxford, 272–80.

2007. A depiction of the organ from Roman Britain, in L. Gilmour (ed), *Pagans and Christians – from Antiquity to the Middle Ages. Papers in honour of Martin Henig, presented on the occasion of his 65th birthday*, BAR International Series 1610, 111–15.

2009. Pottery and the fired clay items, in P. Boyer, J. Proctor and R. Taylor-Wilson, *On the Boundaries of Occupation: Excavations at Burringham Road Scunthorpe and Baldwin Avenue Bottesford, North Lincolnshire*, Pre-Construct Archaeology Monograph 9, London, 37–55.

2010. Face pots and the Roman army: review of Gillian Braithwaite, Faces from the Past. A Study of Roman Face Pots from Italy and the Western Provinces of the Roman Empire, *Journal of Roman Archaeology* 23, 643–50.

2011. Cult pottery from Navenby, in C. Palmer-Brown and J. Rylatt, *How Times Change: Navenby Unearthed*, Pre-Construct Archaeological Services Ltd. Monograph No. 2, Saxilby, 92–100.

2012. Stuffed dormice or tandoori chicken in Roman Britain? in D. Bird, J. Bird and G. Dannell (eds) *Dating and interpreting the past in the western Roman Empire: Essays in honour of Brenda Dickinson*, Oxbow Books, Oxford, 346–57.

2016. Summary of Roman pottery from sites in the Lower City, in K. Steane (ed.) *The Archaeology of The Lower City and Adjacent Suburbs*, Lincoln Archaeological Studies No.4, Oxbow Books, Oxford, 501–12.

unpublished a, The Roman pottery kilns at Market Rasen.

unpublished b, The pottery from the military site at Lake Farm, Wimborne, Dorset.

unpublished c, Residuality- A New Approach.

Brisbane, M. and Darling, M.J. 1994. Experiential learning through work experience, *The Field Archaeologist* No. 20 (Spring 1994), 400–1.

Darling, M.J. and Field, N. 2003. The Roman pottery, in N. Field and M. Parker Pearson, 2003, *Fiskerton An Iron Age Timber Causeway with Iron Age and Roman Votive Offerings,* 115–17.

Darling, M.J. with Gurney, D. 1993. *Caister-on-Sea: Excavations by Charles Green, 1951–55*, East Anglian Archaeology Rep 60, Field Archaeology Division, Norfolk Mus Service, Dereham.

Darling, M.J. with Hartley, K.F. and Dickinson, B. 2000. The Roman pottery, in K. Hunter-Mann, M.J. Darling and H.E.M. Cool, Excavations on a Roman Extra-Mural site at Brough-on-Humber, East Riding of Yorkshire, UK, *Internet Archaeology* 9, 4.0.

Darling, M.J. and Hartley, K.F. 2000. Mortaria, in K. Hunter-Mann, M.J. Darling and H.E.M. Cool, Excavations on a Roman Extra-Mural site at Brough-on-Humber, East Riding of Yorkshire, UK, *Internet Archaeology* 9, 4.3.

Darling, M.J. and Precious, B. 2001. A saltern at Gold Dyke Bank, Wrangle, Lincolnshire, in T. Lane and E.L. Morris (eds) *A Millenium of Saltmaking: Prehistoric and Romano-British Salt Production in the Fenland,* Lincolnshire Archaeology and Heritage Report Series No. 4., Heritage Trust of Lincolnshire, Heckington, 424–5.

Darling, M.J. and Precious, B.J. 2014. *A corpus of Roman pottery from Lincoln*, Lincoln Archaeological Studies No. 6, Oxbow Books, Oxford.

Darling, M.J. and Precious, B.J. forthcoming West Heslerton Roman Pottery, publication report submitted to D. Powlesland, *West Heslerton: Excavation of the Anglian Settlement*, Landscape Research Centre.

Darling, M.J. and Timby, J.R. 1985. Roman Amphorae, in H.R. Hurst, *Kingsholm: Excavations at Kingsholm Close and other sites with an archaeological discussion of the area,* Gloucester Archaeological Publications, Cambridge, Stroud, 72–6.

Darling, M. and Wood, K. 1976. Washingborough Roman Tile Kiln, in M. Darling (ed.) Lincoln Archaeological Trust 1975–1976, *Annual Report of the Lincoln Archaeological Trust*, Lincoln Archaeological Trust, Lincoln, 22–3.

Darling, M.J. and Wood, K. 1981. A Roman tile-kiln near Heighington, in M.J. Jones (ed.) Excavations at Lincoln. Third Interim Report: Sites outside the walled city 1972–1977 *The Antiquaries Journal* 61, 110–12.

Darling, M.J., Rowlandson, I. and Fiske, H.G. with Wild, F.C. and Monteil, G. 2020. Roman pottery, in R. Atkins, J. Burke, L. Field and A. Yates, *Middle Bronze Age and Roman Settlement at Manor Pit, Baston, Lincolnshire: Excavations 2002–2014*, MoLA Northampton monograph, 102–29.

Rowlandson, I.M. with Darling M.J. 2015. The other Roman pottery, in A. Palfreyman and S. Ebbins, Excavations at a Suspected Roman Villa at Heage, Derbyshire 2011–2013, *Derbyshire Archaeological Journal* 135, 62–70.

Wood, K.F. and Darling, M.J. 1977. Heighington, *Lincolnshire Hist Archaeological* 12, 74.

Roberta Sylvia Tomber (1954–2022)

Roberta Tomber at the 2017 SGRP conference at Carlisle. Photo supplied by Alice Lyons.

Even if you had not had the privilege of meeting Roberta in person her name will be familiar to everyone who works in British Roman ceramics through the publication of the

National Roman Fabric Reference Collection handbook undertaken in collaboration with the late John Dore (see *Journal of Roman Pottery Studies* 15) (Tomber and Dore 1998). She was, however, involved in many other diverse projects throughout her career.

Roberta, originally an American citizen of Jewish heritage, was born in the United States in 1954. She attended Brandels University, a private research university in Waltham, Massachusetts, founded in 1948 as a non-sectarian, coeducational institution sponsored by the Jewish community and graduated in 1977 with a degree in Classics. She recognised early on that this was the general field she wished to pursue, although it evolved somewhat towards archaeology and in particular the study of pottery shortly afterwards.

She came to the UK in the later 1970s and was involved in various excavations in Herefordshire and Worcester including Kenchester and Beckford. One of her first published reports is that on the pottery from Kenchester (Tomber 1985). The report is an exemplary example of how a pottery report should be written and typifies the care with which Roberta approached her work. The publication, following a general introduction, includes detailed fabric and forms descriptions, full tabulation and a discussion of the assemblages on an intra and inter-site basis. Roberta's activities in the West Midlands probably introduced her to Severn Valley ware as when she subsequently enrolled at the University of Southampton, she did an MSc on this very topic (Tomber 1980). Roberta, like many others, benefitted by being a student of David (DPSP) Peacock and his influence in her approach to pottery, in particular the discrimination of fabrics through petrology, is manifest throughout her ceramic career.

It was around this time that Roberta had the misfortune to get diagnosed with cancer but, after a short hiatus when she returned to the States for treatment, she came back to Southampton to pursue a PhD. The title of her thesis submitted in 1988 was: *Pottery in long-distance economic inference: an investigation of methodology with reference to Roman Carthage*, reflecting both David Peacock's influence and areas of interest as well as clearly setting the path for some of her later work.

Having successfully completed her PhD in 1988 Roberta became Head of Roman ceramics at the Museum of London. During this time, she authored several publications. One of the most significant contributions of which was to *A dated corpus of early Roman pottery from the City of London* (1994) co-authored with Barbara Davies and Beth Richardson. She also collaborated on an article discussing the pottery from late Roman London with her colleague Robin Symonds (Symonds and Tomber 1991).

Roberta was a great supporter of the Roman Pottery Research Group and was President between 2006 and 2009 during which time there were conferences at Cardiff (2007), Cambridge (2008) and Chichester (2009). She published a number of short articles in the Study Group Journal including the first edition (Tomber 1990; 2003;

Williams and Tomber 1986), as well as being instrumental in the creation of the mortarium bibliography for Roman Britain (*Journal of Roman Pottery Studies* 13, 2006).

In 1992, Roberta was seconded to the British Museum to lead on a project initiated by English Heritage, MoLAS and the British Museum to create a national Roman pottery fabric reference collection. Together with her colleague John Dore a physical reference series was developed, and the resulting monograph published in 1998. This has become one of the standard reference works for current pottery work.

She was made a Fellow of the Society of Antiquaries in 1995. As a leading scholar in the field of ceramic petrology, she was Acting President of The Ceramic Petrology Group between 1999 and 2012 and she served as a member on the Council of the Roman Society in 2019. In 2002 she was appointed Honorary Visiting Researcher at the British Museum in the Department of Conservation and Scientific Research (2002–2022).

At around the same time Roberta re-joined the University of Southampton to undertake research with David Peacock and others on Roman pottery from Egypt and the Red Sea ports. Her name can be found in many key reports including the Roman quarry complexes at Mons Claudianus, Wadi Umm Wikala and Wadi Semna; the settlements at Sabratha, Libya; Carthage, Tunisia; Berenike and Myos Hormos (Queseir al-Qadim), ports on the Egyptian Red Sea coast as well as Wadi Faynan, Jordan. For the Berenike excavations she was chief pottery specialist for the Dutch-American and Polish-American projects shaping their research strategies. Working on these assemblages led her to looking at trade relations in the Eastern Mediterranean and beyond and, in particular, identifying a strong Egyptian-Indian connection from a range of Indian finds at the Red Sea sites particularly for the early Roman period. These included pottery, textiles, beads and archaeobotanical remains (particularly pepper and coconut). This study culminated in her book published in 2008 on the Indo-Roman trade, which brings together for the first time archaeological findings from key ports throughout the Indian Ocean, the Red Sea, South Arabia, the Gulf, India and Sri Lanka. The ceramic and other evidence, both artefactual and documentary, allowed Roberta to build up a picture of the trade whereby ordinary goods were piggy-backed alongside more costly items such as pepper, spices and gems. She continued to publish other articles on this subject (Tomber 2010; 2013) and there are still further to come in the pipeline including her *magnum opus* (Tomber forthcoming).

Roberta's knowledge on Roman pottery from North Africa, the Levant, the Red Sea, South Arabia, Mesopotamia, the Gulf and India was, and will be for many decades to come, unsurpassed. She was a meticulous and very thorough worker and from my own experience working with her in the 1980s in Carthage, Israel and Sicily, demanded very high standards with regard the pottery illustrations, but in the nicest way.

Colleagues have commented that Roberta was a sage person to run ideas and thoughts by for sound council. She was always generous in giving advice and helping others and many people in remembering her have commented on the warmth of her lovely smile.[2]

Jane Timby

Notes

1   Archaeology from the Earth (1954), Oxford Clarendon Press, Preface, v. Thanks to Jenny Mann for accessing Maggi's archive, Christopher Young, Lauren Gale, Martin Henig, Grahame Soffe and Diana Bonakis Webster for the photographs.
2   Compiled by Jane Timby with grateful acknowledgement to information provided by many others including Beth Richardson, Gill Andrews, Iwona Zych, Steve Willis and Jane Faiers.

Bibliography

Davies, B. Richardson, B. and Tomber R. 1994. *A dated corpus of early Roman pottery from the City of London*, CBA Research Report 98. Museum of London and the Council for British Archaeology, York.

Symonds, R.P. and Tomber, R.S. 1991. Late Roman London: an assessment of the ceramic evidence from the City of London, *Transactions of the London & Middlesex Archaeological Society* 42, 59–97.

Tomber, R.S. 1980. *A petrological assessment of Severn Valley ware: kilns and selected distribution*, MSc dissertation, University of Southampton.

Tomber, R.S. 1985. Pottery, in T. Wilmott and S.P.Q. Rahtz, An Iron Age and Roman settlement outside Kenchester (Magnis), Herefordshire. Excavations 1977–1979, *Transactions of the Woolhope Naturalists Field Club* 45, pt 1, 99–133.

Tomber, R. 2007. Rome and Mesopotamia – importers into India in the first millennium AD, *Antiquity* 81, 972–88.

Tomber, R. 2008. *Indo-Roman trade: from pots to pepper*. London, Duckworth.

Tomber, R. 2013. Pots, coins and trinkets in Rome's trade with the East, in P.S. Wells (ed.) *Rome Beyond its Frontiers: Imports, Attitudes and Practices* (J Roman Archaeology Supp 94). Portsmouth Rhode Island, 87–104.

Tomber, R.S. forthcoming. *Local, regional and global: the ceramics from the Ptolemaic and Roman Red Sea ports of Myos Hormos and Berenike*, British Museum.

Tomber, R., Blue, L. and Abraham, S. (eds) 2010. *Migration, Trade and Peoples, Part I: Indian Ocean Commerce and the Archaeology of Western India*, The British Association for South Asian Studies, London.

Tomber, R. and Dore, J. 1998. *The National Roman fabric reference collection. A handbook*. Museum Archaeology Service, London.

Paul Bidwell, OBE, LLB, MA, FSA, MIfA (19 June 1949–5 November 2022)
President of SGRP 1993–1996

Paul's first contact with pottery came when as a teenager he fell off a horse and found himself examining a scatter of

Paul Bidwell in the library at South Shields Roman Fort, 2007. Photo supplied by Alexandra Croom.

pot sherds at close quarters; subsequent research showed he had been in a field containing some 13th–14th century pottery kilns. He read law at Exeter University before changing directions and joining the City's archaeological team, rapidly rising through the ranks to take charge of the excavations of the legionary bath-house and later forum in front of the main entrance to Exeter Cathedral in the 1970s. Paul was equally interested in the structural remains and the pottery, and when he published these excavations they included the detailed type-series for BB1 and other wares common in the south-west that he had researched and written himself.

Paul never lost his love of the south-west, but in 1980 he moved to the north. He worked first at Vindolanda, publishing his excavations there in 1985, which was the first monograph publication of a single excavation on Hadrian's Wall. He then excavated and published excavations on the bridges of Hadrian's Wall at Willowford and Chesters. As well as writing up the structural remains, all his publications included his own pottery reports.

He joined (what is now) Tyne & Wear Archives & Museums (TWAM) in 1983 as an archaeologist, working on a 30-year programme of excavations at South Shields Roman Fort. He led on the series of reconstructions built at both South Shields and Wallsend, starting with the West gate at Arbeia in 1988, and was behind the proposals for the redevelopment of Wallsend Roman Fort, which led to the opening of the new museum there in 2000. In addition, Paul was in many ways one of the creators of what today is known as community archaeology, always ensuring local people were engaged in and enthused by the archaeology beneath their feet and was awarded an OBE for this work in 2012.

Paul retired from TWAM, but not from archaeology, in 2013. He continued to write up excavations, including the Branch Wall, the section of Hadrian's Wall to the west of Segedunum Roman Museum, and the bridge abutment at Chesters. In all these, as well as many other publications, he was untangling and understanding the supply of pottery to the Wall, and in particular the forts in the lower Tyne Valley, with articles on the supply of pottery from the south-east during the third century, and the dating of late Roman wares in the north.

It is clear that many people feel they owed much to Paul for his inspiration, support, guidance and company, but he was in essence an introvert. He was happy engaged in small-scale discussions with archaeological friends down the pub, but being privately immersed in books or classical music were an equal source of great pleasure for him.

Alexandra Croom and William Griffiths

Selected publications on Roman pottery by Paul Bidwell from 2012 onwards

For a full list of Paul's work see 'Bibliography of the published works of Paul Bidwell' in N. Hodgson and B. Griffiths 2022. *Roman Frontier Archaeology – in Britain and beyond: Papers in honour of Paul Bidwell presented on the occasion of the 30th annual conference of the Arbeia Society,* Archaeopress Roman Archaeology 92, Archaeopress, Oxford, 12–17.

2014. The Coarse Pottery, in C. Smart, *A Roman military complex and medieval settlement on Church Hill, Calstock, Cornwall: Survey and Excavation 2007–2010*, British Archaeological Reports British Series 603, British Archaeological Reports Publishing, Oxford, 49–55.

2016. Fifth Century Pottery in Devon and North East Cornwall. Internet Archaeology 41. https://intarch.ac.uk/journal/issue41/1/toc.html.

2017. Rural Settlement and the Roman Army in the North: external supply and regional self-sufficiency, in M. Allen, L. Lodwick, T. Brindle, M. Fulford, and A. Smith, *The Rural Economy of Roman Britain*: New Visions of the Countryside of Roman Britain, Vol 2. Britannia Monograph Series 309, Society for the Promotion of Roman Studies, London, 290–305.

2018. The Roman Pottery, in D.J. Breeze (ed.) The Crosby Garrett Helmet, *Cumberland and Westmorland Archaeological and Antiquarian Society* extra series 48, 66–8.

2020. The external supply of pottery and cereals to Antonine Scotland, in D.J. Breeze and W.S. Hanson (eds) *The Antonine Wall: Papers in honour of Professor Lawrence Keppie*, Archaeopress Roman Archaeology 64, Archaeopress, Oxford, 263–85.

2021. Pottery Supply in Roman Exeter and the South-West, in S. Rippon and N. Holbrook (eds) *Studies in the Roman and Medieval Archaeology of Exeter*. Exeter: a Place in Time 2, Oxbow Books, Oxford, 309–37.

Bidwell, P. with Croom, A. 2012. The Roman pottery, in M. Stephens and P. Ware, *A Roman Pottery Kiln from the Community Primary School, Norton-on-Derwent, North Yorkshire*. MAP Archaeological Practice Ltd Publication 1. MAP Archaeological Practice Ltd, Malton, 8–22.

Bidwell, P. with Croom, A. 2016. The coarse wares, and, Discussion of pottery, in D.J. Breeze, *Bearsden: a Roman Fort on the Antonine Wall,* Society of Antiquaries of Scotland, Edinburgh, 108–29 and 176–81.

Bidwell, P. with Croom, A. 2017. The Roman ceramics, in M. Cook, J. Lawson and D. McLarne, *Excavations and Interventions in and around Cramond Roman Fort and Annexe, 1976 to 1990*. Scottish Archaeological Internet Reports 74, 19–37. https://doi.org/10.9750/issn.2056–7421.2017.74.

Bidwell, P. with Croom, A. 2019. Roman pottery from the excavations in 2012–13 (Area J), in S.J. Sherlock, *A Neolithic to Late Roman Landscape on the North-East Yorkshire Coast. Excavations at Street House, Loftus, 2004–17*. Tees Archaeology Monograph 7, Tees Archaeology, Hartlepool, 132–4.

Bidwell, P. with Croom, A. 2020. The Roman pottery, in M. Kirby, *Excavations at Musselburgh Primary Health Care Centre: Iron Age and Roman discoveries to the north of Inveresk Roman Fort, East Lothian*. Scottish Archaeological Internet Reports 89, 53–83. https://archaeologydataservice.ac.uk/archiveDS/archiveDownload?t=arch-310-1/dissemination/pdf/Magnus_Kirby.pdf.

Glass-working at Mancetter-Hartshill

Caroline M. Jackson

Abstract

This paper examines the nature of glass-working at Mancetter-Hartshill in Warwickshire where, during excavations in the 1960s, a glass-working furnace and glassy waste was recovered. The waste found indicated that glass blowing was taking place, and utilitarian vessels were produced, predominantly in blue-green glass, the most common glass colour of the period. Compositional analysis showed that most of this glass had been recycled many times, the site seemed to have received very little fresh raw glass from the eastern Mediterranean sites. Evidence of furnace re-lining along with the range of different glass compositions, which had a finite lifetime, indicate the furnace was in operation for a period of multiple melts; this was not a single event. Vessel production may also have been periodic, based on demand. This site fits into a picture of small-scale, regional glass-working sites in Britain, outside London, in the mid-2nd century, using cullet as the raw material. Production was relatively low-skilled; they were making utilitarian goods for a relatively local market.

1. Introduction

Britain was a substantial consumer of Roman glass. Some of this arrived as imported vessel glass, but by the 2nd century AD a limited number of small glass-melting furnaces emerged throughout Britain which remelted ready formed glass, made elsewhere in the Empire, and shaped it into simple utilitarian vessels or window glass. These secondary glass-working complexes were often very small and were located where glass was in demand, for instance, in or near towns or military sites, and also where complementary high temperature industries were located (e.g., see Price and Cool 1991; Price 2005; Shepherd and Wardle 2016, 91–7).

This paper examines the nature of glass-working at Mancetter-Hartshill in Warwickshire where, during excavations in the 1960s, a glass-working furnace and glassy waste were recovered. The types of glassy waste found, and the composition of this material are examined to determine what glass was available to the glassworker for remelting, what might have been produced at the site, and assess the scale and possible duration of production. The data may also give an insight into the skill set of the glassworkers operating in Britain in the 2nd century AD. This evidence, compared to that from other glass-working sites in Britain, provides a snapshot of the extent of production and recycling of glass in Britain in the 2nd century AD. A large part of the contextual information given in this paper was provided by Hilary Cool and Jennifer Price in their report on the Mancetter industry the

1990s as part of the Romano-British Glass project (Cool and Price, unpublished report in ADS).

2. Context: The Roman glass industry

In the Roman period, glass was made from sand and an evaporate salt, known as natron or trona, used to flux the glass. Pliny suggests the natron derived from Egypt (Pliny Natural History (NH) XXXI, 107 and XXXVI, 193–4). Archaeological and documentary evidence alongside more recent analytical work on glass compositions suggest there were two primary locations producing Roman glass in the 2nd century AD. These were located in northern Egypt relatively close to the natron supplies, and the Syria-Palestine coastal region where natron would have been imported (Barag 2005; Jackson *et al.* 2016). Here raw glass was produced in large tank furnaces capable of producing up to 20 tonnes of glass in a single firing (e.g., Nenna 2015). Once formed and cooled, this glass was then broken into chunks and shipped to smaller secondary glass-working centres located throughout the Roman empire which shaped the glass (Foy *et al.* 2003; Silvestri 2008). Broken and waste glass collected for remelting known as cullet, was also shipped for re-working at secondary centres (e.g., Silvestri 2008). Many of these secondary glass-working centres produced standard utilitarian goods, others appear to have made specialist goods (Amrein 2001; Wedepohl *et al.* 2003). Martial and Statius (Epigrams I, 1.41.3–5; Silvae 1.6.74) record the

Table 1. *The most common Roman soda lime-silica compositional groups found in the 2nd century AD relative to the period of operation of the Mancetter glass-working furnace (from Jackson and Paynter 2015), discussed in the text. The label 'raw glass' is given to represent a composition that has not been recycled (although mixing like with like cannot be detected compositionally).*

Compositional group	Antimony colourless (raw glass)	Manganese colourless (raw glass)	Manganese blue-green (raw glass)	Antimony-Manganese (recycled glass)
Oxide Wt%				
Al_2O_3	1.97	2.92	2.67	2.4
Fe_2O_3	0.37	0.46	0.31	0.58
MgO	0.48	0.63	0.5	0.58
CaO	5.82	8.48	7.66	6.59
Na2O	19.39	16.81	17.47	18.69
K_2O	0.51	0.68	0.67	0.82
TiO_2	0.07	0.08	0.07	0.09
P_2O_5	0.04	0.11	0.13	0.11
MnO	0.03	1.15	0.34	0.4
PbO	0.04	0.01	>0.01	0.06
Sb_2O_5	0.54	0.04	>0.01	0.35

collection of scrap glass as early as the 1st century AD and it was widespread by the 2nd century AD.

A small number of secondary glass melting and working centres have been found in Britain, but none show evidence of product specialisation. Some remelted the glass in tank furnaces, e.g., at Caistor in Norfolk (Atkinson 1929), and Basinghall Street in London (Wardle *et al.* 2016), and some in crucibles or more accurately glass-melting pots (sometimes suitable domestic pottery) were used to melt the glass in small furnaces. In many cases the choice of melting vessel was determined by what was being made; windows that require large volumes of glass in a single gather would probably need a tank furnace. However, even within tank furnaces, pots could have easily been used in conjunction with tank, potentially holding a different colour of glass, so the distinction between the two types of furnaces is not unequivocal (Taylor and Hill pers. comm.). Evidence from London, which has numerous glass-melting sites producing vessels, suggests that crucible/pot furnaces are a later 3rd–4th century AD phenomenon in Britain. The earlier furnaces at Regis House and Old Bailey in London, indicate that even small furnaces could accommodate a small tank (Shepherd 2015). The early continental evidence is more mixed. Both tank furnaces and 'pot furnaces' have been found throughout the Roman period (e.g., Hochuli-Gysel 2003; Raux *et al.* 2010; Ivanov *et al.* 2021; and summary in Cottam 2018, Appendix 2). The picture of Britain outside London is, as yet, unclear as remains of furnaces, such as that found at Mancetter, are rare; generally only the solidified remains of glass and/or glass-melting pots have been recovered (e.g., at Deansway in Worcester, Blue Boar Lane in Leicester and Wilderspool in Cheshire (May 1900; Price and Cool 1991; Cool and Jackson 2004).

Roman glass was made in a wide range of colours from translucent dark blue to purple and opaque whites, yellows and red, but the most common transparent colours were blue-greens and colourless. Blue green glass is the natural colour of glass that has no colouring additions, the blue-green hue arising from the iron that is naturally found in the raw materials used. Often manganese (MnO) or antimony (Sb_2O_5) from mineral sources, were added to the glass to change the hue of the glass and both could be added to decolourise the glass and make it colourless. Glass with low concentrations of manganese (e.g., less than 1wt%) is often blue-green, at higher concentrations the glass may be colourless. Antimony is a stronger decolouriser and only a small amount is needed to make the glass water clear. These two additions are very important when characterising Roman glass from the 1st–3rd centuries AD as the type and amount of decolouriser (antimony or manganese) varied through time and with glass production location. Manganese-containing glass more readily defines glass that was made in the Syro-Palestine furnaces, whereas antimony decolourised glass was generally produced in Egypt. Both types of glass are found by the 2nd century AD, although antimony colourless glasses had become more common than manganese colourless glasses (Paynter and Jackson 2018).

As raw glass contains *either* antimony *or* manganese, glasses that contain both are the result of recycling (Paynter and Jackson 2016). These 'antimony/manganese recycled' glasses, are most often a range of hues, influenced by the decolourising properties of both elements and the relative concentration of iron, but tend to be blue to green (blue-green). This is because the glassworker remelting the cullet would not know the exact compositions of the glasses he was introducing into the melt. Recent studies have found that much of the glass found in Roman Britain was produced from recycled glass cullet (Jackson and Paynter 2015; Wardle *et al.* 2016). Table 1 shows typical compositions of glass found in the 2nd century AD and whether the compositions indicate if this might be raw glass or recycled glass. The label 'raw glass' is given to represent a composition that has not been recycled (although mixing like with like cannot be detected compositionally).

3. The glass-working site at Mancetter-Hartshill

As demonstrated in reports presented in the Archaeology Data Service, the excavations at Mancetter-Hartshill uncovered a large number of kilns and other associated evidence associated with mortarium production (Hartley 1973a; 1973b). Amongst the pottery kilns a single glass furnace was found in 1964 (Price 2003) (Fig. 1). A large assemblage of blue-green and colourless glassy waste was also recovered, some from around the furnace (M24; site 7) scattered through the filling and stoke hole (45% of the waste glass recovered) and a water channel (M63/64; site 7/20), also 45% of the waste, which may suggest either another possible furnace was in operation or that this glass was dumped (Cool and Price, unpublished report in ADS, and pers. comm.). Although the extent of the glass-working area has not been established most glass waste came from sites 7 and 7/20. This scatter of material appears to be the disposal or tidying up of the site rather than dedicated cullet heaps (Cool and Price, unpublished report in ADS). The importance of the site is because it is the only one to date that has produced glass waste in association with a furnace. The small furnace (65 × 53 cm and 25 cm deep) was clay-lined with a solidified flow of glass on one surviving wall. Excavations in 1969 indicate it had been used more than once as it was relined, possibly up to four times (Warwickshire Historic Environment Record (HER) WA6244). At its maximum it was 0.8 m in diameter.

The vessel and glass waste assemblage recovered was extensive at around 1350 fragments of predominantly blue-green glass (90% of that found), with a few yellow-green or brown, some polychrome and colourless (Cool and Price, unpublished report in ADS). Forty-one percent of this assemblage by number is of melted or bubbly distorted vessel fragments or wasters, possibly failed attempts at vessel manufacture (Fig. 2). Many fragments had broken edges, which may indicate they were crushed for reuse. The rest of the waste consisted of trails/threads of glass, a large quantity of spilled glass drips and lumps, and glass blowing waste (Price and Cool 1991). There is ample evidence that the glass was blown. Collars of glass, knocked off from the end of the blowing iron once the vessels had been removed, called moils, were the most common type of blowing waste found at Mancetter making up a third of the assemblage (apart from miscellaneous heat affected and rounded lumps, Fig. 2). These moils ranged from 15–30 mm in diameter and were often streaked with iron scale. Small round or oval disks, often convex in shape with a shiny upper and rough concave surface, called roundels, were also recovered. These are also typical waste from glass blowing, and again may be associated with the waste knocked off the end of the iron to clean it after vessels production (Price

Figure 1. The Mancetter glass-melting furnace (imperial measurements shown, Photograph courtesy of University of Leeds, and Hilary Cool and Jenny Price).

and Cool 1991). The thin threads, trails and droplet shaped glass waste was probably produced when the glass was pulled out of the furnace to test it or from the application of decorative trails on vessels.

The bubbly, distorted vessel wasters were often found associated with spilled glass drips and solidified lumps. In the waster assemblage Price and Cool (1991, 26) identified distorted tubular rimmed bowls (Isings 44/45, mid-1st–late 2nd centuries AD), collared jars (Isings 67b/c types, late 1st to early 2nd centuries AD), funnel mouth jars and jars with base rings and prismatic and cylindrical bottles (Isings 50/51 types, 1st–2nd century AD) suggesting this was the product of the glass melting (see Isings 1957). These forms are typical of common utilitarian vessels forms of the period in Britain. There is no evidence for bottle production. Most were blue-green or colourless (with a very few in amber or green), mirroring the colours found in the waste assemblage (95% blue-green or colourless; Cool and Price, unpublished report in ADS). The colours of the glass, the forms represented and the dating of the furnace suggest the glass-working activity at Mancetter took place around the mid-2nd century AD (Cool and Price, unpublished report in ADS).

4. Compositional analysis of the glassy waste

The assemblage at Mancetter is an excellent opportunity to view a moment in time for glass re-working in Britain as it contains such an extensive range of glass waste, associated with at least one furnace, and a range of waster vessel forms which were probably made on site. Compositional analysis enhances our understanding of manufacture at the site giving an insight into the supply of glass to the glassworker, the extent of recycling, and the relative duration of vessel production at Mancetter.

The glass was chemically analysed, using a solution method, by Inductively Coupled Plasma – Atomic Emission Spectroscopy (ICP–AES) at the Geology Department, Royal Holloway University of London to obtain major and minor elements. The materials, methods, instrumentation

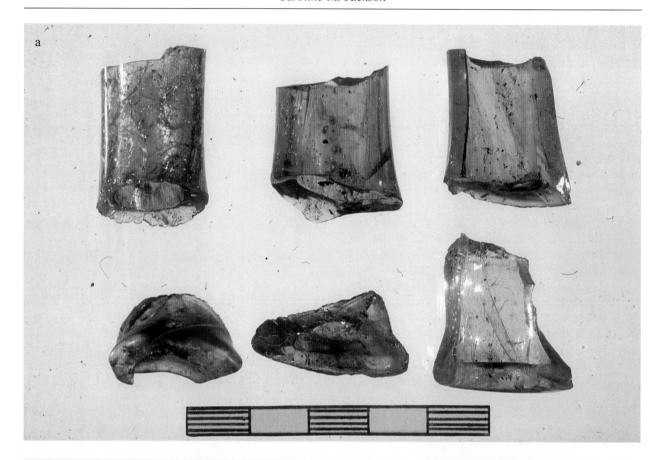

Figure 2. Blowing waste and glass vessel wasters from Mancetter. a: Moils, knocked off ends of the blowpipe. b: Heat distorted vessel fragments (Photographs courtesy of University of Leeds, and Hilary Cool and Jenny Price).

and data validation are given in Jackson *et al.* 2003. This method cannot determine silica in the glass as during glass dissolution in acids the silica is lost through volatilisation. The full dataset is published in Jackson and Paynter 2021 (table 2), and summary tables and figures are provided here. The relative numbers in each compositional group give a flavour of the different compositions identified but do not represent the absolute ratios of different glass types used at the site or in Britain at this time.

5. Findings

5.1. Compositional groups represented in the waste at Mancetter

The Mancetter glass waste reflects the range of glass colours produced in this period throughout the western Roman Empire, and is dominated by blue-green glass. Most of the glass analysed here shows evidence of recycling, containing both antimony and manganese (Table 2). This antimony/manganese recycled glass is predominantly blue-green in colour but some appears to be colourless to the eye. A further indicator that this glass was recycled is in the enhanced concentration of potassium in the recycled glasses, which would arise from fuel ash contamination upon successive remelting (Paynter 2008) (Fig. 3). This glass type is present in the blowing waste (moils and roundels) indicating it was worked at the site into vessels.

Manganese blue-green glass was also present and represented in the blowing waste. This glass may not be recycled glass, although it is impossible to identify recycling compositionally if glasses of the same composition are mixed, which may be the case here. One of these samples appears colourless to the eye. A few samples, appearing visually green, show no evidence of any decolouriser. These too show no signs of recycling.

Table 2. Numbers of analysed glass waste fragments in each of the compositional groups identified by glass colour (top) and also by waste or identified waster (bottom).

	Antimony colourless	Manganese blue-green	Manganese colourless	Antimony-Manganese recycled	No decoloriser (no antimony or manganese) (glass appears green)
Glass colour					
Blue-green		31	1 (high Mn)	57	5
Colourless	1		1	7	
Waste/waster					
Waste	1	18		36	1
Vessel waster		13	2	28	4

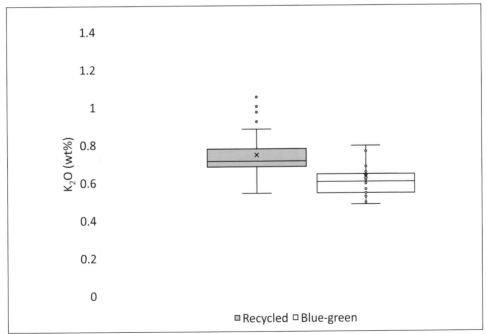

Figure 3. Boxplot showing enhanced potassium oxide concentrations in the recycled manganese/antimony compositions compared to the manganese blue-green glasses as a result of fuel ash incorporation during repeated remelting.

Colourless glass is rare in this assemblage. One sample is of antimony colourless glass, typical of 2nd century AD colourless glass, and another of manganese colourless glass, which is more uncommon, having declined in use after the mid-1st century AD.

One fragment is labelled 'manganese colourless' as it contains relatively high concentrations of manganese at concentrations that would be expected in a colourless glass. However, it is in fact blue-green in colour to the eye, which may indicate it was originally colourless glass that had been recycled many times previously, which made the decolouriser less effective (Jackson and Paynter 2021).

5.2. Glass supply to the furnace

The Mancetter glass waste shows compositions that are typical of the 2nd century AD, indicating that most glass in supply had been recycled, possibly several times. Very little waste was identified that could be identified as chunks of raw glass imported straight from the manufacturing sites in the Mediterranean. The presence of a significant number of fragments of waste in manganese blue-green glass, which would have been in circulation at least by the 1st century AD, suggests the glassworkers at Mancetter had a steady supply of this glass or that it had been recycled from earlier campaigns at the site, and the presence of distorted and bubbly vessel glass in this composition may support this. Glass that had not undergone some form of recycling was scarce by the mid-2nd century AD and so it is likely even this glass had undergone some recycling (Jackson and Paynter 2015). The rest of the glass is predominantly clearly recycled antimony/manganese glass where both blue-green and colourless glasses have been introduced to the melt or that previously recycled glasses, which had already been through a number of melting cycles were used.

Cullet is the main source of glass used in the furnace. This range of compositions seen in the melting and blowing waste most probably reflects a supply network that was dictated by what was available, rather than what was actively sought. This suggests the glassworker may have had to actively manage what he introduced to the melt if he wanted to control the colour and melting properties of each glass batch.

5.3. What was being made?

It is often difficult on glass-working sites to distinguish what was being made from what was brought to the site as cullet, but the distorted vessel wasters at Mancetter suggest a range of utilitarian forms were blown. The vessel wasters match the moils compositionally, indicating that jars, bowls, jugs and containers were produced at the site from recycled cullet (Price 2000, 1; Cool 2003) and both manganese blue-green and antimony manganese recycled compositions are represented throughout the wasters. Bottles do not appear to have been produced,

nor is there evidence for substantial working of colourless high quality glass forms.

5.3.1. The duration of glass-working

The one excavated furnace at Mancetter appears to have been relined at least four times, suggesting glass production was not a single event. There may also have been other furnaces, not found, which were in operation as suggested by the distribution of the waste in two locations, one near a water channel (Cool and Price, unpublished report in ADS).

Further insight into the length of operation may be inferred by the glass compositions represented at the site. Roman glasses produced in Egypt or Syro-Palestine have identifiable compositions, reflecting the local geology of the sands. The supply of specific compositions of glass from these regions also appears to have a finite lifetime (Foster and Jackson 2009; 2010; Jackson and Paynter 2015). Therefore, the circulation of these unadulterated compositions before recycling can help to determine the period and length of operation of a glass facility. As Mancetter has a spread of compositions from manganese to antimony colourless glass, and also green and blue-green glasses with and without manganese, this suggests a lifespan of the complex, which saw different compositions rise or decline. Whilst the exact duration or period of operation cannot be estimated, it does suggest the furnace operated over multiple batches, potentially over an extended period of time in the 2nd century AD. As the pottery industry was long lived, the glass-working installations may also have been operational for part of this time to service the local community.

5.4. Scale of production

The site at Mancetter shows evidence for the relatively limited small-scale nature of glass-working in Britain. The glass furnace is located alongside other high temperature industries and so could utilise shared knowledge of high temperature facilities and fuel. It appears to have been used for multiple glass-working campaigns as it was rebuilt at least four times and a range of glass time-limited glass compositions are represented. No small crucibles or melting pots or evidence of tank fragments (although solidified glass was found on one surviving wall) were recovered, but in either scenario the volume of molten glass would be limited, which in turn would limit what could be produced. Only glass vessels such as the ones seen in the waste material might have been produced rather than windows, which require a higher volume of glass (Wardle *et al.* 2016). The vessels identified in the wasters were utilitarian and predominantly common forms. It is possible therefore that the furnace was not operated continually, but used periodically when glass was needed. Price (2005, 185) suggests glassworkers also may not have been resident, but itinerant, producing vessels at multiple centres that may support the remains at Mancetter.

5.5. Glass-working technology and skill of the glassworker

The debris found at Mancetter suggests blue-green glass was the predominant colour of the products, and that relatively simple utilitarian forms such as jars, bowls and bottles were produced. Blue-green glass or shades of green glass would be the default glass colour when different colours of glass were mixed, suggesting that the glassmakers here may not have segregated different glass colours when making a new batch. Colourless glasses, especially antimony decolourised glass, which typified many high quality tablewares, is relatively rare at Mancetter. Colourless cullet may also have been in short supply. Such colourless glass, even upon remelting, would have required more skill when remelting to retain the colourless hue than a blue-green glass, and either the Mancetter glassmakers were not particularly skilled or there was no demand for high quality tablewares. The colourless glass waste recovered at Mancetter may represent some limited experimentation with colourless glass or the application of colourless glass as decoration (Jackson and Paynter 2021). However, it is more likely that most of the colourless glass was introduced into the batch and became part of the blue-green antimony manganese recycled composition common at the site, potentially added to modify the glass hue, suggesting these glassworkers had some knowledge of glass manipulation to control the colour. It is likely colourless vessels were only produced in a few centres, and these may not typically have been in these regional centres in Britain (Paynter and Jackson 2018).

6. The Mancetter glass-working industry in context

The Mancetter waste glass-working assemblage is one of the largest presently recovered in Britain outside London. It appears to have relied predominantly on recycled glass or at least was using cullet as its raw material for vessel production, which may itself have already been through more than one recycling event. It is possible that production of vessels at the site may have been destined for local consumption only, or alternatively relied upon supply chains developed for the distribution of mortaria. The furnaces may have only been operational periodically when craftspeople were available and there was a demand for glass.

Mancetter is one of a series of small regional glass-working sites in Britain in the 2nd century AD. Others operating in Britain during this period, such as Guildhall Yard, London (2nd century AD), Wildespool, Cheshire (possibly 1st/2nd century AD (May 1900)) and Verulamium (probably mid-2nd century AD (Bayley 1991))

also demonstrate evidence of small-scale melting of glass using cullet. It seems raw glass was not plentiful or readily available. The waste at Mancetter, and at Colchester and Wroxeter, suggests glass was blown into vessels (Price and Cool 1991). However, other British glass-working sites may have been producing window glass for local use as they show no signs of glass-blowing waste e.g., Caistor by Norwich. Production at all of these sites is relatively simple and seems to be unspecialised. The glass-working site at Mancetter, alongside other contemporary and later sites such as Leicester (Jackson and Paynter 2021) and St Algars (Tyson and Lambdin 2014), probably represent a typical picture of small-scale glass-working in Britain outside London.

In London many furnaces have been uncovered, some clustering together, e.g., those in the Upper Walbrook Valley (Shepherd 2015). Some have yielded large volumes of furnace fragments and/or cullet (e.g., Guildhall Yard, Basinghall) (Shepherd 2015). Although these too operated to remelt glass, the structures uncovered are sometimes tank furnaces that could melt much larger quantities in a single firing. The remains at Basinghall Street (also 2nd century AD), part of the Upper Walbrook Valley complex, showed evidence for a minimum of three glass-melting campaigns. The product appears to be tablewares and bottles in different compositions/colours, including manganese blue-green, antimony colourless and manganese colourless (Freestone *et al.* 2016; Shepherd and Wardle 2016, 71–3, 109). Some of these London furnaces, for example Tower Hill and possibly Moorgate, were remelting raw glasses, in addition to cullet (Parnell 1982; Shepherd 2015). The furnaces in London were probably also bringing in cullet from the wider market area; the Guildhall yard dump suggests an accumulation of glass, which is unlikely to have come just from the city (John Shepherd pers. comm). The sites in London appear therefore to be on a supply network that obtained both cullet and, in some cases, unadulterated raw glasses and produced a more extensive range of products and quantity of glassware than other sites presently known in Britain. These glassworks may have had greater access to materials and crafts people who worked colourless glass because of the proximity to the Continent, and also served a more extensive market, including the locally stationed military, who were known as large glass consumers. Shepherd and Wardle (2016, 102, 109) suggest the London furnaces may also have been provisioning hubs for markets elsewhere.

The smaller hub at Mancetter had a greater reliance on the use of recycled glass, and as such probably had a much more limited access to material and possibly craftspeople. Some glassworkers may have been peripatetic, working in London and then moving elsewhere as the market demanded (Price 2005, 185). These glassworkers would produce what was needed at any particular location, only demonstrating higher skill levels when local demand required. Mancetter's glass-working furnaces located in the centre of mortarium production may have allowed some network for distribution of glass in the region, although on a much more limited scale than that of London and with a much more limited range of products, dictated by the local market.

Thus, whilst London furnished its hinterland with a range of glass products, the picture overall of glass-working in Britain – typified by the furnace at Mancetter – was of small scale, fairly low skilled production of utilitarian vessels for a relatively local market. Glassworkers at Mancetter and in Britain generally in the Roman period produced goods to provision a local need.

Acknowledgements

Thanks to Hilary Cool and to the late Jennifer Price of the British Academy Romano British Glass Project for access to the material from Mancetter and their unpublished report and support. Also for photographs of the material (care of Leeds University). John Shepherd is thanked for his insights into the London glass industries, and Mark Taylor and David Hill for their knowledge of furnaces and their operation. The Science and Engineering Research Council are thanked for financial assistance in the form of a PhD grant (SERC 88803864), and Drs J.N. Walsh and S. James of the then NERC ICP–AES facility at Royal Holloway, Egham, for help with chemical analysis of the samples.

Bibliography

Amrein, H. 2001. *L'atelier de verriers d'Avenches: L'artisanat du verre au milieu du 1er siècle après J.-C.*, Cahiers d'Archéologie Romande 87. Aventicum XI, Lausanne.

Atkinson, D. 1929. Caistor excavations 1929, *Norfolk Archaeology* 24, 93–139.

Barag, D. 2005. Alexandrian and Judaean Glass in the Price Edict of Diocletian, *Journal of Glass Studies* 47, 184–6.

Bayley, J. 1991. *Analytical Results for metal and glass-working crucibles from Frere's excavations at Verulamium, Herts*, Ancient Monuments Laboratory Report 68/91. English Heritage, London.

Cool, H.E.M. 2003. Local Production and trade in glass vessels in the British Isles in the first to seventh centuries AD, in D. Foy and M.-D. Nenna (eds) *Echanges et Commerce du Verre dans le Monde Antique*, Monographies Instrumentum 24, Montagnac, 139–45.

Cool, H.E.M. and Jackson, C.M. 2004. Roman vessel glass and glassworking waste, in H. Dalwood and R. Edwards (eds) *Excavations at Deansway, Worcester 1988–9. Romano-British small town to late medieval city*, CBA Research Report 139, York, 439–49.

Cool, H.E.M. and Price, J. unpublished report in ADS. The Roman Glass from Mancetter. Report produced as part of the Romano-British Glass Project. https://archaeologydataservice.ac.uk/archiveDS/archiveDownload?t=arch-3735-1/dissemination/5_Other_finds-Mancetter_Hartshill/Reports/Glass_report-MB/HE7725_glass_report_MB.pdf (last accessed 3-5-2023).

Cottam, S.E. 2018. Developments in Roman Glass Vessels in Italy, France, Britain and the Lower Rhineland c.A.D.40–A.D.110. Unpublished PhD Thesis, Kings College London.

Foster, H. and Jackson, C.M. 2009. The composition of 'naturally coloured' late Roman vessel glass from Britain and the implications for models of glass production and supply, *Journal of Archaeological Science* 36, 189–204.

Foster, H. and Jackson, C.M. 2010. The composition of late Romano-British colourless vessel glass: glass production and consumption, *Journal of Archaeological Science* 37, 3068–80.

Foy, D., Picon, M., Vichy, M. and Thirion-Merle, V. 2003. Caractérisation des verres de la fin de l'Antiquité en Mediterranée occidentale: l'emergence de nouveaux courants commerciaux, in D. Foy and M.-D. Nenna (eds) *Echanges et Commerce du Verre dans le Monde Antique*, Monographies Instrumentum 24, Montagnac, 41–85.

Freestone, I., Gutjahr, M., Kunicki-Goldfinger, J., McDonald, I. and Pike, A. 2016. Composition, technology and origin of the glass from the workshop at Basinghall Street, in A. Wardle and I. Freestone and M. MacKenzie and J. Shepherd, *Glass working on the margins of Roman London. Exacavations at 35, Basinghall Street*, MOLA Monograph 70, London, 75–90.

Hartley, K.F. 1973a. The kilns at Mancetter and Hartshill, Warwickshire, in A. Detsicas (ed.) *Current Research in Romano-British Coarse Pottery*, CBA Research Report 10, Council for British Archaeology, London, 143–7.

Hartley, K.F. 1973b. The marketing and distribution of Mortaria, in A. Detsicas (ed.), *Current Research in Romano-British Coarse Pottery*, CBA Research Report 10, Council for British Archaeology, London, 39–51.

Hochuli-Gysel, A. 2003. L'Aquitaine: Importations et Productions au Ier siècle av. J-C et au Ier siècle ap J.-C., in D. Foy and M.-D. Nenna (eds) *Echanges et Commerce du Verre dans le Monde Antique. Actes du Colloque de l'AFAV Aix-en-Provence et Marseille, 7–9 Juin 2001*, Monographies 'Instrumentum' 24. Editions Monique Mergoil, Montagnac, 177–93.

Isings, C. 1957. *Roman Glass from Dated Finds*, Wolters, Groningen.

Ivanov, M., Cholakova, A. and Gratuze, B. 2021. Glass furnaces from Serdica – and example of Roman practice of glass mixing. *Annales du 21e Congrés de l'Association International pour l'Histoire du verre 3–7 Septembre 2018*, Istanbul, AIHV, Italy.

Jackson, C.M. and Paynter, S. 2015. A Great Big Melting Pot. Patterns of Glass Supply, Consumption and Recycling in Roman Coppergate, York, *Archaeometry* 58, 68–95.

Jackson, C.M. and Paynter, S. 2021. Friends, Romans, Puntymen, lend me your irons, in C. Höpken, B. Birkenhagen and M. Brüggler (eds) *Römische Glasöfen – Befunde, Funde und Rekonstruktionen in Synthese*, Denkmalpflege im Saarland 11, Landesdenkmalamt Saarland, Schiffweiler, 253–77.

Jackson, C.M., Joyner, L., Booth, C.A., Day, P.M., Wager, E.C.W. and Kilikoglou, V. 2003. Roman Glass-Making at Coppergate, York? Analytical Evidence for the Nature of Production, *Archaeometry* 45, 435–56.

Jackson, C.M., Paynter, S., Nenna, M-D. and Degryse, P. 2016. Glassmaking using Natron from el-Barnugi (Egypt); Pliny and the Roman glass industry, *Anthropological and Archaeological Sciences* 10, 1179–91. DOI 10.1007/s12520-016-0447-4.

May, T. 1900. Supposed glass furnaces, in Excavations at Wilderspool, *Transactions of the Historical Society of Lancashire and Cheshire 52*, 32–42.

Nenna, M.-D. 2015. Primary glass workshops in Graeco-Roman Egypt: preliminary report on the excavations of the site of Beni Salama, Wadi Natrun (2003, 2005–9), in J. Bayley, I.C. Freestone and C.M. Jackson (eds) *Glass of the Roman World*, Oxbow Books, Oxford, 1–22.

Parnell, G. 1982. The excavation of the Roman city wall at the Tower of London and Tower Hill, 1954–1976, *Transactions of the London and Middlesex Archaeological Society* 33, 85–133.

Paynter, S. 2008. Experiments in the reconstruction of Roman wood-fired glassworking furnaces: waste products and their formation processes, *Journal of Glass Studies 50*, 271–90.

Paynter, S. and Jackson, C.M. 2016. Re-used Roman Rubbish: a thousand years of recycling glass, *Post-Classical Archaeologies 6*, 31–52.

Paynter, S. and Jackson, C.M. 2018. Clarity and Brilliance: antimony in natron colourless glass. *Archaeological and Anthropological Sciences 11*, 1533–51.

Price, J. 2000. Late Roman Glass Vessels in Britain and Ireland from AD 350 to 410 and Beyond, in J. Price (ed.) *Glass in Britain and Ireland AD 350–1100*, British Museum Occasional Paper No. 127, British Museum, London, 1–31.

Price, J. 2003. Broken bottles and quartz-sand: glass production in Yorkshire and the North in the Roman period, in P. Wilson and J. Price (eds) *Aspects of Industry in Roman Yorkshire and the North*, Oxbow Books, Oxford, 81–93.

Price, J. 2005. Glass-working and glassworkers in cities and towns, in A. MacMahon and J. Price (eds) *Roman working lives and urban living*, Oxbow Books, Oxford, 167–90.

Price, J. and Cool, H.E.M 1991. The evidence for the production of glass in Roman Britain, in D. Foy and G. Sennequier (eds) *Ateliers de verriers de l'Antiquité à la période pré-industrielle. Association Française pour l'Archéologie du Verre*, AFAV, Rouen, 23–30.

Raux, S., Breuil, J.-Y. and Pascal, Y. 2010. Un four de verrier de la toute fin de IIe ap. J.-C. sur le site du 'Parking Jean Jaurès' à Nîmes (Gard, F). Actes des 24e Rencontres de l'A.F.A.V., Fréjus, novembre 2009. 24e Rencontres de l'A.F.A.V., Fréjus, France, 71–9.

Shepherd, J. 2015. A Gazetteer of Glass Working Sites in Roman London, in J. Bayley and I. Freestone and C.M. Jackson, *Glass of the Roman World*, Oxbow Books, Oxford, 33–43.

Shepherd, J. and Wardle, A. 2016. The Basinghall glass in context, in A. Wardle and I. Freestone and M. MacKenzie and J. Shepherd, *Glass working on the margins of Roman London. Excavations at 35, Basinghall Street*, MOLA Monograph 70, London, 91–110.

Silvestri, A. 2008. The coloured glass of Iulia Felix, *Journal of Archaeological Science 35*, 1489–501.

Tyson, R. and Lambdin, C. 2014. Overview of the Roman glass from excavations at St Algar's Farm, Somerset, 2010–2013, *Glass News 36*, 8–11.

Wardle, A., Freestone, I., MacKenzie, M. and Shepherd, J. 2016. *Glass working on the margins of Roman London. Exacavations at 35, Basinghall Street*, MOLA Monograph 70, London.

Warwickshire Historic Environment record 6244. Mancetter Glass Furnace. http://timetrail.warwickshire.gov.uk/detail. aspx?monuid=WA6244 (last accessed 6-1-2017).

Wedepohl, K.H., Gaitzsch, W. and Follmann-Schulz, A.-B. 2003. Glassmaking and Glassworking in Six Roman Factories in the Hambach Forest, Germany. *Annales du 15e Congrès de l'Association Internationale pour l'Histoire du Verre*. New York, Corning 2001, Nottingham, 56–61.

Fifty years (or perhaps 49) of the Study Group for Roman Pottery

Christopher Young

Abstract

This paper is a personal and impressionistic review of the first half-century of the Study Group for Roman Pottery. The Group developed out of a meeting in March 1971 to plan a Council for British Archaeology (CBA) conference on recent work on Romano-British pottery. The first annual meeting of the Group was held at Colchester in January 1972. The early years of the Group were led by Graham Webster, supported by Alec Detsicas but, since 1986, it has been led by a committee and elected officers. Apart from its annual meetings, the Group has undertaken, or supported, many other initiatives and provided a forum for the development of Roman pottery studies and of expertise among practitioners, whether professional or non-professional.

The Group's growth and development have paralleled that of archaeology as a whole. In the next 50 years, the Group must continue to champion the need for expertise and the fundamental importance of pottery evidence to the wider archaeological community, and to knowledge of our past. As part of this process, it would be good to develop a better understanding of its history, starting with the collection and securing of its archives as the basis for further historical work.

1. Introduction

This is a revised version of a paper originally delivered at the 2021 virtual conference of the Study Group for Roman Pottery at the invitation of the organisers. It is a personal recollection of the first 50 years of the Study Group, based on my memory (principally of the first and last decades as in between I was preoccupied with other tasks) and input from other sources. I have only been able to do this with help from many people who have provided anecdotes and memories, occasional documents, pictures, and have almost completed my electronic run of Newsletters from 1988 onwards with very few gaps, to all of whom I am most grateful. Any errors in the paper are entirely the responsibility of the author. This paper is therefore in no way a definitive history of the Group and this remains to be written.

2. Beginnings of the Study Group

The Study Group for Romano British Coarse Pottery was conceived in March 1971 near Wolverhampton and born in January 1972 in Essex. Its age has been uncertain ever since, celebrating its 21st anniversary in 1992 at Lincoln, its 40th in Glasgow in 2012, and now, its 50th in the

ether in 2021. It is the oldest by a few years of the three specialist archaeological pottery groups in the UK.

The origins of the Study Group lie in a weekend meeting organised by Graham Webster to plan a conference on recent research on Romano-British coarse pottery. Graham was of course one of the outstanding figures of Romano-British archaeology and one of his many special interests was pottery. The meeting was arranged by the Extra-Mural Department of the University of Birmingham at the request of the Iron Age and Roman Research Committee of the CBA (Webster 1973, 162 fn1).

The meeting was held at Pendrell Hall, near Wolverhampton, which was, at that time, an extramural study centre of the University of Birmingham. The 16 attendees are listed in Table 1, based on discussions with survivors of those who were there. One name, however, is uncertain and it has not been possible to locate any definitive list. The participants were drawn from across those working then on Romano-British pottery and ranged from those with long experience to those who were mere neophytes, such as the present author. I had, I think, met Graham Webster once, and possibly Brian and/or Kay Hartley because my supervisor was Sheppard Frere. Otherwise, Roman pottery was still very new to me, as a research

Table 1. Attendees at Pendrell Hall meeting 1972.

1	Joanna Bird
2	Geoff Dannell
3	Maggi Darling
4	Alec Detsicas
5	Ray Farrar
6	John Gillam
7	Brian Hartley
8	Kay Hartley
9	Val Rigby
10	Vivien Swan
11	Malcolm Todd
12	Graham Webster
13	Peter Webster
14	John Peter Wild
15	Christopher Young
16	? Rachael Shaw

student just 18 months into my grant and having spent most of that time in the Ashmolean Museum pottery store.

In the event, the CBA conference was planned very quickly and, to quote Vivien Swan:

[...] following an initiative from Graham Webster, the group spent the rest of the weekend discussing the future of Roman pottery studies in Britain. The participants agreed that there was a universal desire for a gazetteer of pottery kilns and kiln sites in Roman Britain, and agreed to establish a small specialist seminar group of those actively engaged in research on Roman pottery, to act as a forum for debate and facilitate the exchange of information. A small list of serious researchers was compiled and a week-end colloquium was planned. Graham Webster was to act as Chairman of the group. Alec [Detsicas] volunteered to act as Secretary (Swan 2004, 129).

The 1972 CBA Conference took place at New College, Oxford, from 24–26 March 1972. The proceedings were published very rapidly as a summary of the current state of research on Romano-British pottery (Detsicas 1973).

3. Annual meetings

Even before the Oxford conference, the first meeting of the fledgling Group had happened over the first weekend of January 1972 at the University of Essex in Colchester. There were 31 attendees accommodated in one of the tower blocks at the University (along with a number of mice who appeared to come with the accommodation). The programme for the weekend (Fig. 1) contained sessions of lectures, a civic reception at Colchester Castle, a museum visit to examine pottery, and a business meeting.

Topics discussed at the business meeting (Fig. 2) included an update on work in hand on a colour chart for the description of pottery, the revision of the CBA Student's Guide to Romano-British coarse pottery, the need for a symposium between pottery specialists and geologists, the development of a collection of coarse pottery at the London Institute of Archaeology, and Vivien Swan's work on kilns. Many of these have become hardy perennials in the work and discussions of the Group.

Since then, the annual conference has been a key part of the Group's activities and it has generally followed the shape of the first Colchester meeting: dissemination of knowledge through lectures, handling pottery (sometimes even at breakfast), discussion of various projects in the business meetings, a visit to a museum and/or a relevant archaeological site, and socialising. Almost all the comments received about the history of the Group have been about the conferences, which clearly play a great part in members' experience and memories.

It has taken some effort to develop the definitive list of annual conferences (Table 2) as no one list existed and there were differing views among the various members consulted. The conference has been held in all areas of England and twice in both Cardiff and Glasgow. Other places visited twice include Carlisle, Chichester, Norwich, Nottingham and Worcester, whilst only London has hosted three meetings. The Group has ventured abroad to the Netherlands, Belgium and northern France. The annual meeting remains a thriving part of the Group's activities though in some years it is a one-day conference with the option of an overnight stay. There have also been periods when regional meetings have flourished.

4. Organisation

In its early years, the Group was informal in its structure; led by Graham Webster and with all the administration done by Alec Detsicas, an archaeologist and schoolmaster in Kent. For some years a strict rule was applied that new members had to be invited or approved by other members. Even in those years, membership was drawn from a wide spectrum of academics, researchers, museum curators, staff from archaeological units, consultants and other specialists, and amateurs, some of whom were experts in their own right. Eventually this situation changed as the numbers of people working on Roman pottery increased and the Group has long been open to anybody with an interest in the subject, with current membership standing at around 150.

The character of the Group has changed through the first 50 years of its existence, along with British archaeology as a whole. In the early days most members of the Group knew many other members, often over long periods. As numbers increased so relationships within the group changed and developed. The study of Roman pottery became a matter of interest and livelihood for many

STUDY GROUP FOR ROMANO-BRITISH COARSE POTTERY

Colchester Seminar, 7-9 January, 1972

P r o g r a m m e

Friday, 7 January: p.m.   Dinner. (6.45 p.m.)

Reception by the Mayor of Colchester
at the Castle.

Saturday, 8 January: a.m.   M.R. Hull: The Colchester Kilns.

(Breakfast: 8.30 a.m.)   Coffee (10.30 a.m.)

K.T. Greene: Sources of pre-Flavian fine
wares in Colchester.

Lunch. (12.30 p.m.)

p.m.   Visit to Colchester & Essex Museum.   2.00

Dinner. (7.00 p.m.)

G. Dannell: The native potter Indivixus.

J.P. Wild: The Longthorpe Kilns.

Sunday, 9 January: a.m.   P. Woods: The Rushden Kilns.

(Breakfast: 8.30 a.m.)   Coffee. (10.30 p.m.)

D. Peacock: Amphorae in late Roman Britain.

Lunch. (12.30 p.m.)

Business Meeting.

M. Brassington: The Derby Racecourse Kilns.

Tea (3.30 p.m.)

Dear Member,

I enclose the programme of the Colchester seminar. Accommodation
has been booked at the Eddington Tower (Flats 4 and 5; single rooms), University
of Essex, Wivenho Park, Colchester, Essex; the charge will be £3.50 per day, with
an additional charge of 20p for coffee/tea. I suggest arrival not later than 6.15
p.m. Please enquire at the Information Centre whence you will be directed to the
accommodation tower.

Looking forward to seeing you,

Sincerely,

20.xii.71

Figure 1. Programme for the first SGRP meeting at Colchester January 1972 (with thanks to John Peter and Felicity Wild for providing the document).

STUDY GROUP FOR ROMANO-BRITISH COARSE POTTERY

MINUTES of the Business Meeting held on January 9th, 1972, at the University of Essex, Colchester.

1. The Accounts for 1971 were presented and accepted.

2. It was reported that work was in progress towards the publication of a colour chart suitable for use in the description of coarse pottery. Dr. D.P.S. Peacock pointed out that the identification of mineral grains was essential and that he had devised a key for the use of students at Southampton University which may be suitably published. Further progress will be reported at the next conference when arrangements will be made for the topic to be fully discussed.

   The C.B.A. Student's Guide on Romano-British Coarse Pottery is being revised, and Dr. G.W. Webster said that comments were invited; it was suggested that a glossary of continental terms should be included, and Miss C. Johns kindly agreed to undertake its compilation.

   Mr G.B. Dannell stressed the need for the scientific analysis of known kiln groups, and the need for integrated research projects to avoid unnecessary duplication.

   It was felt that it would be of great advantage if a symposium could be arranged for archaeologists and geologists interested in coarse-pottery studies, and Mr. C. Young agreed to enquire into the possibility that the Oxford Laboratory might be interested in organising it.

   Some progress had been made in the collection of coarse pottery at the Institute of Archaeology, University of London, and individual contributions of material would be welcome.

   Progress has also been made in the compilation of a check-list of kiln-groups in museums and private collections, and Mrs. V.G. Swan is compiling a list of known kiln materials on the basis of the O.S. card index.

   Dr. G.W. Webster reported on the question of a possible publication of stratified groups from published excavation reports. Some progress has been made, though difficulties concerned with printing have been met; it was agreed to explore this matter further.

3. It was agreed that an invitation should be extended to a number of scholars to be associated with the Study Group, though not as full members, and Dr. G.W. Webster undertook to approach Professor S.S. Frere, Professor W.F. Grimes and Mr. F.H. Thompson.

   It was further agreed to invite Messrs. B. Barr, G.C. Boon and A.B. Sumpter to become Group members.

4. It was reported that advance bookings for the C.B.A. Oxford Conference were very promising, and members were urged to apply in good time.

5. It was agreed to hold the next Conference at Cardiff in January 1973.

                                              A. P. Detsicas.
                                              (Hon. Secretary.)

Figure 2. Minutes of the Business Meeting at the first annual SGRP meeting, January 1972 (with thanks to John Peter and Felicity Wild for providing the document).

Table 2. Definitive list of annual meetings.

Pendrell Hall (Wolverhampton)	1971
Colchester	1972
Cardiff	1973
York	1974
Winchester	1975
Preston Montfort	1976
Alnwick Castle	1977
London	1978
Norwich	1979
Chester	1980
Cirencester	1981
Nottingham	1982
Exeter	1983
Knuston Hall (Wellingborough)	1984
Leicester	1985
Newcastle	1986
Clacton-on-Sea/Colchester	1987
Glasgow	1988
Southampton	1989
Lancaster	1990
Swansea	1991
Lincoln	1992
Birmingham	1993
Durham	1994
Chichester	1995
Hull	1996
Ipswich	1997
Arras	1998
Carlisle	1999
Writtle College (Chelmsford)	2000
Liverpool	2001
Winchester	2002
Tyne and Wear Museums (Wallsend)	2003
London	2004
Worcester	2005
Ghent	2006
Cardiff	2007
Cambridge	2008
Chichester	2009
Nottingham	2010
Amsterdam	2011
Glasgow	2012
London	2013
Worcester	2013

(Continued)

Reading	2014
Norwich	2015
Peterborough	2016
Carlisle	2017
Oxford	2018
Atherstone	2019
None	2020
Zoom (Newcastle University)	2021
Leicester (hybrid)	2022
Milton Keynes (hybrid)	2023

Table 3. Presidents of the SGRP

Vivien Swan	1986–90
Val Rigby	1990–3
Paul Bidwell	1993–6
Maggi Darling	1996–9
Rob Perrin	1999–2003
Steven Willis	2003–6
Roberta Tomber	2006–9
Jane Evans	2009–12
Paul Booth	2012–15
Christopher Young	2015–18
Rob Perrin	2018–22
Alice Lyons	2022–

more people, often working in commercial archaeology, and its pressures and disciplines have influenced those working on pottery.

By the mid-1980s, increasing membership meant that it was no longer possible to manage the Group so informally. The result was the 'formalisation' of the Group with the adoption of a constitution and the election of a President, Secretary, Treasurer and Committee members, who work hard to manage the Group's business. The first president was Vivien Swan (1943–2009) who served from 1986 to 1990 (see Table 3 for list of presidents). From the formalisation in 1985 (and indeed previously), Vivien was a leading personality within the Group, and highly influential. Her energy and determination to get things done achieved much. A further development was the production of the Newsletter, officially from 1988. The Committee has expanded over the years with new roles, and since 2019, the Group has been a registered charity.

5. Achievements of the Group

While the annual meeting is the major occasion in its programme, the Group has carried out many other activities. A selection of what has been achieved in the last 50 years includes the pottery colour chart published in

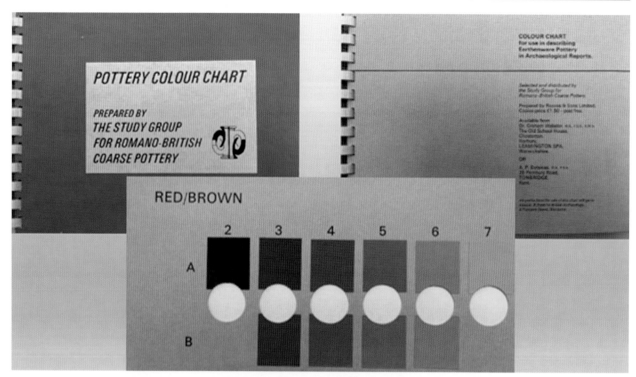

Figure 3. Pottery Colour Chart 1973.

1973 (Fig. 3) as an aid to pottery descriptions, although, sadly, the colours proved to be too pure and bright for most pots. There was input to the third edition of the interim revision of *Romano-British coarse pottery: a student's guide* (Webster 1976), and the Group also worked towards a final full revision, which has never been completed.

The Group has also branched out in many other directions to support the study of Roman pottery and those who work on it. The Group has acted on behalf of Roman pottery specialists in discussions with the Directorate of Ancient Monuments and Historic Buildings, then with English Heritage, and now with Historic England. A good example of this were the discussions on the Fulford/ Huddleston report on the state of Romano-British pottery studies (Fulford and Huddleston 1991).

The Group has worked on guidance documents, beginning with *Guidelines for the processing and publication of Roman pottery from excavations* (Young 1980), guidance on archiving Roman pottery (Darling 1994), and leading, most recently, to *A Standard for Pottery Studies in Archaeology* (Barclay *et al.* 2016), produced jointly by the Prehistoric Ceramics Research Group, the Study Group for Roman Pottery, and the Medieval Pottery Research Group. The Group started discussions of a national fabric reference collection at the Colchester meeting in 1972, and the online version of the *National Roman Fabric Reference Collection* (Tomber and Dore 1998) is now freely accessible on the Group's website.

The Group has also developed research strategies for Roman pottery. The first *Research Framework for the*

Study of Romano-British Pottery was produced in 1997, following two years of work (Willis 1997). Following updates in 2002 (Willis 2002) and 2004 (Willis 2004), Rob Perrin prepared *A Research Strategy and Updated Agenda for the Study of Roman Pottery in Britain* in 2011 (Perrin 2011). The Group has also taken responsibility for digitising the record of known Roman kiln sites in Britain first compiled by Vivien Swan (1984) and periodically updating it with new discoveries (see https:// romankilns.net).

Dissemination of information is another vital task performed by the Group. This is done through the website (https://romanpotterystudy.org.uk), and an electronic newsletter, both of which have become increasingly effective over the years. As noted above the website now houses the online version of the *National Roman Fabric Reference Collection* and other useful resources. The most recent addition is the link to the website of the *Kay Hartley Mortarium Archive Project*, developed by the Group and housed by the Archaeology Data Service (ADS). This will be enormously useful to anyone who works regularly with stamped mortaria.

Most significantly, in 1986, the Study Group launched the *Journal of Roman Pottery Studies*, which is now up to Volume 20. The journal is peer reviewed and has achieved European Reference Index for the Humanities (ERIH) PLUS status. Some volumes have been devoted to just one site or topic, such as amphorae, while others have published a wide range of articles dealing with Roman pottery and production sites. There has been periodic work on the development of pottery bibliographies published in successive volumes of the *Journal*. The development of the *Journal* is another major achievement for the Group and thanks are due to its successive editors.

6. Conclusion

This paper is, as stated at the outset, a personal and impressionistic view of the development of the Group over the last 50 years. The Group began in response to the need to gain recognition of the significance of Roman pottery at a time when archaeology was expanding out of its traditional homes – academia, museums, and local societies – with the growth of rescue archaeology. It was also a time when new ideas were gaining ground on the usefulness of Roman pottery for more than just dating deposits. There was a need to make others aware of the potentials of Roman pottery and to ensure that the specialists existed to exploit that potential.

The Group's growth and development have paralleled that of archaeology as a whole. Many of the problems are still there albeit in different forms. There is still the need to convince others of the importance of pottery, to develop pottery expertise among those working in the modern world of commercial archaeology, and to disseminate information and knowledge. In the next 50 years, the Group will change and develop further and will, it is hoped, continue to champion the need for expertise and the fundamental importance of pottery evidence to the wider archaeological community and to knowledge of our past.

As well as looking forward, it is also necessary to look backwards at the history of the Group. What has happened in the past has helped to shape the Group and its activities in the present and will continue to do so into the future. At the moment our past is not well understood in any detail. This paper does not fulfil that need, as it is essentially the personal views of one individual drawing on the memories of others and on some documentation. From at least 1988 onwards, the Newsletters provide a great deal of information, but it has not yet been possible to find one complete run of them. There may be earlier newsletters which have not yet been located. Some archives of the Group do survive and there is an urgent need to evaluate and catalogue these and to collect or copy any material in the hand of members of the Group to include in the archive. There would also be merit in recording the views and memories of long-term members and more recent of the Group. There is a need to provide secure storage for any archives the Group does have. Doing so would provide the basis for writing a more thorough history of the Group's development.

Bibliography

Barclay, A., Knight, D., Booth, P., Evans, J., Brown, D. H., Wood, PCRG, SGRP, and MPRG 2016. *A Standard for Pottery Studies in Archaeology*, [England]: Medieval Pottery Research Group on behalf of the Prehistoric Ceramics Research Group, the Study Group for Roman Pottery and the Medieval Pottery Research Group.

Darling, M. (ed.) 1994. *Guidelines for the Archiving of Roman Pottery*, Study Group for Roman Pottery, London.

Detsicas, A. (ed.) 1973. *Current Research in Romano-British Coarse Pottery*, CBA Research Report 10, London.

Fulford, M.G. and Huddleston, K. 1991. *The current state of Romano-British pottery studies*, English Heritage Occasional Paper 1, London.

Perrin, R. 2011. *A Research Strategy and Updated Agenda for the Study of Roman Pottery in Britain*. Study Group for Roman Pottery Occasional Paper No. 1.

Swan, V. 1984. *The Pottery Kilns of Roman Britain*, Royal Commission on Historical Monuments Supplementary Series 5, London.

Swan, V. 2004. Alexander Peter Detsicas, MA, D Litt, FSA, a ceramic perspective, *Journal of Roman Pottery Studies* 11, 129.

Tomber, R. and Dore, J. 1998. *The National Roman Fabric Reference Collection: a Handbook*, Museum of London Archaeological Service Monograph 2. https://romanpotterystudy.org.uk/nrfrc/base/index.php (last accessed 25 August 2023).

Webster, G. 1973. Summing Up, in Detsicas 1973, 161–2.

Webster, G. (ed.) 1976. *Romano-British Coarse pottery: a student's guide*, CBA Research Report 6, 3rd edition, London.

Willis, S. (ed.) 1997. *Research Frameworks for the Study of Roman Pottery*, Study Group for Roman Pottery.

Willis, S. (ed.) 2002. *Research Frameworks for the Study of Roman Pottery*, rev edn, Study Group for Roman Pottery.

Willis, S. 2004. The Study Group for Roman Pottery: Research Framework Document for the Study of Roman Pottery in Britain, 2004, *Journal of Roman Pottery Studies* 11, 1–17.

Young, C. (ed.) 1980. *Guidelines for the processing and publication of Roman pottery from excavations*, Directorate of Ancient Monuments and Historic Buildings Occasional Report 4, London.

Article 3: Reflections on the past and considerations for the future on the objectives of the SGRP

Fiona Seeley

Abstract

This paper is a personal reflection on the support and strengths of the Study Group as I have experienced them since I joined in the early 1990s and how I see this aligns with its objectives, in particular those of Article 3 of the Constitution. With an emphasis on the open and inclusive nature of the organisation, this paper will evidence some of the tangible contributions it has made to the study of Roman pottery and its importance for the future especially in regard to people entering the profession.

My initial response to Eniko's request for a paper on my 'personal experiences, memories, and any thoughts on where the Group might be in the future' was one of hilarity on remembering (mostly) unscheduled events from attending SGRP conferences for the past 29 years. Once I had recovered my composure, I realised that my overwhelming memory of being a member of the Group and of years of attendance at the annual conferences is one of enjoyment, support and an egalitarian openness by a genuinely diverse and immensely knowledgeable community of individuals who are passionate about their subject and sharing their knowledge. In this paper I would like to show some examples of that inclusivity and how it is manifested through the object of the SGRP Constitution (Article 3) (SGRP 2022).

The object of the Study Group as defined in the 2022 revised edition of the Constitution is:

> To promote and encourage the general education of the public in the study of ceramics, to promote Roman pottery studies, disseminate the results, and further the appreciation of Roman pottery across all possible audiences.

So, this objective has four elements that I would like to explore in more detail, showing examples of how the Study Group has fulfilled these in its activities and ways of operating.

All four of these elements are exemplified in the SGRP website and I am only going to mention a few items here of the multiple resources available there that are essential for anyone interested in the subject. The website is often how people first encounter the group and where they seek guidance on the study of Roman ceramics. There are an ever-increasing number of resources for all stakeholders irrespective of what brings them to the study of Roman pottery. As part of its remit to promote Roman pottery studies over the years, the Group has produced or jointly produced a number of Guidelines that visitors will now find online. I think it is important to stress that these are the Guidelines for our profession, as with the other ceramic interest groups the SGRP sets the standards for this discipline. One of the most recent examples of this is the publication, *A Standard for Pottery Studies in Archaeology*, jointly produced by the Study Group with the Prehistoric Ceramics Research Group and the Medieval Pottery Research Group (Barclay *et al.* 2016). Funded by Historic England, this is for use by all ceramicists working on excavated and survey collected material whether they be from community groups, universities or commercial units. With the Study Group, you have an organisation that has a very broad membership that it actively encourages but is also one that produces professional technical guidelines for the industry.

Included in the links on the website is one to the digitised gazetteer of *The Pottery Kilns of Roman Britain* (Swan 1984) that is the result of an ongoing Study Group project to make this important work available to a wider audience and update the resource as new kiln sites are discovered. Increasingly, the website is either actively involved in creating or facilitating access to essential resources, many of which are out of print, such as the aforementioned kilns volume or the *National Roman Fabric Reference Collection* (Tomber and Dore 1998). It is not that long ago that if one was interested in studying

Roman pottery they would need to amass a large library of books and journals, the most popular of which would quickly sell out due to short print runs. The Study Group's utilisation of the potential of online resources meant that far more people can access key resources at no cost.

The egalitarian philosophy of the Group is seen in the membership policy as stated on the Study Group website:

> Membership is open to all those interested in the study of Roman Pottery, whether actively working in, researching, interpreting or teaching the subject of Roman ceramics – both professionals and amateurs.

Membership does not require you to be nominated by an existing member or to have your membership approved by a committee (though in the past, as with other bodies and societies that took themselves seriously, this had been a condition prior to c. 1990). For a modest annual cost anyone interested in the study of Roman pottery can join. In the past, there have been a few examples of demonstrating a hierarchy in the Group. For example, at the 25th anniversary conference at Hull (1996) there was a strict seating plan at a horseshoe-shaped table based on how long you had been at the Group with those with the longest service at the middle and those who had most recently joined at the ends – you can see that Louise Rayner and myself are just hanging on the end there, giggling with the single glass of wine we were all offered for the occasion (Fig. 1).

In 2004, following a proposal and vote at the Group's AGM, an annual prize was established – the John Gillam Prize – named after one of the founders of the Group. The eligibility for this prize is broad and encompasses all published and unpublished work as specified on the website:

> A wide range of work that has had an impact on pottery found in Roman Britain and the Continent is eligible, so long as it was completed within the last two years. Nominations can include pottery reports (both published and grey literature), site reports, monographs, synthetic studies, websites, student dissertations, digital projects, theses and so on. Any nomination must highlight specific aspects of Roman pottery from a technological, regional or thematic perspective.

To date a total of 16 prizes have been awarded. Examining the Gillam Prize by publication type it is interesting to note the range of avenues that are represented with only half being either traditional hard copy books or journal articles and online resources increasingly apparent (Fig. 2).

If we look at the recipients, although half are pottery specialists working commercially or in museums, four have been awarded to students for their academic work (Fig. 3). This is important not only to have their work recognised for its merit and contribution to the discipline, but also to help those researchers who may want to develop a career in ceramic studies and do not have access to those platforms that established specialists have to disseminate

Figure 1. 25th Study Group Conference celebratory dinner table plan (no scale).

their work and build their reputations. I have been very fortunate in my career to be trained by very experienced specialists and to have had the time to develop my skills surrounded by a team of ceramicists of all periods. Although there have been notable exceptions such as the Chartered Institute for Archaeologists finds bursaries, which addressed loss of skills within the industry and the advent of workplace initiatives such as the Trailblazer Apprenticeships (Institute for Apprenticeships), there are limited opportunities for early career entrants to get the relevant dedicated training and experience to further their careers. Additionally, even if early career entrants do get opportunities to pursue their professions in a commercial environment as a trainee, they may not necessarily be working alongside specialists within their preferred historic period. This is where the Study Group is crucial to provide a professional support network.

The website can arguably come under the objective of disseminating the results but also there is the *Journal of Roman Pottery Studies*. Included in the modest annual membership fee, the journal was first published in 1986 and a total of 19 volumes have now been produced. The level of professionalism and high academic quality is maintained through peer review and the Editorial Board in addition to the journal now having achieved ERIH PLUS status (European Reference Index for the Humanities and Social Sciences). The format is wide-ranging, with most volumes consisting of short papers on various topics from contributors from the UK and abroad, some of whom are members of the Study Group but not exclusively; and some volumes are single topic reports such as Volume 8 on the Roman pottery from excavations at *Durobrivae* (Perrin 1999) and Volume 9 on pottery from Rossington Bridge (Buckland *et al.* 2001). There are volumes comprising papers from conferences such as Volume 10 based on a two-day conference on amphorae held at the Museum

of London in 1994 (Plouviez 2003) and resource-based volumes such as the mortarium bibliography for Roman Britain (Hartley and Tomber 2006). Currently volumes 1–12 are open access on the Group's website with further editions to follow in due course.

The last element of Article 3 is to further the appreciation of Roman pottery across all possible audiences, the main conduit for which is, arguably, through the Group's conferences. I think the first SGRP conference I attended was at Durham in 1994, so my recollections are from the last 29 years. However, despite the friendliness experienced at the conferences, it took me a few years to pluck up the courage to actually give a paper and I have to admit that I was terrified, which is something I always recall when hearing papers given by new entrants to the Group. My paper was met with kind comments and helpful advice and although I won't be mentioning many of the Group by name in this paper, I will make an exception here for the late Vivien Swan. I was probably not alone in finding Vivien to be formidable in her knowledge and passion for her subject, so was not a little apprehensive when she put up her hand to comment on my lecture, especially as the subject was a kiln site, a topic of study in which she could arguably be seen as the foremost expert. Vivien could not have been kinder or more generous in her advice and she continued her support over the years when I later wrote the site publication. I offer this as an example of how the Study Group provides the opportunity for specialists starting their careers to be supported by the collective experience and knowledge of the members.

Open to members and non-members, each conference is organised and managed by individual members of the Group and with an understanding that, to ensure that the event is as affordable and accessible as possible, the attendance fees are kept to a minimum. Over the years the cost of the conference has been substantially lower than other archaeology conferences and this is in keeping with the SGRP's membership policy of

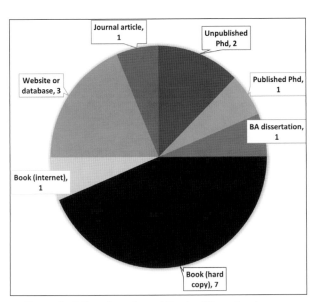

Figure 2. Gillam Prize by publication/dissemination type.

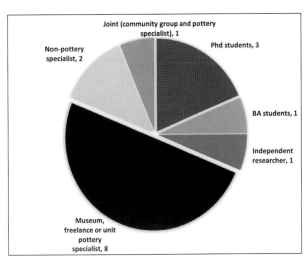

Figure 3. Gillam Prize recipients.

embracing all interested parties. There has always been the understanding that many of the attendees will be paying for the event themselves and not be supported by an employer. Additionally, there is a lower rate for students and the Graham Webster bursaries (also initiated following a vote at the AGM in 2004). These two bursaries, named after one of the founders of the Study Group, provide 50% of conference fees and 50% of travel costs up to a maximum of £100. The eligibility requirements are quite broad and recognise the breadth of the audience as they are open to students, part-time researchers, those who are retired or between posts. The modest cost of the conferences belies the high standard of papers, visits and events. The residential conference includes a trip, usually on the Saturday afternoon, highly enjoyable and frequently exhausting. These visits anchor the conference in the history and archaeology of the region and give context to the talks. I am sure I am not alone in looking forward to us resuming these trips and peering through a rain-splattered coach window, trying to ascertain if the ditch the cow is standing in is one of the Antonine Wall earthworks.

As well as the outings, the schedules included wine receptions held in museums or in town halls such as at Arras in 1998, an audience and welcome by the Mayor of Glasgow in 2012, Roman kiln construction and firings such as at Nottingham in 2010 (Fig. 4) and Carlisle in 2017 (Fig. 5). There is also the care and attention to detail such as at the Norwich conference when one of the tours was to one of the Saxon shore forts, Burgh Castle; our walk to the monument was structured so that we only saw the very impressive remains once we turned through a gap in a hedge, so you got the full impact of the structure. Nice bit of theatrical staging!

By convention these two-day residential conferences would be held annually and in different parts of the United Kingdom and abroad (Arras, Ghent and Amsterdam). Over the last few years this format has been adapted to a biennial residential conference alternating with a single day event in the intervening year. This change reflected the increasing costs of the conference facilities, especially those at universities and the amount of work that is required to put together a successful conference. During the late 1980s and 1990s there were also twice-yearly meetings held by the Regional Groups that allowed for pottery viewings and papers concentrating on local sites and ceramic industries. These meetings, usually held on Saturdays, were well attended and were open to all interested parties.

In 2019 Jane Evans and Jane Faiers organised the very successful conference in Atherstone, which was centred on a collaborative project on the Mancetter-Hartshill Roman pottery kilns archive (WAAS and Hartley 2020). The project and conference were inspired by the enthusiasm

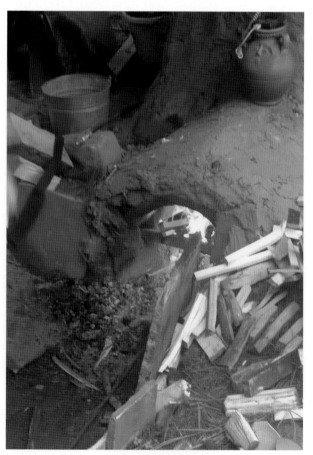

Figure 4. Experimental Roman kiln firing by Beryl Hines at the Nottingham SGRP conference 2010.

Figure 5. Experimental Roman kiln firing by Graham Taylor at the Carlisle SGRP conference 2017.

and energy of the Atherstone Civic Society, Friends of Atherstone Heritage and, in particular, Margaret Hughes, who presented a paper. Many of the local community attended this event. We have always had members of local archaeology or community groups attend the conferences and help us with opening facilities or laying out pottery, but I think this is the first when they were very much at the centre of the event. Looking to the future this model could be one that the SGRP should embrace and develop so that we are open to new audiences by including them from the inception of the conference.

Most recently, in 2021, as a response to the pandemic, we had our first online-only conference through Newcastle University's platform, and in 2022 at Leicester there was an option to attend online or in person. As I mentioned earlier there is a real sense of enjoyment to these meetings of the Group especially the residential conferences and I know that I am not the only person to look forward to them but also realise having been involved in their organisation just how much time it takes to create a successful, enjoyable and informative conference.

I hope that I have demonstrated some of the ways in which the SGRP has fulfilled the promise of Article 3, how it has developed and adapted over the last 50 years to meet financial and societal changes as well as those within the archaeological sector. Indeed, how some of the initiatives, such as those seen at the Atherstone conference, could be developed in the future for our Group to continue to become more inclusive and embrace different audiences. Despite the huge changes over the last 50 years within all areas of the archaeology sector – community, commercial, research and museums – the Study Group has remained relevant, open and welcoming in its 'objective to promote and encourage the general education of the public in the study of ceramics, to promote Roman pottery studies, disseminate the results, and further the appreciation of Roman pottery across all possible audiences'.

Bibliography

Barclay, A., Knight, D., Booth, P., Evans, J., Brown, D. H., Wood, PCRG, SGRP, and MPRG 2016. *A Standard for Pottery Studies in Archaeology*, [England]: Medieval Pottery Research Group on behalf of the Prehistoric Ceramics Research Group, the Study Group for Roman Pottery and the Medieval Pottery Research Group.

Buckland, P.C., Hartley, K.F. and Rigby, V. 2001. The Roman pottery kilns of Rossington Bridge excavations 1956–1961, *Journal of Roman Pottery Studies* 9.

Hartley, K.F. and Tomber, R. 2006. A mortarium bibliography for Roman Britain, *Journal of Roman Pottery Studies* 13.

Perrin, J.R. 1999. Roman pottery from excavations at and near to the Roman small town of Durobrivae, Water Newton, Cambridgeshire, 1956–8, *Journal of Roman Pottery Studies* 8.

Plouviez, J. (ed.) 2003. Amphorae in Britain and the western Empire, *Journal of Roman Pottery Studies* 10.

SGRP 2022. https://sgrp-wordpress-offload.s3.eu-west-2.amazonaws.com/wp-content/uploads/2023/01/01171227/SGRP_Constitution_June_2022.pdf. [accessed March 2023].

Swan, V.G. 1984. *The Pottery kilns of Roman Britain*, Institute for Apprenticeships https://www.instituteforapprenticeships.org/developing-new-apprenticeships/trailblazer-group/. [accessed March 2023].

Tomber, R. and Dore, J.N. 1998. *The national Roman fabric reference collection*, MoLAS Monograph Series 2, London.

Worcestershire Archive and Archaeology Service and Hartley, K.F. (2020) *Mancetter-Hartshill Roman Pottery Kilns Archive Project* [data-set]. York: Archaeology Data Service [distributor] https://doi.org/10.5284/1079019. [accessed March 2023].

Why study Roman pottery? Surely the men have done it all already!

Kayt Hawkins

Abstract

The study of Roman Britain has historically been dominated by male academics, whilst several recent sector-wide surveys have shown that the study of Roman artefacts is female dominated. With the arrival of the 50th anniversary of the Study Group for Roman Pottery's foundation it seemed appropriate to delve into this apparent gender division in more detail. A survey was sent out to all SGRP members in 2021, to gain a snapshot of gender equity in the type of work SGRP members undertake, and who, how and where that research is disseminated. These results were first presented at the 50th anniversary conference, and this paper elaborates further on the survey findings by exploring some of the common perceptions, and potential structural biases, within British archaeology that perpetuate inequality in terms of gender across the profession, and specifically Roman pottery studies.

1. Introduction

The origins of this paper lie in a passing comment from the prominent social anthropologist, Sheila Kitzinger, who asked the author why she studied Roman pottery when, 'Surely the men have done it all already?'

This exchange occurred a decade before the SGRP anniversary conference, held in 2021. On reflection it is painfully easy to see why this would be a common perception of not just Roman pottery studies but archaeology in general; alongside the classic stereotypical white, male, archaeologist beloved of the film industry (Killgrove 2021). Even within our own discipline this bias is acknowledged when statements like the following have appeared in print:

> …Finally, the vast majority of Romano-British archaeologists in this century have had one thing in common: we have been men. (Jones 1987, 95)

Certainly, men have traditionally been more visible as archaeologists, and the quote above was published three years prior to the publication of *Public Policy Guidance note 16 on archaeology and planning* (PPG 16) (Department of Environment 1990) and the ensuing significant changes within commercial archaeological practice in the UK (Bryant and Willis 2016). The number of women entering the archaeological profession has been steadily increasing over the past two decades, however, we know that women are still to be found in larger proportions of certain study areas, and within particular employment divisions,

pottery studies being one of these (Aitchison 1999; 2014; 2017; Aitchison and Edwards 2003; 2008; Aitchison and Rocks-Macqueen 2013; Aitchison *et al.* 2021).

With the arrival of the 50th anniversary of the Study Group for Roman Pottery's foundation, it seemed appropriate to delve into this question of gender in more detail. The paper presented at the conference and now elaborated on here set out to explore gender equity in the type of commercial and academic work SGRP members undertake, and by whom, how and where that research is disseminated. As highly academically and technically skilled professional pottery specialists (many of whom hold accreditation with the Chartered Institute of Archaeologists), visibility in terms of our individual publication profile is key to demonstrating these skills to colleagues and the wider world. Linked to this are questions around the future of Roman pottery studies and how accessible and inclusive an image we present to students, early career researchers and the public. To gain a picture of the current situation, a survey was sent out to all SGRP members in 2021, the results of which are presented here, followed by a wider discussion.

2. The survey

The survey was circulated to all SGRP members by email and promoted within the SGRP newsletter between 12 May 2021 and 1 June 2021. In total, 95 responses were received, out of a membership at the time of 158, equating to a 60% response rate. Confidentiality was key; all responses were anonymous, and respondents were able to opt out of individual questions, or out of the survey, at any point. The survey comprised 19 questions, relating to group demographics, employment, qualifications, outreach and publication, and concerns for the future of Roman pottery studies. Additional information was recorded on members' geographical location and research interests and how the committee communicates with the wider membership; these results have been shared with the committee but are not reported on in detail here.

3. Gender, age and ethnicity

In discussions of gender within this paper, there is a recognition that it is purely at a basic binary division of male/female and lacks any aspects of intersectionality in terms of exploring gender alongside race, dis/ability, sexuality or socio-economic background (Crenshaw 1989; 1991). Lack of diversity within the UK archaeology sector is a known and well documented situation (Cobb 2015; Aitchison *et al.* 2021) and reflected in this survey with 96% of respondents identifying as *White: English / Welsh / Scottish / Northern Irish / British / Irish / Gypsy or Irish Traveller / Any other White background*, the remaining 4% preferring not to answer. When asked about gender, 51% of respondents identified as female, 48% as male and 1% preferred not to say. Respondents were not asked if their gender matches that assigned at birth due to the small size of the target audience and concerns over potential individual identification. Whilst it is recognised that women are more inclined to respond to surveys than men, as are individuals who are white, affluent, educated

and younger (Smith 2009), the prevalence of women over men within finds studies has been a constant in several studies to date (Aitchison 2017; Hawkins 2019).

A basic binary gender division was also used in the sector-wide *Profiling the Profession* surveys up until the latest survey in 2020 (Aitchison *et al.* 2021), where even then, the number of individuals indicating other genders were so low that data was merged into a single group to again preserve anonymity of respondents (*ibid.*, section 2.4). When comparing the reported proportion of men and women across these surveys, some trends are very noticeable. The 2020 *Profiling the Profession* survey recorded 53% of respondents identifying as male and 47% as female, which for the first time correlates with the wider UK workforce (*ibid.*, section 2.4), a situation that the survey authors observe has taken decades to achieve; in their 1997 report, women comprised 35% of the archaeological workforce (Aitchison 1999). This increasing trend can be seen by going back further to the Institute for Archaeology (now Chartered Institute for Archaeology) member survey in 1991, where just 26% of respondents were women (Morris 1992). A 2017 Survey of Archaeological Specialists however reveals a different picture, with 45% of respondents identifying as male, 55% as female (Aitchison 2017, 24). Within this latter report the different specialist categories are broken down further and within 'Archaeological Finds Survey' 330 respondents identified as finds specialists, of which 36 specified Romano-British pottery. This small group in turn show an even more pronounced gender divide of 35% male and 65% female (Fig. 1).

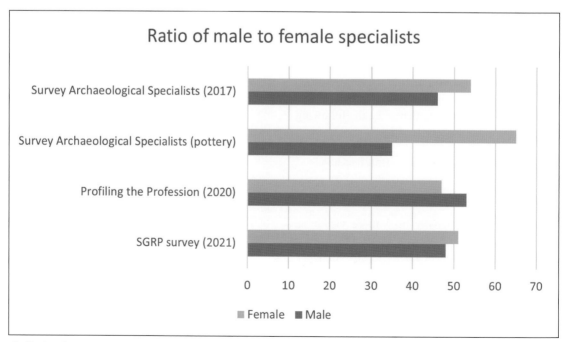

Figure 1. Ratio of men to women reported across the Survey of Archaeological Specialists 2016–2017, *including a sub-set of respondents identified as Roman pottery specialists (Aitchison 2017),* Profiling the Profession 2020 *(Aitchison* et al. *2021) and the SGRP survey (2021).*

The patterning of gender division across UK archaeology has been highlighted since at least the early 1990s and here we see it again, with finds study reversing the trend seen in the wider profession. The large-scale picture presented in sector-wide surveys cited above of more women entering the profession masks more disturbing patterns. Whilst there are indeed more women choosing a career in archaeology, which in itself is reassuring, this does not illustrate an increase in diversity when these are primarily cisgender white women (Heath-Stout 2020). In addition, despite the presence of more women and contrary to the findings of *Profiling the Profession*, the trend of women leaving the sector identified by Morris (1992) is still holding, as illustrated by Pope and Teather in their re-analysis of the most recent *Profiling the Profession* survey data (Pope 2021; Pope and Teather in prep.). Thus, we have a situation, still, where men retain the more senior roles in the profession as a whole. Whether this scenario occurs in Romano-British pottery studies is discussed below.

When the SGRP survey results for age and gender are combined, we see that younger women do form a larger cohort compared to their male peers within the SGRP membership, however the best represented age category for both is 65 and older. Half of the male respondents are aged 65 or older, compared to 35% of women. The worry, expressed by respondents both in this survey and in an earlier membership survey (Peachey 2009), of an ageing specialist workforce, appear well grounded with 79% of the respondents within the SGRP, at the time of this survey, aged 45 or over (Fig. 2).

4. Employment

Given the evidence, that women leave archaeology in their 30s (Andrew *et al.* 2020; Pope and Teather in prep.) this does not seem to be the case in Roman pottery studies, where women here outnumber men in both the 35–44 and 45–54 age categories (13%:11%, and 23%:11% of respondents respectively). These ratios are also significant for another reason, that of earnings. The Survey of Archaeological Specialists revealed the charge out rates across all specialisms for male specialists were higher than for women, with a mean charge out rate of £273 for men compared with £218 for women (Aitchison 2017, section 4.5). Within the specialist categories they identified, archaeological finds study was the third lowest paid specialist area, above those of archives and illustration, sectors which also employ a high number of women (Morris 1992; Aitchison 2017; Pope 2021). The conclusion from this is that those fields where significantly more women are employed are also those that are the lowest paid. Within the SGRP survey, salary brackets unfortunately overlap between the recommended pay minima set by the Chartered Institute for Archaeologists (CIfA) for those working at Associate and Member level for the most common pay bracket for female respondents (£26,500 to £35,400), where they outnumber male respondents (28% and 12% respectively). These figures are reversed for earnings over £35,500, with 6% of women and 21% of men in the pay categories above £35,500 (Fig. 3). Given the proportion of members working as specialists, a role which would correspond with CIfA Member level

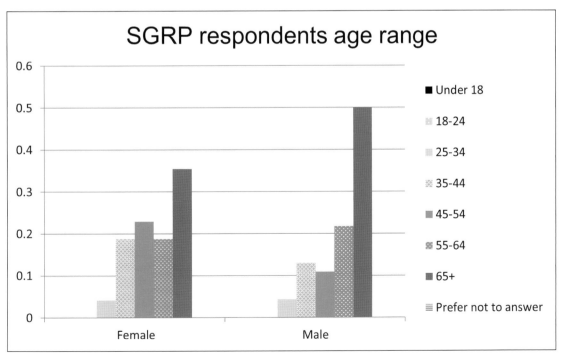

Figure 2. Percentage of SGRP survey respondents by age group and gender (n=95).

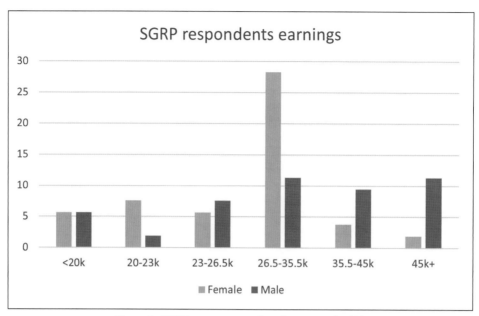

Figure 3. SGRP survey respondents' earnings (n=92).

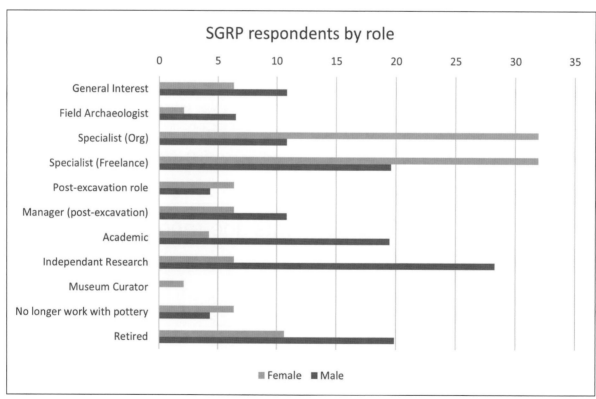

Figure 4. Job roles within the SGRP membership (n=93).

competencies, it is unclear if specialists in these roles are being remunerated in accordance with the CIfA minima (CIfA 2023).

Looking at the type of employment positions held by members of the SGRP (Fig. 4), revealed that just under two thirds of women hold either specialist roles within commercial organisations (32%), or work as freelance specialists (32%). Conversely men are more prevalent in managerial or academic roles, twice as likely to be managers in archaeological organisations and at least four times more likely to hold academic positions or class themselves as independent researchers, reflecting the trend seen in the wider archaeological workforce.

A divergence from the sector and UK-wide figures, is with regard to full-time and part-time working (Aitchison *et al* 2021, table 2.2.5). The figure for women

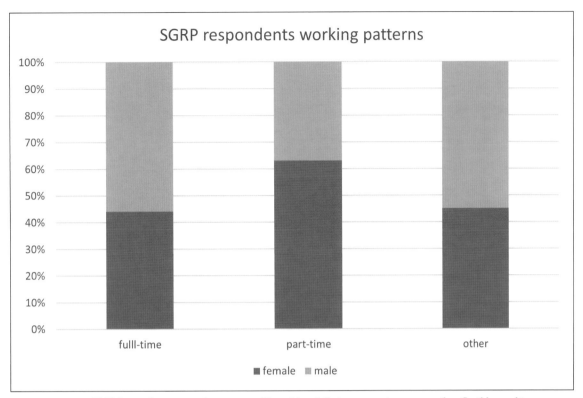

Figure 5. Proportion of SGRP members in employment working either full-time, part-time or on other flexible working arrangements (n=63).

working full-time in archaeology is stated at 79% and part-time 21%; within the SGRP, of those members currently employed 47% work full-time, with 39% of women working part-time and a further 13% on some form of flexible working pattern (Fig. 5). This compares to 60% of SGRP male respondents in full-time employment, 24% part-time and 16% on flexible working patterns. In addition, 15% of employed women in the SGRP undertake freelance work alongside paid work, a figure that rises to 23% for men. Just under a third of respondents are not currently employed (32%). There is more parity between these groups when looking at carer responsibilities, with 31% of SGRP respondents having carer roles, only slightly above the national and sector-wide average of 29% (*ibid.*, section 2.9).

When asked about the highest educational qualification held, 24% of respondents are educated to degree level, 30% hold a Master's degree, and 29% have PhDs. Just 4% of respondents are not educated to degree level. This latter figure may be a reflection of the age demographic in the group and also that a small number of respondents are interested in but have not been/are not employed in Roman pottery studies.

5. Presentations and publications

When asked about public engagement and outreach, men were again four times more likely to have given five or more papers that were either pottery based or that included

an element of Roman pottery research, during the period 2016–2021 (Fig. 6). It is recognised here that this period includes the 2020 lockdown, and the biased detrimental impact of this on women archaeologists (Hogarth *et al.* 2021), although it is beyond the remit of this paper to explore the relationship between this and the rise of online participation opportunities. Gender bias in terms of conference presentation has been identified in a number of different disciplines (Jones *et al.* 2014). The hostile environment to which women can be exposed to when they do speak up or out in archaeology has been previously reported (Scott 1998; Pope 2011; Perry 2019), yet there are real career-based implications from this lack of participation. Presenting at conferences, whether local society, regional or international conference level, enhances the visibility of that researcher, and increases the likelihood of citation. Participation also provides important networking opportunities, particularly for those who are self-employed. Is it that men who tend to hold more senior positions or who are retired have both the time and financial resources to prepare and present their research? Is it that those working in commercial organisations are not, for whatever reason, either being given the opportunities or encouragement to participate in conferences? With more women holding specialist roles and more likely to work part-time, the additional resources required when presenting is often voluntary, and when working under time constraints, it can easily be seen how these factors could contribute a significant additional mental and financial burden.

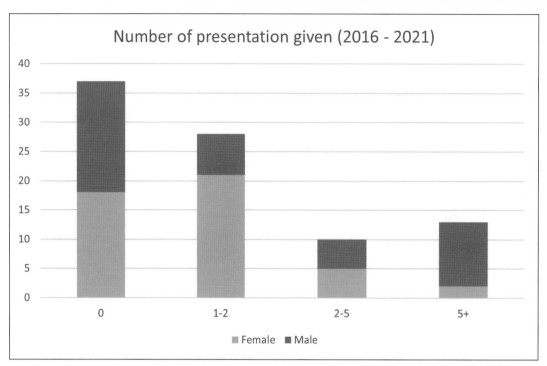

Figure 6. Number of presentations given, by gender. Categories have been grouped into two presentations or less, and more than two presentations (n=89).

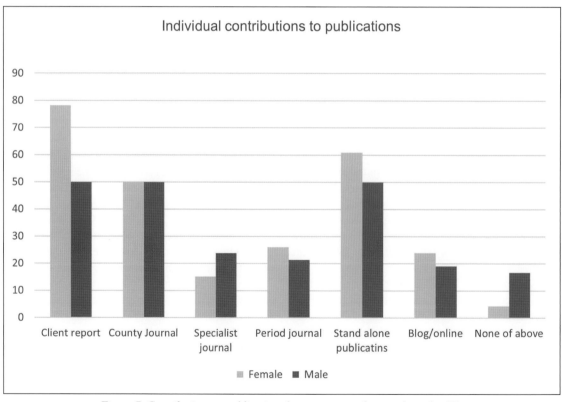

Figure 7. Contributions to publications by percentage of respondents (n=89).

SGRP members were asked two questions on the subject of publication: the first looking at specialist contributions to a range of publication formats (Fig. 7), the second asking about primary authorship in these publications (Fig. 8). Respondents were asked which of the following types of publication they had contributed to in the previous five year period: Client report, county journal, specialist subject journal, specialist period journal, standalone publication (e.g., monograph), online resource/blog, or none of these.

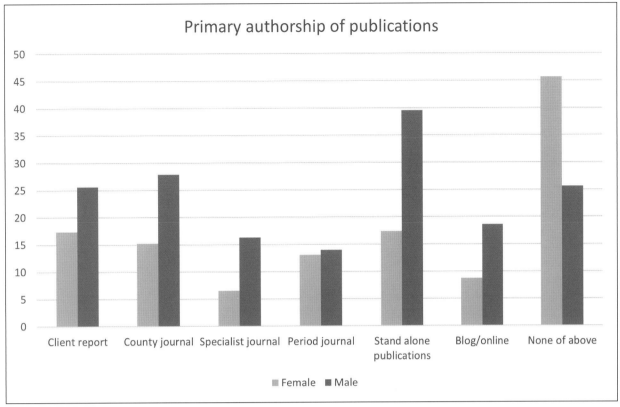

Figure 8. Percentage of respondents as primary author in publications (n=89).

As almost two thirds of women in the SGRP are working as specialists, either within an organisation or in a freelance capacity then a significant publication turnout by these individuals might be expected. For both men and women, the three most common types of publication contribution were client reports (64%), standalone publications/monographs (55%) and county journals (50%), reflecting again the publication forms most associated with specialist work. Whereas the ratio between these types of publication was relatively stable for men (at 50% across all three types), there was a greater diversity amongst women, with client reports the primary contribution (78%).

This division became even more apparent when asked about primary author contributions (Fig. 8): men scored more highly across all the publication categories except one, that of no primary authorship (26%), whereas for women this figure was significantly higher (46%). Women may be contributing to more client reports (78%); however, few (17%) have been a primary author of such reports.

6. Future concerns

When asked for their top three concerns for the future of Roman pottery studies, respondents were given a free text field, and a total of 80 individuals used this opportunity to record their concerns. By far the most commonly expressed of these revolved around a lack of specialists and fears over succession in pottery studies, in terms

of both the shortage of new specialists and problems of retention. Training, or rather the lack of, was closely allied to these concerns, ranging from perceived poor university coverage of pottery studies, opportunities for new specialists, mentoring and ongoing training for existing specialists. Despite various initiatives that have been undertaken over the last two decades to provide specialist training, the most recent being the Level 7 Specialist Apprenticeship (Historic England 2023), training provision remains a major concern. Collections and resources also figured highly, primarily in terms of lack of access to existing resources and the backlog of archives awaiting deposition. Worries around potential, or experienced, negative attitudes towards specialist contributions included having to justify the value of pottery studies, a preoccupation by colleagues with spot dating and chronology (linked to a decline in the appreciation of pottery studies and analysis) and a lack of funding for research beyond the demands of client reports. Standards were also flagged, particularly the need for sector wide conformity in all aspects of recording to ensure compatible research datasets.

7. Discussion

The SGRP survey described above, by focusing on a discrete and specialist area of archaeological studies, has highlighted, quite starkly, broad trends that have been observed within the wider archaeological profession; the high proportion of women in finds study, the lack of diversity, poor pay, lack of visibility and continued prevalence of men in senior positions. Although a specialist interest group, which inevitably includes individuals with a general interest in the subject, the SGRP nevertheless also serves as the primary membership organisation for those engaged in the paid work of Roman pottery studies in the UK, offering a window into this specialist world. The often-spoken concerns over an ageing specialist population can quite clearly be seen to be justified (Fig. 2). Clearly, if left un-addressed, this poses severe long-term implications for the profession primarily, but not only, in the loss of highly specialist knowledge. The lack of diversity in terms of race within the survey is likewise in accord with the wider profession. This is contrary to the situation at university level where surveys such as Digging Diversity (Cobb 2015) has shown that archaeology courses are far more diverse in terms of race, dis/ability, sexuality, gender and socio-economic backgrounds, yet this level of diversity does not progress beyond the classroom, to the detriment of our discipline (Cobb and Croucher 2016; Dave 2016). Add to this factors of low pay (Stanton-Greenwood *et al.* 2022), significant gender pay gaps across archaeological organisations (Bryan *et al.* forthcoming), job insecurity, and the expectation to acquire voluntary experience, and it becomes easy to see why archaeology in general remains the preserve of a small sector of society.

Feminist critiques of the wider archaeological discipline have been drawing attention to the poor representation of women within archaeological research and also inequalities within the archaeological workplace for decades (for some examples see Conkey and Spector 1984; Gero 1985; 1988; Kramer & Stark 1988; Gilchrist 1991; Scott 1993a; 1993b; 1998; Moore and Scott 1997; Champion 1998; Sørensen 2000; Croucher *et al.* 2014; Cobb and Croucher 2016; 2020). These concerns can be viewed broadly as two different threads termed by Alison Wylie (1991) as *Content Critiques* and, relevant to this paper, *Equity Critiques*. The work so far undertaken has highlighted the androcentric emphasis of our discipline-wide historiographies, however, within Romano-British archaeology the situation is at least as poor, if not worse. Colin Wallace, writing in 2002, observed that there was no mention at all of women within *The archaeologists of Roman Britain*, the paper from which the quote at the start of this paper was taken (Jones 1987). Yet if we look specifically at Roman pottery, one of the still key texts, *Roman Pottery in Britain* by Paul Tyers (1996) provides a concise history of Roman pottery studies and women are cited, albeit in small numbers, with reference made to Kathleen Keynon's Jewry Wall report (1948), and into the 1960s and 1970s works by Vivian Swan and Kay Hartley (Tyers 1996, 18–23). Some prominent women researchers of Roman Britain have been highlighted, such as Grace Simpson,

through the work of the TrowelBlazers project (www.trowelblazers.com) yet more can and should be done to raise the profile of those women who have contributed significantly to this area of study.

When comparing Roman pottery studies with the wider profession, the gender disparity is also strikingly obvious, in terms of the number of women working in this field and in their working patterns. Whilst gender parity is now the norm in terms of much commercial fieldwork (Andrew *et al.* 2020; Aitchison *et al.* 2021), to avoid falling foul of the 'Leaky Pipeline' (Toren 1993; Griffith 2010) many women find themselves being given the advice to 'get a specialism', thus perpetuating the 'Woman-at-home archaeologist' who must 'fulfil her stereotype feminine role by specialising in the analysis of archaeological materials....She will have to do the archaeological housework' (Gero 1985, 344).

Herein lies another pitfall encountered by female specialists; too much specialist knowledge may then hinder future opportunities to move into senior managerial or curatorial posts, due to having concentrated a narrow field of experience within the sector (Evans 2019), although why that should impact female specialists more than male specialists is unclear. To quote one SGRP survey respondent 'many women tend to graduate towards finds work which has proved to be a backwater in terms of the more senior field posts'. The placement of women in finds work, effectively removes them from experience in the decision-making process, experience that is key to accessing more senior managerial roles (Scott 1998, 139).

Returning once again to Jones (1987):

> ...There have been many women interested and knowledgeable in Roman Britain, but most have written as specialists on some class of objects or another and have not written works of synthesis. (Jones 1987, 95)

There are several points here relevant to the survey findings. Firstly, the acknowledgement that women have always been engaged in Romano-British studies, although why writing about artefacts does not equate to being a 'Romano-British archaeologist' is not explained, perhaps this is an example of women being accepted into the discipline yet still not treated as equal (Diaz-Andreu and Sørensen 1998). Is there an argument to be had here over whether finds work is still viewed by parts of the profession as a form of 'archaeological housework', along the lines of Gero (1985)? Do the women engaged in finds work themselves recognise this stereotype?

The second theme to take from this quote, is that of a lack of syntheses works by women. Is this through choice or circumstance, by having become structurally and habitually embedded in our work processes? There are certainly a number of women in Roman pottery studies who have written both as a pottery specialist and more widely in Roman studies, for example Grace Simpson and Vivian Swan to name just two such specialists with comprehensive and varied bibliographies (both have significant publication lists searchable on the Archaeology Data Service website). The phenomenal bibliography of Kay Hartley, now almost 20 years out of date (Dannell and Irving 2005) shows just how much of a contribution to wider studies individual specialists can make.

Fulkerson and Tushingham (2019) in their review of archaeological publishing in north America showed that a disproportionate number of women are producing significant amounts of archaeological knowledge through technical report writing yet are poorly represented in higher prestige peer-reviewed publications (Fulkerson and Tushingham 2019, 392). That can certainly be seen in these results, with the large proportion of women's contributions to client reports, and lack of primary authorship illustrated above (Figs 7 and 8). In addition, in recent years specialists have raised concerns that they are not always being credited for their work where it forms a contribution to a larger report (Cattermole 2017). It is also important to mention here that although increasingly these unpublished reports are available and accessible via the Archaeological Data Service (www.archaeologydataservice.ac.uk), the

contributions by women remain largely invisible, due to reports being indexed by primary author only; the most recent OASIS form, the mechanism by which information is uploaded to the website, now includes the option to list contributors, which will hopefully rectify this situation.

Turning attention towards specialist journals, what is the situation in terms of gender in our own publication, the *Journal of Roman Pottery Studies*? A basic count of papers by a binary gender split of authors, with a third category for papers with two or more authors of either gender, was undertaken across all volumes, excluding the site-specific volumes (Fig. 9). Overall, 62% of single authored papers across the remaining volumes are by men, with parity being reached in volume 12 (2005). Thereafter women are noticeably more present in terms of the proportion of published papers (except for volume 17).

The extent to which men dominate publications in 'prestige' (e.g., peer-reviewed) publications and grant awards has been critiqued in a number of papers since first being highlighted in the mid-1980s, one of the most recent being Heath-Stout's survey, which explored not just gender but the intersectionality of gender with other forms of discrimination (Heath-Stout 2020). Within the range of publications reviewed by Heath-Stout,

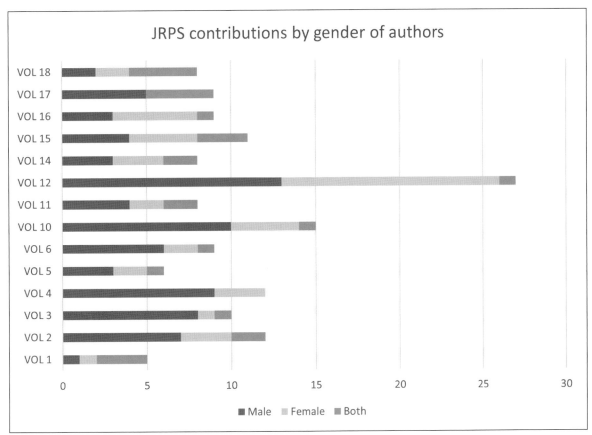

Figure 9. Number of contributions to individual volumes of JRPS by gender of author (male, female, combined authorship of male/ female).

two journals are published in the UK, the *Cambridge Archaeological Journal* and *Antiquity*. Both publications were shown to have high rates of male authorship, at 62% and 67% respectively (*ibid.*, 414, table 2). In 2019, the editorial team of the *Journal of Roman Studies* undertook a review to explore any potential gender-bias within their peer-reviewed published contributions (Kelly *et al.* 2019). Their study looked at published contributions over a 15-year period (2005–19) and revealed that the low rate of articles by female authors (28%) was largely concomitant with the number of submissions by women (30%) during the period 2009–19, and, they concluded, not the result of bias within the Journal (*ibid.*, 444–5). More recently still, an exploration of intellectual property in developer-led archaeological projects showed similar trends of male dominated authorship across a range of publication types and showed not just a gender bias in terms of authorship, but also wider restrictions in terms of who gets to contribute or be visible, such as field archaeologists, early career researchers and specialists (Mazzilli *et al.* forthcoming).

8. Conclusion

The SGRP survey has shown that men in Roman pottery studies are not 'doing it all'. Their narratives, however, for one reason or another, are still dominating the wider discourse. For the record, I do not believe this is intentional on the part of male colleagues, rather the pressures cited as concerns by the SGRP membership in the survey have created an environment where we all as practitioners subconsciously conform to the structural biases we have inherited, and which permeate through the wider profession. Over the last 50 years the SGRP has played a key role in establishing Roman pottery studies within the sector. There is a phenomenal amount of knowledge contained within our specialism and yet Roman pottery studies as a resource appears in need of protection, and somewhat bizarrely, further promotion still within the archaeological sector as the emphasis on chronology over wider narratives still dictates much output.

The SGRP is well placed to use its voice to help support members, through collaboration with industry bodies such as CIfA in discussions around pay, recognition and with the university sector in support for new specialists. Improving accessibility to key texts (many of which are now out of print) on which students of Roman pottery depend and facilitating attendance at conferences help open the area of study. Working with the likes of Trowelblazers, the SGRP can raise the profile of those women who have made contributions to both pottery studies and the wider discipline.

The results of this survey have provided new and valuable insights into the structural biases governing our discipline to the detriment of individuals and to our subject area. It has provided a specific dataset beyond that of generic sector wide research that the SGRP committee and wider membership can use to address known challenges and voiced concerns as the SGRP embarks on the next 50 years.

Bibliography

Aitchison, K. 1999. *Profiling the Profession: A survey of archaeological jobs in the UK*, Council for British Archaeology, English Heritage, Institute of Field Archaeologists, London.

Aitchison, K. 2014. *Heritage Market Survey 2014*, Landward Research (for the Chartered Institute of Archaeologists/ Federation of Archaeological Managers and Employers, Sheffield. Available at: http://www.archaeologists.net/sites/ default/files/Heritage_Market_Survey_2014_final_report.pdf (last accessed 8 May 2023).

Aitchison, K. 2017. *Survey of Archaeological Specialists 2016– 17* [data-set], Archaeology Data Service, York [distributor] https://doi.org/10.5284/1043769 (last accessed 8 May 2023).

Aitchison, K. and Edwards, R. 2003. *Archaeology Labour Market Intelligence: Profiling the Profession 2002/03*, Cultural Heritage National Training Organisation and Institute of Field Archaeologists, Bradford and Reading.

Aitchison, K. and Edwards, R. 2008. *Archaeology Labour Market Intelligence: Profiling the Profession 2007–08*, Institute of Field Archaeologists, Reading.

Aitchison, K. and Rocks-Macqueen, D. 2013. *Archaeology Labour Market Intelligence: Profiling the Profession 2012–13*, Landward Research, Sheffield.

Aitchison, K. German, P. and Rocks-Macqueen, D. 2021. *Profiling the Profession 2020*, Landward Research. Available at: https://profilingtheprofession.org.uk/profiling-the-profession-2020-introduction/ (last accessed 8 May 2023).

Andrew, J. Bryan, J. and Watson, S. 2020. *Getting our House in Order: Archaeologists' responses to Prospect's Workplace Behaviours Survey*. Available from: https://members.prospect.org.uk/your-prospect/branch/181/document/7028 (last accessed 8 May 2023).

Bryan, J., Foreman, P., Phillips, I. and Watson, S. forthcoming. Union activism and #MeToo in UK contracting archaeology, in H. Cobb and K. Hawkins (eds) *The legacy of #MeToo in Archaeology*, Archeopress, Oxford.

Bryant, S. and Willis, J. 2016. Before, during and after: life pre-PPG16, its impact after 1990 and the current struggle to retain its legacy, *The Archaeologist* 98, 4–8.

Cattermole, A. 2017. Review of the standard of reporting on archaeological artefacts in England. Unpublished report for the Chartered Institute for Archaeologists, funded by Historic England. Available at: https://www.archaeologists.net/sites/ default/files/7090FinalReport.compressed.pdf (last accessed 8 May 2023).

Champion, S. 1998. Women in British Archaeology: visible and invisible, in M. Diaz Andreu and M.-L. Stig Sørensen (eds) *Excavating Women: A history of women in European archaeology*, Routledge, London, 175–97.

Chartered Institute for Archaeology 2023. Statement on pay minima. Available at: https://www.archaeologists.net/practices/ salary (last accessed 8 May 2023).

Cobb, H.L. 2015. A diverse profession? Challenging inequalities and diversifying involvement in British archaeology, in

P. Everill and P. Irving (eds) *Rescue Archaeology: Foundations for the Future*, RESCUE, Hereford, 226–45.

Cobb, H. and Croucher, K. 2016. Personal, Political, Pedagogic: Challenging the binary bind in archaeological pedagogy, *Journal of Archaeological Method and Theory* [Special Issue: 'Binary Binds': Deconstructing Sex and Gender Dichotomies in Archaeological Practice] 23(3), 949–69. http://dx.doi.org/10.1007/s10816-016-9292-0.

Cobb, H. and Croucher, K. 2020. *Assembling Archaeology; teaching, practice and research*, Oxford University Press, Oxford.

Conkey, M.W. and Spector, J.D. 1984. Archaeology and the Study of Gender, *Advances in Archaeological Method and Theory* 7, 1–38.

Crenshaw, K. 1989. Demarginalizing the Intersection of Race and Sex: A Black Feminist Critique of Antidiscrimination Doctrine, Feminist Theory, and Antiracist Politics, *University of Chicago Legal Forum* 1989(1), 139–67.

Crenshaw, K. 1991. Mapping the Margins: Intersectionality, Identity Politics, and Violence against Women of Color, *Stanford Law Review* 43, 1241–99.

Croucher, K., Cobb, H. and Casella, E. 2014. Feminist Pedagogy: implications and practice. In M.J. Rodriguez-Shadow and S. Kellogg (eds) *Género y Arqueología en Mesoamérica: Homenaje a Rosemary Joyce. Lomas de Plateros,* Centro de Estudios de Antropología de la Mujer, Mexico, 121–36.

Dannell, G. and Irving, P. 2005. An Archaeological Miscellany: Papers in honour of Kay Hartley, *Journal of Roman Pottery Studies* 12.

Dave, R. 2016. Archaeology must open up to become more diverse, *The Guardian* 23/05/2016 https://www.theguardian.com/culture-professionals-network/2016/may/23/archaeology-must-open-up-become-more-diverse [accessed 24-04-2023].

Diaz-Andreu, M. and Sørensen, M.-L.S. 1998. Excavating Women; towards an engendered history of archaeology, in M. Diaz-Andreu and M.-L.S. Sørensen (eds) *Excavating Women, A history of women in European archaeology*, Routledge, London, 1–30.

Department of Environment 1990. Planning Policy Guidance Note 16: Archaeology and Planning. HMSO, London. https://webarchive.nationalarchives.gov.uk/ukgwa/+/http:/www.communities.gov.uk/publications/planningandbuilding/ppg16.

Evans, J. 2019. Take three girls (development of finds work since 1980s seen through the careers of three pottery specialists at the Herefordshire and Worcestershire County Archaeology Service), unpublished conference paper, The Finds Group at 30: celebrating the past, reviewing the present, planning the future https://archaeologists.net/civicrm/event/info?reset=1&id=31.

Fulkerson, T.J. and Tushingham, S. 2019. Who Dominates the Discourses of the Past? Gender, Occupational Affiliation, and Multivocality in North American Archaeology Publishing, *American Antiquity* 84, 379–99. doi: https://doi.org/10.1017/aaq.2019.35.

Gero, J.M. 1985. Socio-politics and the woman-at-home ideology, *American Antiquity* 50(2), 342–50.

Gero, J.M. 1988. Gender bias in archaeology: here, then and now, in S.V. Rosser (ed.) *Feminism within the Science and Health Care Professions: Overcoming Resistance, The Athene Series*, Pergamon Press, Oxford, 33–43.

Gilchrist, R. 1991. Women's archaeology? Political feminism, gender theory and historical revision, *Antiquity* 65(248), 495-501. doi: https://doi.org/10.1017/S0003598X00080091.

Griffith, A.L. 2010. Persistence of minorities in STEM field majors: is it the school that matters? *Economics of Education Review* 29(6), 911–22.

Hawkins, K. 2019. Demographics of the Finds Group and results of our survey, unpublished report and conference paper at The Finds Group at 30, Chartered Institute of Archaeologists day conference, September 25th 2019. Available at: https://archaeologists.net/civicrm/event/info?reset=1&id=31 [accessed 24-04-2023].

Heath-Stout, L.E. 2020. Who Writes About Archaeology? An Intersectional Study of Authorship in Archaeological Journals, *American Antiquity* 85(3), 407–26. https://doi.org/10.1017/aaq.2020.28.

Historic England 2023. Apprenticeships in the Heritage Sector. Available at: https://historicengland.org.uk/services-skills/training-skills/work-based-training/heritage-apprenticeships/ (last accessed 8 May 2023).

Hogarth, J.A., Batty, S., Bondura, V., Creamer, E., Ebert, C.E., Green-Mink, K., Kieffer, C.L., Miller, H., Ngonadi, C.V., Pilaar Birch, S.E., Pritchard, C., Vacca, K., Watkins, T.B., Zavodny, E. and Ventresca Miller, A.R. 2021. Impacts of the COVID-19 Pandemic on Women and Early Career Archaeologists, *Heritage* 4, 1681–702. doi: https://doi.org/10.3390/heritage4030093.

Jones, R.F.J. 1987. The archaeologists of Roman Britain, *Institute of Archaeology Bulletin* 24, 85–98.

Jones, M., Fanson, K.V., Lanfear, R., Symonds, M.R.E. and Higgie, M. 2014. Gender differences in conference presentations, a consequence of self-selection? *PeerJ* 2, e627 doi: https://doi.org/10.7717/peerj.627.

Kelly, C., Thonemann, P., Borg, B., Hillner, J., Lavan, M., Morley, N. and Whitton, C. 2019. Gender Bias and the Journal of Roman Studies: JRS EDITORIAL BOARD, *Journal of Roman Studies* 109, 441–8. doi: 10.1017/S0075435819000935.

Kenyon, K.M. 1948. *Excavations at the Jewry Wall Site, Leicester*, Society of Antiquaries of London, London. https://doi.org/http://dx.doi.org/10.26530/OAPEN_1004997.

Killgrove, K. 2021. The Enduring Myths Of Raiders of the Lost Ark, *Smithsonion Magazine*, 08/06/2021 https://www.smithsonianmag.com/arts-culture/enduring-myths-raiders-lost-ark-180977923/ [accessed 24-04-2023].

Kramer, C. and Stark, M. 1988. The status of women in archaeology, *Anthropology Newsletter* 29(9), 1, 11–12.

Mazzilli, F., Hawkins, K. and Watson, S. forthcoming. Intellectual Property in developer-funded archaeology projects from the Roman periods in Britain, *Britannia*.

Moore, J. and Scott, E. 1997. *Invisible People and processes; writing gender and childhood into European Archaeology*, Leicester University Press, London.

Morris, E. (ed.) 1992. *Women in British Archaeology*, IFA Occasional Paper 4. Institute of Field Archaeologists, Birmingham.

Peachey, A. 2009. Urning a Living: a survey of the opinions and concerns of Roman pottery specialists, *The Archaeologist* 58, 15.

Perry, S. 2019. Foreword, in H. Williams, C. Pudney and A. Ezzeldin (eds) *Public Archaeology, arts of engagement*, Archaeopress Publishing, Oxford, XI–XIV.

Pope, R.E. 2011. Processual archaeology and gender politics: the loss of innocence, *Archaeological Dialogues* 18(1), 59–86.

Pope, R.E. 2021. Women in the past, Women in the present. Keynote lecture for 'Modern' women of the past? Unearthing gender in antiquity, 5th March 2021. Available at: https://www.youtube.com/watch?v=hJe6388wmSY. (last accessed 8 May 2023).

Scott, E. (ed.) 1993a. Introduction: TRAC (Theoretical Roman Archaeology Conference) 1991, in E. Scott (ed.) *Theoretical Archaeology Conference: First Conference Proceedings*, Avebury, Aldershot, 1–4.

Scott, E. 1993b. Writing the Roman Empire, in E. Scott (ed.) *Theoretical Archaeology Conference: First Conference Proceedings*, Avebury, Aldershot, 5–22.

Scott, E. 1998. Tales from a Romanist: a personal view of archaeology and equal opportunities, in C. Forcey, J. Hawthorne and R. Witcher (eds) *TRAC 97: Proceedings of the Seventh Annual Theoretical Roman Archaeology Conference Nottingham 1997*, Oxbow Books, Oxford, 138–47.

Smith, W. 2009. Does Gender Influence Online Survey Participation? Available at: https://files.eric.ed.gov/fulltext/ED501717.pdf [accessed 07-07-2022].

Sørensen, M.L.S. 2000. *Gender Archaeology*, Polity Press, London.

Stanton-Greenwood, L., Connolly, D., Tideswell, L. and Hughes, G. 2022. Archaeologists in Financial Crisis: Poverty Impact Report. Available at: 03-04-2022].

Toren, N. 1993. The temporal dimension of gender inequality in academia, *Higher Education* 25(4), 439–55.

Tyers, P. 1996. *Roman Pottery*, B.T. Batsford, London.

Wallace, C. 2002. Writing disciplinary history, why Romano-British archaeology needs a biographical dictionary of its own, *Oxford Journal of Archaeology* 24, 4, 381–92. doi: https://doi.org/10.1111/1468-0092.00173.

Wylie, A. 1991. Gender Theory and the Archaeological Record Why is There No Archaeology of Gender?, in J.M. Gero and M.W. Conkey (eds) *Engendering Archaeology: Women and Prehistory*, Social Archaeology. Basil Blackwell, Cambridge, Massachusetts, 31–54..

National initiatives in archaeological archiving

Duncan H. Brown

Abstract

This paper originated as a talk given to the 50th anniversary conference of the SGRP and represents, as such an occasion warrants, a review of past initiatives, together with a consideration of the current situation. The text is in two parts, the first of which looks at the general situation in archaeological archiving nationally, especially the response to the recommendations that stemmed from the Mendoza Review into museums in England. The second part attempts to relate archiving practice to the development of Roman pottery studies, from 1991 to the 2016 publication, in ground-breaking collaboration with the two companion pottery study groups, of A Standard for Pottery Studies in Archaeology.

1. Introduction

The invitation to deliver this talk to the 2021 conference of the SGRP is perhaps an indication of how, in the last ten years or so, issues around archaeological archives have increased in prominence. The occasion of an anniversary conference seemed like a good vehicle for a review and the invitation was one the author was happy to accept. As the title indicates, that talk itself consisted of an update on various national initiatives, finishing with a look at the progress of archaeological archiving in relation to Roman pottery studies. At the time of writing, a year later, most of those national initiatives have moved along and much of what was said would now be out of date. The same might apply in the days between completing this draft and final publication so it is worth setting out the current state of play, if only to provide some background to the section written from a Roman pottery perspective.

A definition of an archaeological archive would be a good place to start, and the most universally accepted version can be found in the standard produced by the Europae Archaeologiae Consilium (EAC):

> An archaeological archive comprises all records and objects recovered during an archaeological project and identified for long term preservation, including artefacts, ecofacts and other environmental remains, waste products, scientific samples and also written and visual documentation in paper, film and digital form. (Perrin *et al.* 2014, 20)

This definition is significant in that it clearly relates an archaeological archive to an archaeology project, thus establishing it as the product of a planned programme

of work, which, at least in theory, makes it easier to assimilate archive guidance and standards into project management. Several recent initiatives are about improving archive practice but before considering those, perhaps some wider background would be useful.

2. Background

The most recent developments in addressing issues around archaeological archives stem from the Mendoza review of museums in England. As the webpage describes:

> This Review was undertaken in response to the Culture White Paper in 2016, which called for 'a wide-ranging review of national, local and regional museums, working closely with Arts Council England (ACE) and the Heritage Lottery Fund (HLF)'. It looks at what the national infrastructure for museums is and what it could and should be; the museums sponsored directly by government; and the challenges and opportunities for all of England's museums. (DCMS 2017)

Neil Mendoza made a number of recommendations, including asking Historic England (HE) to: 'Work with key stakeholders to produce recommendations for DCMS early in 2018, which will improve the long-term sustainability of the archaeological archives generated by developer-funded excavations' (*ibid.*, 16). The response from HE was to formulate an action plan that was endorsed by the Department for Culture, Media and Sport (DCMS) and has now become the Future for Archaeological Archives Programme (FAAP; Historic England 2022).

Among the original recommendations to DCMS from HE were the following, which are most relevant to this discussion:

- A feasibility study of the viability of establishing additional publicly accessible repositories for archaeological archives.
- Recommend to museums that they should consider charging for the deposition and curation of archaeological archives.
- Action plan to improve the sustainability of archaeological archives.
- Relieve museums of the expectation that they should attempt to curate digital archive material from archaeological projects.

The feasibility study was completed as an options appraisal (Cambridge County Council / DigVentures 2021), and Arts Council England (ACE) and HE are preparing a business case to take to DCMS for funding to develop a network of museum collections based around a national storage facility.

The other recommendations have now been incorporated into the FAAP Action Plan, which comprises various work packages, that include these action points:

- Professional Standards and Guidance
- Best practice in planning
- Advice on the costs of archival deposition, storage and curation
- A 'digital first' approach to archaeological archives
- Digital archives and museums
- Framework for legal ownership
- Joint sector best practice guidance
- New approaches to selection
- Museums collecting archives
- Patterns and frequency of archaeological archive usage
- Archive retention reviews.

Various documents have been produced, or initiatives set in train, to address these, including: a programme of revision of Chartered Institute for Archaeologists (CIfA) Standards and Guidance; an Association of Local Government Archaeology Officers (ALGAO) report, commissioned by HE, entitled *Planning for Archives* (Donnelly-Symes 2019); an HE project to examine possible alternative models for calculating deposition costs for archaeological archives (HE 9108); CIfA's 'dig digital' toolkit (Archaeological Archives Forum / DigVentures 2021); the Society for Museum Archaeology (SMA) *Standard and Guidance in the Care of Archaeological Collections*, which advises museums not to collect digital material, in favour of working with a Trusted Digital Repository (SMA 2020); an HE project that is using advice from a QC on ownership of

archaeological material and a model deed of transfer prepared to create guidance on planning for transfer of title; the CIfA selection toolkit (CIfA 2019); an HE funded project for the SMA to conduct three consecutive annual reviews of museums collecting archaeological archives (SMA 2016; 2017; 2018a); two HE funded projects that will collect information on the frequency of visits to curated archaeological archives (UAUK 2022; HE Project 8478); and an HE funded project leading to SMA guidance on the rationalisation of museum archaeology collections (SMA 2018b).

A few of those projects merit closer consideration as a way of setting the scene in greater detail. *Planning for Archives*, for instance, attempted to gather information on the quantity of project archives that found their way into museum collections, concluding that:

> The reality shown by the results of the Planning for Archives survey and the 2017 SMA survey indicates that 'useful' archives are not currently being produced in all areas of the country due to accessibility and deposition problems. 27.5% of respondents for this projects survey indicated that all or some of the archaeological archives produced in their area is not currently collected. Three of these respondents indicated that 95% or more of the archive produced in their area is not currently collected. (Donelly-Symes 2019, 14)

Those numbers are not entirely attributable to museums that are no longer collecting archaeological archives and many museum curators will know the problems of getting contracting archaeologists to deposit with them. For digital archives, the picture is much worse:

> … comparing the number of digital archives deposited with the ADS with the number of OASIS records created within the 2013–2018 timeframe [shows that] c.36,000 records have been created by archaeological units on OASIS. This figure is broadly in line with the number of WSIs approved and suggests only 1.2% of projects where an OASIS record has been created have been archived with a digital repository. For c.34,500 of these records the Digital Archive Recipient was marked as either blank or an organisation that does not hold a Core Trust Seal as an accredited digital archive. (*ibid.*, 22).

If it is true that very few digital archives have been transferred for curation, it is possible that this reflects the rate of archive transfer overall and there are many physical project archives that have not been transferred to a repository, even where it is possible to do so. Many repository curators who still receive archives know of several that, even years after project completion, have not been deposited with them. This is unlikely to be a problem on the scale of undeposited digital material but in a similar vein, it is a difficult situation to resolve.

The SMA surveys of 2016, 2017 and 2018 (SMA 2016; 2017; 2018a) highlight the additional problem of museums that are no longer collecting archaeological archives. The 2016 survey showed that of 154 collecting museums, 35 have stopped collecting, while 61 estimate that they will have run out of space within five years and a further 16 within 10 years. In addition, 101 museums do not have a specialist curator of archaeology. That picture did not change much in the surveys of 2017 and 2018 and the prospect is that by 2026, 112 museums will no longer be able to collect archaeological archives. A new survey was planned for 2021 but that has been delayed while museums recover from the lockdowns and temporary closures that resulted from the threat of COVID-19. By early 2023 it still had not commenced but it will be interesting to see how many of the 61 who anticipated running out of space by 2021 have actually done so.

One way of improving the rate of deposition of archives is to simplify the means of effecting transfer of title. Advice sought by HE from a QC has clarified our understanding of the legal basis for owning archaeological finds. It is suggested that settling an in-principle agreement for the landowner to transfer title to a repository at the beginning of a project will make it easier to settle what often becomes an outstanding issue. To that end, HE commissioned a solicitor to produce a Deed of Transfer that will be made available, with supporting guidance, to landowners, developers, planning officers and contractors.

Part of the case being made to DCMS for supporting the development of a national archive facility is that the compiled products of archaeology projects are worthy of collection and long-term curation. The introduction of the CIfA Selection Toolkit (CIfA 2019) is one way of ensuring that project managers evaluate the archival significance of documentary and material elements. It encourages conversations with repository collections personnel, finds specialists and others in agreeing a selection strategy as part of project planning. The strategy can be modified in response to unexpected discoveries during data-gathering and the overall aim is to ensure that there is agreement between all parties that the final archive contains everything that it should to reflect the aims of the project, to inform future research and to meet the requirements of the repository.

An additional assurance that must be made is that archaeological archives have future value. HE commissioned University Archaeology UK (UAUK) to review the numbers of academic research projects that were based on information gathered from museum collections (UAUK 2022). The results are summarised as follows:

> Of a total of 590 completed theses within the geographical and disciplinary scope of this project, 438 were available online and analysed. 186 of these were found to have used materials archives held in museums and other repositories (42%) at an estimated cost over 10 years of over £11M at current levels of UKRI doctoral studentship funding. (UAUK 2022, 1)

Those numbers are encouraging, and it is hoped that a parallel project that the SMA is about to commence, with HE funding, will gather information from museums about the frequency of visits to museum collections for any reason over the next two years. These surveys should strengthen the argument that archaeological archives have research value, as well as social and communal importance, which will support the case being made for investment in their preservation for the future.

The documents and initiatives set out above represent a very full list and as it works through its action plan, the FAAP is bringing together an extensive resource that will inform archive practice in the future. A parallel initiative is the upgrading of OASIS (https://oasis. ac.uk/), the online system for reporting archaeological investigations. The new version, OASIS V, includes the facility to enter archive information and allows the tracking of progress in compiling and transferring archive components.

The overall picture is that progress is being made in archaeological archiving at a faster rate and with more likelihood of positive outcomes than ever before. If all those plans are realised, there will be:

- Sufficient storage and curatorial capacity
- Confidence that what is being collected is what should be curated
- Consistent procedures for archaeological archiving that include:
  ○ Tracking archive progress
  ○ Management of digital data
  ○ Documentation
  ○ Selection of materials for archive
  ○ Approaches to packing and boxing
  ○ Transfer of ownership
  ○ Costs of archive deposition
  ○ Making archives accessible.

3. Archive practice and Roman pottery studies

The second part of this paper attempts to relate the current national strategic programme for archaeological archives to the development of Romano-British pottery studies. An early starting point is the review carried out for English Heritage in 1991 by Fulford and Huddleston, *The current state of Roman-British pottery studies* (Fulford and Huddleston 1991). Their report was based on the results from a questionnaire sent out to pottery specialists and includes a single paragraph on 'archive reports', which may as well be written out here in full:

> What do you understand by an 'archive' pottery report?
>
> An archive was generally agreed to be an unpublished report containing context-by-context lists of the fabrics and forms of each sherd present (with quantification, although a lack of definition was seen, for which English Heritage was blamed. Archive reports formed the basis of the shorter, synthesised published reports. It was also commonly held that archive material, especially that of other Units, was difficult to access, often lost, and even if available, was difficult to use because of the lack of standardisation. Computers were mentioned by a few as being the means to improve archives and their accessibility, while claimed to dislike their use (for no apparent reasons). The impression gained from the respondents was of dissatisfaction, both with the construction of their own archives, and with the fact that under project-funding, they would never have time fully to use material which they themselves had presented, let alone the work of others. Indications of possible future research projects (e.g. possible fabric and form trends, or deposits of unusual character) noted in the archive during its compilation, were felt to be unrealisable opportunities, although offering the sort of ideas which most pottery workers would wish to have the chance occasionally to pursue. (*ibid.*, 20)

The focus is very much on the content and accessibility of reports that were intended for archive rather than general dissemination. No mention is made of archive tasks such as the identification and ordering of record sheets or the packaging and organisation of sherds. That is not surprising, because those tasks were not regarded as relevant to, or indeed appropriate for specialists. Elsewhere, however, there are interesting insights into the practice of sampling assemblages. As one would expect, there is no mention of a selection strategy, which today is recommended as a way of ensuring that pottery is retained in accordance with various specialist and project-based requirements.

In 1991, the emphasis was more on guiding practice to ensure enough of an assemblage was recorded. This amounted to 50% of a 'large' assemblage, although it was stated that 'no minimum or optimum size for a sample can be isolated, now or ever, owing to the nature of archaeological data' (*ibid.*, 10). At the same time, it was noted that

> increasing economic constraints are making the option of sampling all large pottery assemblages more attractive, [so] before sampling can become an accepted part of the methodology, a comprehensive investigation into the

> different sampling methods must be undertaken. One method must be chosen as the standard, to prevent further inconsistencies in methodological approaches occurring. (*ibid.*, 10)

It is also recognised that the whole assemblage size must be stated in any report, so that the validity of any interpretations of a sampled fraction can be understood. This could be viewed as the pre-cursor to the current emphasis on developing a selection strategy for each project and is in some ways quite far-sighted, especially given that this report was written before the emergence of PPG16 and competitive tendering. Indeed, in Section 4, 'Current Aims and Objectives' sampling re-appears, with recommendations that, certainly for rural sites, a 'sampling policy' could be advanced before the commencement of excavation (*ibid.*, 45). Other sections consider sampling on urban sites, kiln sites and in post-excavation, all aimed at ensuring that resources are focused on analysing material from meaningful contexts.

It was not until 1994 that 'the archive' was introduced as an entity, when the SGRP produced 'Guidelines for the Archiving of Roman Pottery' (SGRP 1994). This was seen as an important response to the publication by English Heritage of *Managing Archaeology Projects* (otherwise known as MAP2; English Heritage 1989), as indicated in their definition of an archive:

> The archive must contain sufficient data to allow interrogation leading to an understanding of its archaeological and ceramic significance. It should be sufficient to facilitate a MAP2 assessment without overlapping into a research archive. (*ibid.*, 1)

The emphasis is again on the quality of the record and the extent of an assemblage, rather than the ordering and packing of archive elements and accessibility:

- All assemblages, whether from excavations, watching briefs, evaluations, field walking or other forms of archaeological intervention should be recorded to the level defined above.
- All pottery, irrespective of stratification, should be included in the archive, unless an academic case can be made for its exclusion.
- Exclusion of unstratified material could be a case in point, but all such material should be examined to ensure its exclusion will not detract from the evidence available for the site and its pottery. (*ibid.*, 2)

That section is headed 'The Extent of the Archive' and there seems to be a persistent confusion between the collection of data and the compilation of an archive as part of a project. There is no doubt, however, that the aim is to produce something that will inform future research, as the recommendations for a minimum archive show, an agreed minimum archive would:

- promote good practice and high standards of work
- facilitate the interchange of data between specialists
- set standards for Museum collections, particularly for any dispersal of material
- specify archive levels for contract archaeology to maintain standards and promote equitable tendering. (*ibid.*, 2)

The 2011 SGRP research strategy (Perrin 2011) echoes those concerns. The section on 'museums and other archives' in the summary of the main issues, lists the following points:

- National database of pottery collections lodged in museums, with CAOs [contracting archaeological organisations], with individuals and elsewhere
- Issues relating to access to pottery collections
- Criteria for retention and disposal of pottery. (Perrin 2011, 37)

Also recommended is 'closer collaboration with museums over aspects including selection and retention, access to collections, educational use of collections' (*ibid.*, 37), all of which indicates a concern with accessing museum collections and the selection of pottery for curation, rather than securing the stability of pottery assemblages through the use of appropriate packaging and making material accessible in museum stores by ordering boxes sensibly. It is notable, however, that the term 'sampling' has given way here to 'selection', as is firmly established in Objective 11B: 'The SGRP believes that the successful completion of its other objectives will provide the framework for a policy on the retention or disposal of Roman pottery and help towards initiatives such as sustainable local collection policies' (*ibid.*, 53). Those other objectives are centred on concerns with the issues of storage capacity that the FAAP was created to resolve:

Many museums do not have the capacity to take new archives, while some have actually shut or are not taking any new material; most CAOs and some universities now hold archaeological archives. Some archives, wherever they are housed, either temporarily or permanently, are not stored in ideal conditions. Various initiatives have been undertaken to try to address this parlous situation, with little actual progress: currently, for example, the idea of regional resource centres appears to have stalled. The SGRP will liaise with other interested parties to try to keep the debate alive and to press for a resolution to the problems. (*ibid.*, 53)

The debate remains very much alive and as has been shown, has moved on considerably since 2011. In terms of standards for archive practice, the 2016 publication of *A Standard for Pottery Studies in Archaeology* by the prehistoric, Roman and medieval pottery study groups (PCRG *et al.* 2016) offers more guidance than any of the earlier documents discussed above. Solely as a collaboration between the three groups, the Standard is ground-breaking, but it also represents the most comprehensive manual yet produced for the recovery, processing, analysis and reporting of pottery assemblages. An additional novelty is the prominence of archiving within the Standard, which is brought out early on, in the section on collection and processing: 'The aim is to compile a stable, clean, ordered and documented assemblage suitable for analysis and comprising 100% of all the pottery found in every contextual unit' (*ibid.*, 9).

A comprehensive section on archive, extending over four pages, follows substantial discussion of assessment, analysis and reporting and identifies archiving tasks during project stages such as planning, data-gathering, analysis, reporting and archive compilation. The Standard is not aimed wholly at ceramicists but also project managers, monitors and finds personnel, so some of the tasks relate to the wider project team and it is recognised that the final tasks of archive compilation and transfer will not usually be the responsibility of pottery specialists. They are though, charged with ensuring the consistency and accessibility of the data they create in accordance with the requirements of the project data management plan. This echoes the concerns of those earlier guidelines, which promoted the value of creating datasets that facilitated comparative studies. The use of computers may now be universally accepted, in contrast to the situation in 1991 but that has only intensified the necessity of producing well-ordered, comprehendible information that can readily be shared. The Standard asks for compliance with a data management plan which, with its necessary focus on file-naming, folder structure and the addition of metadata, will ensure that the digital record is easy to access and understand.

The issue of selection is also considered in some detail, mainly emphasising the importance of involving a specialist in developing and updating project selection strategies:

It is not the function of the Standard to describe the creation and development of a selection strategy, nor to state categorically what pottery finds can or cannot be excluded from selection. Selection should be based, however, on the premise that every pottery find has the potential to inform future research and a strong case has to be made for not selecting pottery for archive. It is advised that in most cases, pottery that has been analysed, or has the potential to reward analysis or re-analysis, should be selected for archive. (*ibid.*, 21)

Indeed, in the section on project planning, the principle of strategic selection of pottery is clearly stated:

> A project design or written scheme of investigation must include a strategy for pottery recovery on site; the standard requirement is to recover for analysis 100% of the pottery present in every contextual unit. (*ibid.*, 8)

While

> All the pottery found in every contextual unit must be collected in accordance with the strategies agreed during project planning. Unexpected finds, such as waster dumps, may lead to the modification of strategies for collection, sampling or selection. (*ibid.*, 9)

Use of the CIfA Selection toolkit, which was created after the pottery Standard, will formalise and facilitate the involvement of specialists in producing a selection strategy as a regular part of project planning. It seems that the aspirations of those earlier guides and standards are finally being realised.

4. Conclusions

Since the formation of the Archaeological Archive Forum in 2004, the profile of archive practice has improved hugely, while the appearance, and subsequent updating, of their guide to best practice (Brown 2011) has accelerated that progress. We are now at the point where more and more resources are available to all archaeologists to enable them to plan for archive work and help them through the whole archiving process. The importance of consulting with pottery specialists in developing approaches to selection has long been recognised and the CIfA Selection toolkit provides a framework for doing that. National initiatives, such as the plan to develop solutions to the decreasing collecting capacity of museums, have been driven in part by that raised profile, which has contributed to the involvement of people beyond the confines of the archaeological profession, for instance in the completion of the Mendoza Review (DCMS 2017). The trajectory is upwards and outwards, and it is certain that, if vital issues such as storage capacity (often called the archive crisis) are to be resolved, then archaeologists need to engage the interest of a broader congregation. Calls for investment have to be backed with evidence that archaeological material merits preservation and public support will be vital to winning that argument.

Many pottery specialists are well practiced in connecting with a variety of audiences and there is no reason why they should not be mobilised when the case for public investment is being made. If the recommendations of a succession of guides and reviews, culminating in the *Standard for Pottery Studies*, are followed then specialists will also have more to contribute to archaeology projects, from beginning to end. From the early 1990s,

the emphasis has been on making data available and easy to share, and also selecting what to analyse and preserve. Specialists can now call on a wide range of resources to support their work. Most of those discussed here relate to archive practice but in addition, there are CIfA toolkits for recording and reporting, while the *Standard for Pottery Studies* will also be made available in a more interactive online format. All this, it is hoped, will make it easier to achieve objectives that should be considered just as important as any others. Those are to train future generations of pottery specialists and educate more widely in the value and importance of pottery studies.

Bibliography

Archaeological Archives Forum / DigVentures 2021. Dig Digital. Available at: https://www.archaeologists.net/digdigital (last accessed 18 August 2023).

Brown, D.H. 2011. *Archaeological Archives: A guide to best practice in creation, compilation, transfer and curation*, Archaeological Archives Forum. Available at: https://archives.archaeologyuk.org/aaf_archaeological_archives_2011.pdf (last accessed 18 August 2023).

Cambridge County Council / DigVentures 2021. Options for Sustainable Archaeological Archives. Available at: https://www.artscouncil.org.uk/research-and-data/options-sustainable-archaeological-archives

CIfA 2019. Toolkit for Selecting Archaeological Archives. Available at: https://www.archaeologists.net/selection-toolkit (last accessed 18 August 2023).

DCMS 2017. The Mendoza Review: an independent review of museums in England. Available at: https://www.gov.uk/government/publications/the-mendoza-review-an-independent-review-of-museums-in-england (last accessed 18 August 2023).

Donnelly-Symes, B. 2019. Planning for Archives. Available at: https://historicengland.org.uk/images-books/publications/planning-for-archives/ (last accessed 18 August 2023).

English Heritage 1989. *Managing Archaeology Projects*, English Heritage, London.

Fulford, M.G. and Huddlestone, K. 1991. *The current state of Romano-British pottery studies*, English Heritage Occasional Paper No. 1. Historic Buildings and Monuments Commission for England, London.

Historic England 2022. Future for Archaeological Archives Programme. Available at: https://historicengland.org.uk/research/support-and-collaboration/future-for-archaeological-archives-programme/ (last accessed 18 August 2023).

Perrin, K., Brown, D. H., Lange, G., Bibby, D., Carlsson, A., Degraeve, A., Kuna, M., Larrson, Y., Pálsdóttir, U., Stoll-Tucker, B., Dunning, C. and Rogalla Von Bieberstein, A. 2014. A Standard and Guide to Best Practice for Archaeological Archiving in Europe, EAC. Available at: https://www.europae-archaeologiae-consilium.org/_files/ugd/881a59_dc8871c3c9d84100a17ac3b763a7f407.pdf (last accessed 18 August 2023).

Perrin, R. 2011. A Research Strategy and Updated Agenda for the Study of Roman Pottery in Britain. Available at: https://romanpotterystudy.org.uk/strategy/ (last accessed 18 August 2023).

Prehistoric Ceramics Research Group, Study Group for Roman Pottery and Medieval Pottery Research Group 2016.

A Standard for Pottery Studies in Archaeology. Available at: https://romanpotterystudy.org.uk/wp-content/uploads/2016/06/Standard_for_Pottery_Studies_in_Archaeology.pdf (last accessed 18 August 2023).

Society for Museum Archaeology 2016. Museums Collecting Archaeology (England) REPORT YEAR 1: November 2016. Available at: http://socmusarch.org.uk/socmusarch/gailmark/wordpress/wp-content/uploads/2016/07/HE-SURVEY-2016-FINAL.pdf (last accessed 18 August 2023).

Society for Museum Archaeology 2017. Museums Collecting Archaeology (England) REPORT YEAR 2: November 2017. Available at: http://socmusarch.org.uk/socmusarch/gailmark/wordpress/wp-content/uploads/2018/04/HE-SURVEY-2017-FINAL.pdf (last accessed 18 August 2023).

Society for Museum Archaeology 2018a. Museums Collecting Archaeology (England) REPORT YEAR 3: November 2018. Available at: http://socmusarch.org.uk/socmusarch/gailmark/wordpress/wp-content/uploads/2019/04/HE-SURVEY-2018-TEMPLATE-FINAL.pdf (last accessed 18 August 2023).

Society for Museum Archaeology 2018b. Guidance on the Rationalisation of Museum Archaeology Collections. Available at: http://socmusarch.org.uk/projects/guidance-on-the-rationalisation-of-museum-archaeology-collections/ (last accessed 18 August 2023).

Society for Museum Archaeology 2020. Standards and Guidance in the Care of Archaeological Collections. Available at: http://socmusarch.org.uk/training/smart-project/ (last accessed 18 August 2023).

Study Group for Roman Pottery 1994. Guidelines for the Archiving of Roman Pottery. Available at: https://romanpotterystudy.org.uk/wp-content/uploads/2015/05/GuidelinesArchivingRomanPot.pdf (last accessed 18 August 2023).

University Archaeology UK 2022. A Report on the Use of Archaeological Material Archives in Research in England (2010–2020), HE Research Report Series 16/2022. Available at: https://historicengland.org.uk/research/results/reports/16-2022?searchType=research+report&search=16%2F2022 (last accessed 18 August 2023).

Pure and sample: An assessment of the impacts of sampling on the interpretation of a Roman pottery assemblage from the A14C2H excavations

Lanah Hewson

Abstract

Sampling, especially regarding bulk finds, is a vital tool for professional units that can alleviate the financial pressures and resource demands that they face. However, there are many theoretical issues with sampling pottery assemblages owing to how many transformations an assemblage has already faced (i.e., depositional or taphonomic processes) and how further transformations (i.e., through sampling) may impact data and the interpretations drawn from these. This research critically assesses an experimental, purposive, *sampling strategy employed in one landscape block of the A14 Cambridgeshire to Huntingdon Improvement Scheme excavations led by MOLA Headland Infrastructure, which involved sampling sherds from features of interest that would contribute to the broader understanding of site occupation, without needing to assess the entire archaeological assemblage. The strategy was employed on c. 205 kg of Late Pre-Roman Iron Age (LPRIA) and Roman pottery and has demonstrated a method that has the potential to decrease the financial burden and demand of resources placed on professional units processing large quantities of pottery on infrastructure projects whilst maintaining the informational value of the assemblage, thus changing the ways pottery is processed by these units.*

1. Introduction

Pottery is one of the most common classes of artefacts recovered archaeologically from Roman sites and can make up a large percentage of bulk finds. This is particularly relevant as more and more large infrastructure projects are being conducted, producing huge quantities of bulk finds that need processing. Consequently, professional units are under considerable pressure to process and analyse pottery as efficiently, or cost effectively, as possible. The fact that many large developer-funded projects usually request 'grey literature reports' as their final outcomes, means specialists can be somewhat limited in how assemblages are analysed, and this hinders sites from being viewed within broader systems and landscapes (Doherty *et al.* 2013, 13). Time and financial pressures are often the driving factors of these limitations and prevent more detailed publications (Fulford and Holbrook 2011, 334). Hence, it is important to acknowledge not only the necessity, but also the benefits, of an effective sampling strategy that may be employed in these circumstances.

Many specialists do employ sampling in some form, though the methods used are neither frequently nor explicitly described in publications. This can lead to issues in understanding what effects these strategies can have on data, and subsequently, how it is interpreted. For example, 'key groups' (a form of *purposive sampling* that allows for the analysis of key assemblages or wares that represent the full population) are a well-established and widely accepted sampling strategy within the specialist community. As a result, it is not often disclosed what criteria assemblages must fulfil to be included within these groups as a general understanding of the concept and its implications is assumed owing to widespread use (for example cf. Timby 2000, 180; Percival with Williams 2007, 52; Anderson with Montiel 2013, 299). Therefore, what is left is a dataset that has been influenced by sampling, without any explicit explanation as to how or why, nor any discussion of how this influence may change the interpretation of the assemblage. This demonstrates how it is not always clear in literature what relationship a sample may have with the 'full population' and thus to what degree sampling may influence how data is interpreted. This is particularly concerning when the sustainability of data is considered, an important concept in the present era of Big Data projects. Such comprehensive studies often draw from large databases generated by (sometimes multiple) past works and a lack of standardised or structured documentation can severely hinder further analyses (Fulford and Holbrook 2011, 327; Doherty *et al.* 2013, 14). Thus, the data drawn must be sustainable, meaning it was recorded in a way that is accessible and understandable for the future use of institutions and individuals who may not have been involved in the initial gathering of said data (Colley and Evans 2018). This does not simply mean the data itself must be clearly presented, but that any factors potentially influencing the way it is interpreted must be entirely transparent. This includes the selection of data, and the methods and criteria of any sampling strategy employed. Examples of the importance of this transparency can be seen in the 'Town and Country in Roman Britain' project, which involved the selection of assemblage data from multiple excavations within one area (Doherty *et al.* 2013, 14; Doherty 2015, 4), and the 'Rural Settlement of Roman Britain' project, which sourced over 2,575 grey literature reports from England and Wales for data to be included in the project (Fulford and Brindle 2016, 10). While the 'Town and Country in Roman Britain' project was successful in drawing together and utilising multiple works, the 'Rural Settlement of Roman Britain' project was unable to make use of the pottery data acquired, owing to issues with a level of standardisation and interregional comparability of data (Fulford and Brindle 2016, 12–14). The inability to effectively utilise and compare pottery reports from different regions highlights the detriment of non-standardisation and a lack of transparency in literature (Rippon 2017, 337).

Whilst sampling in and of itself was not a substantive issue in incorporating interregional data in the 'Rural Settlement of Roman Britain' project, the general lack of transparency in the numerical aspects of pottery studies is a broader issue that needs to be considered generally before sampling can be discussed in isolation. Numerical aspects in this context not only include the implementation of sampling and retention policies, but also methods of quantification (ENV, MNV, EVE, sherd count, etc), and statistical analysis done after data collection. By not being transparent about the methods and approaches used when facing these numerical aspects, there becomes a risk of creating data that are not able to be compared on an interregional level or utilised by other individuals and organisations in the future. Data can be made sustainable through clearly stating how and why certain numerical aspects have been implemented and the current lack of transparency could stem from both subsumed and assumed knowledge (i.e., regarding key groups which are so widely accepted that justification of their use is not deemed necessary), and/or a general discomfort when it comes to discussing, and perhaps understanding, the more complex numerical aspects of methods utilised. Therefore, open discussions of methodologies must be facilitated within the context of numerical understanding and statistical theory. By doing so and encouraging this as a standard of study, specialists will be able to ensure the data they

produce are sustainable and available to benefit future works, rather than producing reports that can only be understood within the context of that particular project. Therefore, one of the aims of this paper is to present a clear methodology for a sampling strategy where any influences on data are transparently discussed, and that may be utilised by specialist when desired and appropriate.

As sampling is such a necessary component of archaeological study, an approach has been devised by A14 specialists that should allow for reliable results to be drawn from a smaller assemblage. The sample drawn equates to c. 60% of the full assemblage by weight, significantly reducing the amount of pottery that requires specialist processing. The reliability of the sampling strategy proposed is discussed through comparing the results of various analytical approaches to those of the full dataset. Comparison was made through initially assessing and then fully analysing both the sampled and non-sampled data, which resulted in a complete dataset where the sample could be considered individually without influence, or directly compared to the full assemblage. Through doing so, it has been possible to investigate how differently the assemblage could be interpreted when using the sampled data, and thus how reliable the sample was within the context of the full- an opportunity not often provided to studies of this nature. As the methods and results of analysis are discussed openly, and within the context of statistical significance testing, the project has been conducted in a way that merges archaeological and numerical discussion. The importance of this approach is that it not only allows for the reliability of this strategy to be tested, but also demonstrates the importance of complete methodological transparency and numerical discussion for understanding and utilising the results of this study. This should allow for the creation of a sustainable dataset from a large-scale project that could be utilised in the future by other studies like those discussed above. Essentially, this paper will critically evaluate whether sampling can be conducted without compromising the results of a study and, if successful, the method can be adopted by professional units working on large infrastructure projects in the future.

The full assemblage discussed in this project has been produced from excavations on the A14 Cambridge to Huntington Improvement Scheme lead by MOLA Headland Infrastructure (MOLA-HI) and comes from three TEAs (Targeted Excavation Areas 14, 15 and 16), which form one landscape block. The landscape block (henceforth the West of Ouse or WoO landscape block) demonstrates an extended chronology of occupation and activity, ranging in date from Bronze Age to post-medieval, though most material comes from the Roman or Late Iron Age (LIA) periods (Fig. 1). Thus, the assemblage was diverse, and produced high-quality data from the large amounts of pottery recovered, meaning it was ideal for this kind of study. Several key features were included within the landscape block and aided in determining key groups for sample selection.

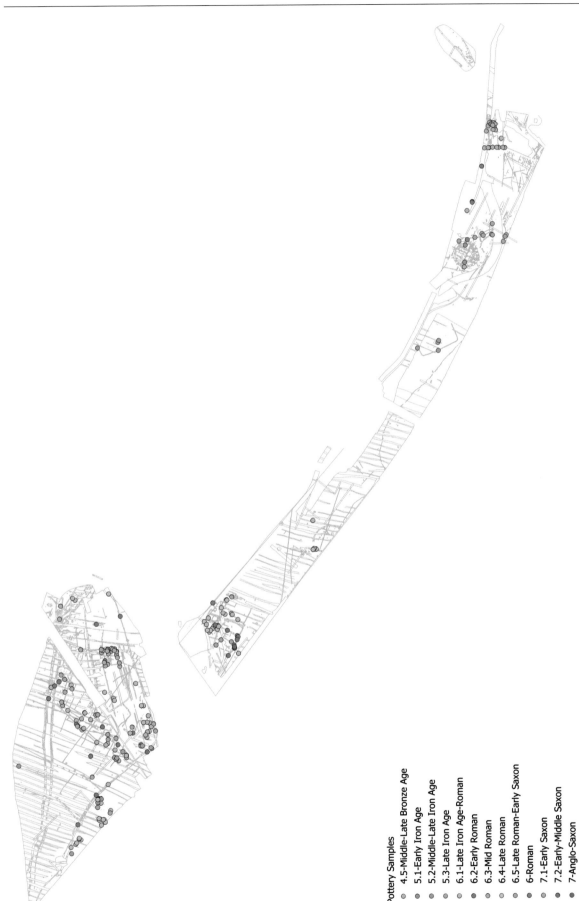

Pottery Samples
- 4.5-Middle-Late Bronze Age
- 5.1-Early Iron Age
- 5.2-Middle-Late Iron Age
- 5.3-Late Iron Age
- 6.1-Late Iron Age-Roman
- 6.2-Early Roman
- 6.3-Mid Roman
- 6.4-Late Roman
- 6.5-Late Roman-Early Saxon
- 6-Roman
- 7.1-Early Saxon
- 7.2-Early-Middle Saxon
- 7-Anglo-Saxon
— WestOfOuse_Survey

Figure 1. Map of pottery samples taken from TEA 14 (top left), TEA 15 (central) and TEA 16 (bottom right), which form the West of Ouse landscape block, copyright MOLA Headland Infrastructure.

These included monuments, kiln structures, and settlement activity. Sampled wares from these features were flagged and recorded separately by specialists Adam Sutton (Iron Age wares) and Eniko Hudak (Roman wares), while the unsampled wares were recorded by the author.

2. *Purposive sampling* on the A14

2.1. *The theory of sampling*

As previously discussed, sampling pottery comes with challenges. One common issue raised is that assemblages are inherently samples to begin with. This is because archaeological work is often with sherds rather than complete vessels, meaning there is no known complete 'population' at the outset, rather, an unintentional sample that we call the 'complete' assemblage (Orton 2000, 40). Furthermore, the life course of artefacts means that this unintentional sample goes through several phases of sub-sampling before reaching excavation and the specialist. There are many processes that may account for movement between assemblage phases, but the phases themselves are standard. While the vessel is in use it is part of the *life assemblage*, but once it is broken and stops being used, it is considered part of the *death assemblage* (Tyers 1996, 24). Once vessels join the *death assemblage*,

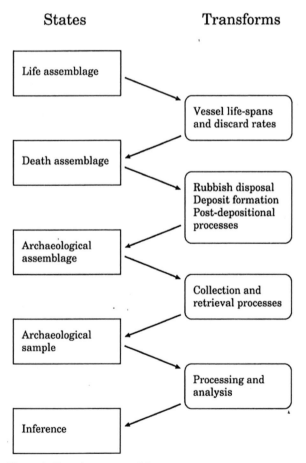

Figure 2. Transformations of the pottery assemblage (from Tyers 1996, 24).

a non-random sample of these enter the *archaeological assemblage* through deposition (Fig. 2). Only a proportion of what is in these deposits is actually excavated and recovered, and so not only do archaeologists not have a complete population to begin with, but this population has also been subject to multiple levels of sampling before even reaching this point. In fact, some degree of this sub-sampling is deliberately applied by archaeologists (i.e., through the selection of which contexts or percentage of contexts are excavated or assessed, often being influenced by third party factors such as council or government policies), meaning the sample itself is further distanced from the original life assemblage. Due to this, many archaeologists are sceptical about further sampling and argue the only way to be truly representative is to include as many sherds as possible for assessment (Rice 2015, 269). This is not always possible, for developer funded projects especially, as time and financial constraints can prevent this ideal large-scale sampling. Furthermore, as the *archaeological assemblage* is already a sample of the *death assemblage* and the *life assemblage*, the validity of considering it as a full population that any further sampling must perfectly represent should be queried. Instead, the sample in this study was considered as a method of representing the life assemblage.

A form of *purposive sampling* was employed for this project owing to the selective nature of the research aims. *Purposive* is one of two techniques outlined in the *representative method* (with the other being *random sampling*, which assumes all units in a given population have equal chance of selection) and refers to an approach where sampled units are selected according to values that relate to variables being studied (Bowley 1926 as cited in Neyman 1934, 559; Campbell *et al.* 2020, 654). *Purposive sampling* was deemed most appropriate for this project as it was necessary to answer specific research aims and include contexts outlined on the landscape block 'wish list' (a list of contexts that were deemed essential to sample given their relevance to fulfilling project wide or Landscape Block-specific aims) whilst reducing the amount of pottery studied rather than exclusively aiming to reduce what was excavated. The working theory was that key features or 'parent contexts' (these can be a range of things, such as a number referring to a layer, or to a relationship such as a cut) would form the primary unit at which sample selection took place. All the constituent contexts from within a parent context would be either included or omitted from the overall sample. This approach would therefore allow for the *purposive* method to be utilised, whilst only necessitating that the sample represent the feature population, thus meaning the broader assemblage profile should be well represented.

The sustainability of this data could be questioned within the context of limitations posed by Neyman (1934) who argued the absolute superiority of the *random* method in this regard (Orton 2000, 15). In his influential work, Neyman noted that when samples are drawn due to specific research aims, the resulting data will not be as appropriate for future use as that gained from *random* sampling, should future research aims differ from those influencing the sampling practice (Neyman 1934, 572). Despite this being an important limitation to bear in mind, Neyman only had two major case studies to consider and frequently acknowledged a lack of transparency within the methods of these. Furthermore, the issues with bias and reliance on hypotheses that Neyman discussed were theoretical, and at the time it was not possible to directly compare the two strategies due to the stark differences in what was considered a population.

To address these challenges, this project not only utilised *purposive sampling*, but also directly compared the sampled data to the full dataset. Thus, any discrepancies or biases were not only identified, but actively considered and critically evaluated. As the prime requirement of any sample is to provide an accurate representation of the wider population (Neyman 1934, 560; Orton 2000, 20; Rice 2015, 267), this study will contribute to the discussion of statistical theory by providing an opportunity to directly comment on the actual (rather than theoretical) representativeness of the methods used.

2.2. Methodology

All pottery from the WoO landscape block was recorded and quantified at the assessment stage. This was 19,871 sherds weighing 207.9 kg deriving from an estimated 4,049 vessels and equating to 213.7 EVEs. Of this, 12,170 sherds weighing 134.2 kg deriving from an estimated 2,051 vessels and equating to 136.7 EVEs were included in the sample. The intention of this study was to compare and contrast the ways in which the landscape block could be interpreted when using either the full or sampled dataset. In this way it would be possible to directly compare the interpretations drawn from the data to determine the effectiveness of a c. 60% by weight sample.

2.2.1. Sampling wares

The *purposive sampling* strategy was employed in two stages. Firstly, the aims of the landscape block research design were considered to generate 'wish list' contexts. It was essential that these were sampled given their relevance to fulfilling these aims (Hudak in prep.; MOLA Headland in prep.; Sutton in prep.). Secondly, samples were retrieved using a 'bulk sample' method, which considered the size of pottery groups (through a minimum weight threshold) and the informational value associated with the context a group was produced from (through a minimum information value) (Hudak in prep.; MOLA Headland in prep.; Sutton in prep.). Thus, to be accepted as part of the bulk sample, a pottery group must adhere to the following:

- Derive from a parent context that produced a minimum of 700g of pottery;

- Derive from a feature that was, **at the very least**, assigned to both a Settlement (here denoting land use) and a Period during the stratigraphic analysis (though in most cases more information was able to be assigned to accepted pottery groups).

This did result in some settlement periods being under-represented, some of which were deemed important to the project's research aims and for the establishment of a chronological pattern. For these reasons, some settlement periods were included in the sample in their entirety (Hudak in prep.; Sutton in prep.). The equivalent of 65.5% of the Iron Age and Roman pottery was initially sampled through the criteria expressed above. Whilst exceeding the target 60% sample, this did include kiln pottery that had already been recorded in order to characterise the products of the Lower Ouse Valley kilns in advance, and thus facilitate recognition of these wares in the rest of the assemblage. When this was excluded the sample size was reduced to 52.8%, thus removing the problematic nature of the sample size, which was now within the limits of the project resources.

Once 'wish list' contexts were sampled, the vessel assemblages associated with them were considered entire populations. In this sense, the samples from these contexts represented 100% of the populations of the features of interest rather than a percentage of the population of the TEA or landscape block. Rice (2015, 267) argues that the purpose of sampling is to gain the most information possible from a sampled sherd and, through focusing on areas of interest, this strategy gathered the most valuable information for answering specific questions from a smaller sample size. In this way, it would be possible to achieve the primary goal of sampling in a method that required less material from excavations, thus reducing the financial demands placed on professional units. However, whilst this was the case, at this point of the study it was not certain to what extent the sample reflected the full assemblage, which required further testing to determine. Therefore, the following methods were applied.

2.2.2. Identification and quantification

Once samples had been selected and retrieved, sherds were subject to general identification and quantification as is standard practice for pottery specialists (Barclay *et al.* 2016, 16–17). This was done through assessing sherds as hand specimens, with the additional use of a microscope (10x magnification) when necessary, to identify fabrics and forms. A new fabric and form type series for Cambridgeshire was produced for this project, which was utilised, and additional research was conducted as and when needed. In addition to form and fabric, sherds were assessed for the following information:

- Sherd count
- Weight in grams

- Rim Diameter
- Estimated Vessel Equivalent (EVE; through summation of rim diameter)
- Decoration

The information gained from this assessment was recorded in the Oracle database used by MOLA, which enforced a consistent set of codes during recording. This meant data input was standardised across all three people working on the wares and could be easily compared. Thus, the data used in this project was sustainable as it was digitally accessible and would be easy to understand and apply to projects in the future (Colley and Evans 2018).

2.2.3. Comparison of sampled and full datasets

The West of Ouse landscape block hosted six Settlements (0–5) and several ungrouped contexts, though only four of these Settlements (1–4) contained stratigraphic phases dateable to the Iron Age or Roman periods and were thus relevant for this project. For this reason, Settlements 0 and 5 were omitted from the sampling process. Settlements 1 and 2 were not sampled, but have been included in some analysis questions to provide wider context for the results.

In order to assess the effectiveness of the sample in terms of accurate representation, the initial reports of the sampled data (Smith *et al.* 2020; Hudak in prep.; Sutton in prep.) were used to determine five key inferences about pottery production and consumption in the landscape block. These inferences were then used to analyse the full dataset and determine whether the same conclusions could be drawn from the full and sampled datasets. The questions considered the representation of fabrics and industries; forms and finewares; the chronology of the local industries; and intrinsically interesting wares omitted from the sample. As each question considered a unique aspect of pottery studies, multiple analytical techniques had to be employed. For example, direct comparisons were made between the quantities of wares found within each settlement, distributions were mapped, and statistical analysis was run in the form of chi-squared goodness-of-fit-tests using methods outlined by Shennan (1997). All techniques used the data available on the MOLA SharePoint to ensure everything used was up to date. The results of each question will be discussed below, and the interpretations are examined in the following discussion. All statistics are by weight in grams unless specifically stated otherwise and all fabric codes used are outlined in Appendix 1.

3. Results

Before discussing the results of the study, the phasing and morphology of settlements should be outlined. As discussed above, the assemblage was comprised of pottery from TEAs 14, 15 and 16, which indicated activity throughout multiple phases of occupation. Most material recovered was dated to the Late Iron Age and Roman phases, which have been outlined below.

- Period 5.2, Middle to Late Iron Age (c. 350 BC–AD 70)
- Period 5.3, Late Iron Age (c. 50 BC–AD 70)
- Period 6.1, Late Iron Age to Early Roman (c. AD 43–70)
- Period 6.2, Early Roman (c. AD 70–200)
- Period 6.3, mid-Roman (c. AD 150–300)
- Period 6.4, Late Roman (c. AD 250–410)
- Period 6.5, Late Roman to Early Saxon (c. AD 400–500)

Settlements 1 and 2 were located within TEAs 14 and 16 respectively, with both demonstrating occupation across Periods 5.2 and 5.3. Settlement 3 spanned TEAs 14 and 15 and demonstrated occupation throughout the entirety of the Roman period (Periods 6.1 to 6.5). Settlement 4 was located within TEA 16, and also spanned most of the Roman period (Periods 6.2 to 6.4).

3.1. Fabrics and industries: Is the prominence of a locally driven industry in Settlements 3 and 4 illustrated in both the full and sampled datasets?

To discuss this question, the fabric categories of Settlements 3 and 4 were assessed separately to determine whether the prominence of local fabrics and industries flagged in the sampled data was also illustrated in the full dataset. Local products included industries immediate to the area such as the Lower Ouse Valley (LOV) and Godmanchester (GOD) industries. While the Horningsea (HOR) industry is often considered local within the area, it was considered a regional import for this study as wares were produced c. 30 km from the landscape block. Similarly, fabrics that could not be provenanced or allocated to one particular industry (bucket code fabrics) such as sandy grey wares which show no evidence to indicate being non-local, were also not included as only definitely local wares were the focus.

3.1.1. Regional and continental imports

Only a small quantity of continental imports was identified across both settlements. Samian (SAM) only accounted for 2.4% of the full dataset by weight and 3.0% of the sample in Settlement 3, and 0.5% in both datasets for Settlement 4. Amphorae (AMPH) were even less common, accounting for 0.5% and 0.1% of Settlement 3, and not being identified at all in Settlement 4. While regional imports were more common, they still only accounted for a small percentage of the overall assemblage. The most prominent of these were the Horningsea industry (7.6% and 11.6% of Settlement 3, and 12.3% and 14.2% in Settlement 4) (Table 1). Thus, both the sampled and full dataset demonstrate the use and consumption of primarily local industries, and a preference for regional imports over continental imports, with minimal variation between the two.

Table 1. Quantification of continental and regional imports from Settlements 3 and 4 by weight (g).

	Settlement 3		Settlement 4	
	Wt. %	*Wt. %*	*Wt. (g)*	*Wt. (g)*
	(Full Dataset)	*(Sample)*	*(Full Dataset)*	*(Sample)*
Continental Imports				
SAM	2.40%	2.90%	0.50%	0.50%
AMPH	0.50%	0.10%	N/A	N/A
Regional Imports				
HOR	7.80%	11.60%	12.30%	14.20%
LNV	3.10%	2.10%	3.80%	4.00%
VER WH	6.30%	7.90%	0.30%	0.40%
DOR BB 1	0.00%	0.00%	1.20%	1.40%
Main Local Industries				
LOV	18.80%	29.40%	51.40%	60.40%
GOD WH	1.10%	0.30%	0.20%	N/A

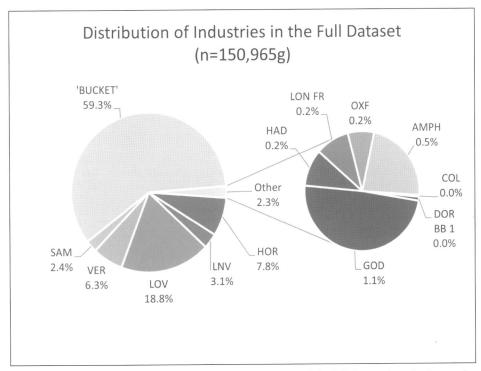

Figure 3. Chart illustrating the prominent fabric categories of the full dataset from Settlement 3.

3.1.2. Local industries

Lower Ouse Valley (LOV) wares were by far the most significant of any industry across both settlements. In Settlement 3, of the 41% of wares in the full dataset that could be attributed to known industries, 18.8% of those were identified as LOV wares (Fig. 3). The prominence of locally produced pottery was also illustrated in the sample (accounting for c. 30%), though a c. 10% discrepancy is notable (Fig. 4). In Settlement 4, LOV wares continued to dominate, making up over half of the full dataset with 51.4% and 60.4% of the sampled data (Figs 5 and 6). While the general trends of Settlements 3 and 4

were reflected in the sample, a c. 10% discrepancy in the quantity of LOV products between the full and sampled datasets was noted in both. Additionally, the full dataset of Settlement 3 demonstrated a high quantity of fine sandy grey wares (FSGW) compared to the sample which are probably an LOV (or local) product and may illustrate the effects of interobserver variation on the study. The significance of this shall be examined in the discussion.

3.1.3. Statistical significance

Goodness-of-fit chi-squared tests (χ^2 tests) were run to compare the observed sample distribution to a pre-specified

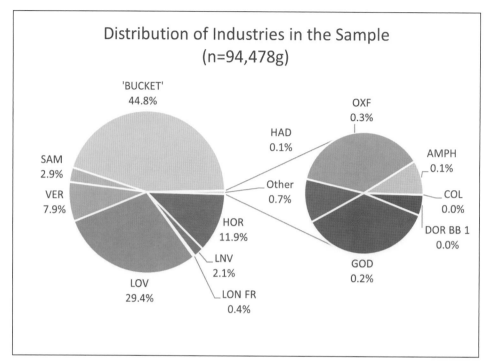

Figure 4. Chart illustrating the prominent fabric categories of the sampled data from Settlement 3.

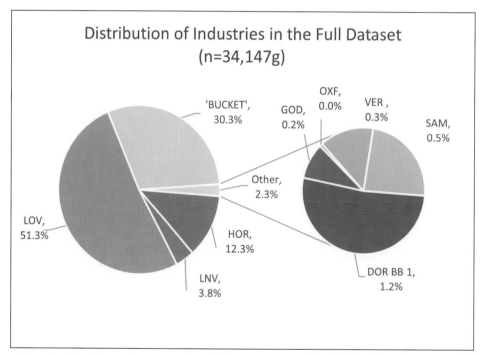

Figure 5. Chart illustrating the prominent fabric categories of the full dataset from Settlement 4.

theoretical population (the full dataset) in order to determine if there was any statistical significance to the distributions. Two tests were run per Settlement, one measuring sherd counts and the other measuring weights, which could be compared to reduce bias in the results. Both tests for Settlement 3 indicated statistically significant differences between the distribution of the sampled wares and those of the full data set (sherd counts: χ^2 (9, n=9,262) = 80.0, $p > 16.9$; sherd weights: χ^2 (9, n=94,478) = 755.5, $p > 16.9$). Likewise, both tests for Settlement 4 indicated statistically significant differences in distribution (sherd counts: χ^2 (7, n=1,907) = 54.2, $p > 14.067$; sherd weights: χ^2 (7, n=29,042) = 916.9, $p > 14.067$). As the visualisations demonstrated very similar trends, it was unlikely that the

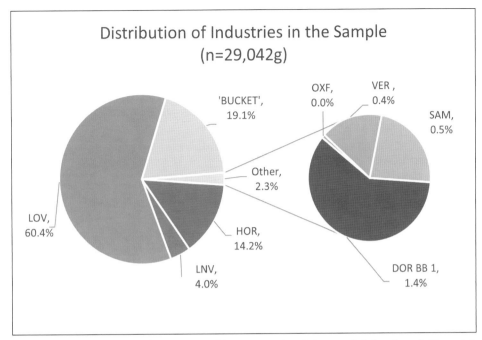

Figure 6. Chart illustrating the prominent fabric categories of the sampled data from Settlement 4.

Table 2. Quantification of Lower Nene Valley colour-coat forms from Settlements 3 and 4.

	Settlement 3, LNV CC				Settlement 4, LNV CC			
	Full Dataset		Sample		Full Dataset		Sample	
	EVE	Ct.	EVE	Ct.	EVE	Ct.	EVE	Ct.
Forms								
-	0	84	0	38	0	36	0	19
Beaker	1.29	13	0.87	8	0.6	15	0.27	4
Bowl	1.13	9	1.13	7	0.65	4	0.65	4
Flagon	0.81	3			1.8	6		
Jar	2.26	15	2.03	12	0.49	3	0.16	1
Lid	0.4	1	0.4	1				
Open Form	0.05	3	0	2				
Platter/Dish	0.96	10	0.68	6	0.88	5	0.2	2

discrepancies were as severe as the test results suggest and may have been the result of discrepancies in smaller fabric categories. Though, the higher proportion of LOV fabrics identified in the sample were also a likely contributor.

3.2. Forms and vessel classes: Do fineware vessel forms and classes remain limited with the exception of an increase during the middle Roman period for Settlement 3 (c. AD 150–300)?

For this assessment, both local and imported finewares were considered (i.e., Samian, colour-coated vessels, and LON FR). This is a similar criterion to that used by Booth in his discussion of ceramics as indicators of site status (1991, 5). However, amphorae and mortaria were not considered despite often representing imported wares,

due to the low quantities yet relatively high weights of these wares which would potentially skew the statistical significance results of the datasets. It was believed that these wares would influence the analysis results in a way that was not truly representative of what the assemblage suggests. In addition, Lower Nene Valley colour-coated wares (LNV CC) have been considered finewares for this assessment due to the high proportions of beakers when compared to other wares, which is more indicative of the early industry's production of finewares than the change in repertoire to predominantly utilitarian wares after the later third century (Booth 1991, 1; Table 2). Finally, Settlements 1 and 2 were not sampled and so could not be used for this comparison, though neither demonstrated any wares considered finewares in this assessment regardless.

3.2.1. Settlements 3 and 4

A drastic increase in the quantity of finewares identified in Settlement 3 was noted when compared to previous settlements, particularly the introduction of colour-coated wares (2.8% and 3.3% by weight of the full and sampled data respectively), which were the most prominent fineware group within the settlement (Table 3). However, this was still relatively limited as finewares only account for 5.4% and 6.6% of the total assemblage for Settlement 3. Finewares were also identified in Settlement 4 but remained in small quantities. Colour-coated wares were the most prominent, though it is debatable to what extent these wares can actually be termed 'finewares' (see above). This could also be queried as the settlement produced far less beakers (a product more associated with the fineware repertoire of the LNV CC industry) and more bowls (a more utilitarian product) than Settlement 3 (Table 2). Additionally, flagons dramatically increased, fine reduced wares were not identified at all, and Samian products appear to have drastically reduced.

Settlements 3 and 4 saw the introduction of new forms such as flagons, lids, amphora and specialist forms. Of the diagnostic forms, those that dominated were jars (64% of the full dataset by EVEs and 68% of the sample for Settlement 3; 19.4% and 29.5% for Settlement 4). In order to interpret the form profile of the settlements, a similar method was used to that of Evans (2001, 26) to differentiate urban from rural assemblages. Evans found that higher proportions of jars than tableware forms were often seen in rural sites while the reverse was true for urban and villa sites, and roadside settlements. The observations regarding vessel form predominance support a correlation between site type and pottery consumption which was used to discuss the limited finewares associated with these settlements. Evans also noted that the disparity between urban and rural is much more pronounced in the early Roman period. Whilst both settlements demonstrated occupation during this time, Settlement 3 had a greater focus of deposition in Period 6.2 than Settlement 4, which primarily indicated deposition in the mid-Roman period. Regardless, as the settlements are broadly contemporary and thus comparison is like to like, the results of this section should not be largely affected by chronological

factors. The proportions of jars to tableware forms (bowls, dishes, and platters) from both Settlement 3 and Settlement 4 indicated similarities to utilitarian-driven rural assemblages which overall lack in finewares (Fig. 7). This was true for both the full and sampled datasets, meaning that the distribution of wares could be interpreted in the same way when using this model.

3.3. Chronology and local industries: Is the decline of the local industry (particularly the LOV industry) by the end of Period 6.3 demonstrated and the discrepancy in what replaces it in Settlements 3 and 4 shown?

The consumption of different industries was assessed through plotting assemblage makeup for Settlements 3 and 4 across Periods 6.1, 6.2, 6.3 and 6.4. This allowed a visualisation of consumption throughout the chronology of the landscape block and was done for both the full and sampled databases. The five most prominent fabrics from each settlement were included in the data visualisation and for clarity all others were included in an 'Other' category (Fig. 8).

3.3.1. Periods 6.1 and 6.2

Only Settlement 3 demonstrated occupation in Period 6.1, and so this was the only settlement assessed. No fabrics of interest were identified as the assemblage consisted entirely of Iron Age wares and no regional or Continental imports were identified in either the full or sampled data. Both Settlements 3 and 4 had occupation periods that extended into Period 6.2, though Settlement 4 was omitted due to a small assemblage size (933 g). Local industries were notable components of the Settlement 3 assemblage in this period with LOV products being the most abundant named industry (42% of the full assemblage by weight and 53% of the sample). Thus, the prominence of the local industry was demonstrated in both datasets (Fig. 8).

3.3.2. Period 6.3

In Settlement 3, a marked decline of LOV wares was illustrated, reducing to 15% of the full assemblage by weight and 24% of the sample. This decline was more

Table 3. Quantification of fineware fabrics from Settlements 3 and 4.

	Full Dataset				Sampled Data			
	Ct.	Ct. %	Wt. (g)	Wt. %	Ct.	Ct. %	Wt. (g)	Wt. %
Settlement 3	**700**	**4.60%**	**8206**	**5.40%**	**450**	**4.90%**	**6212**	**6.60%**
CC	437	2.90%	4263	2.80%	278	3.00%	3115	3.30%
FNRD	40	0.30%	335	0.20%	40	0.40%	335	0.40%
SAM	223	1.50%	3608	2.40%	132	1.40%	2762	2.90%
Settlement 4	**125**	**5.10%**	**1216**	**3.60%**	**85**	**4.50%**	**1059**	**3.70%**
CC	100	4.10%	1032	3.00%	68	3.60%	904	3.10%
SAM	25	1.00%	184	0.50%	17	0.90%	155	0.50%

extremely illustrated in the sample which could be due to no instances of LOV oxidised ware being identified, or an increase in sample size which may have resulted in a wider array of fabrics being identified. The reverse was true for Settlement 4, where the prominence of LOV products dramatically increases to 56% of the full assemblage (previously being 0.5%) and 60% of the sample (previously 16%). While regional imports could also be seen in this period for Settlement 4 (Horningsea products contributing to 13% and 14% of the assemblages), this was to a lesser extent than in Period 6.2. However, the sample sizes for Settlement 4 have radically increased

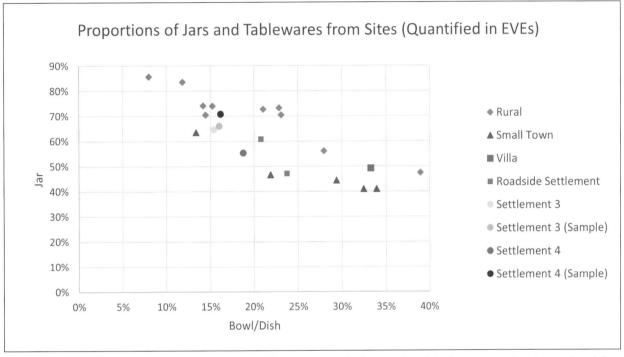

Figure 7. Graph illustrating the proportions of jars and tablewares in Settlements 3 and 4 when compared to data gathered from various sites from across the Central Belt region of Britain (namely Northamptonshire, Cambridgeshire and Oxfordshire). Sites and references listed in Appendix 2.

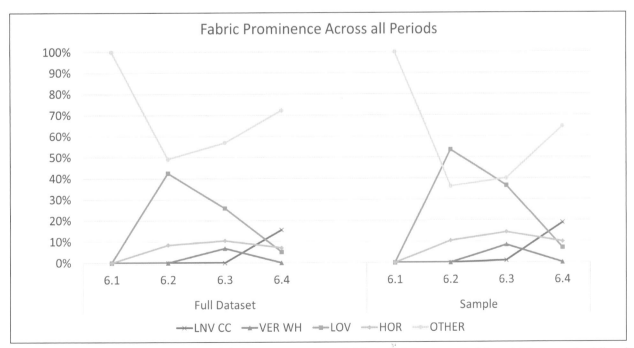

Figure 8. Chart illustrating the growth and decline in prominence of different fabrics (quantified by weight) across the full and sampled datasets.

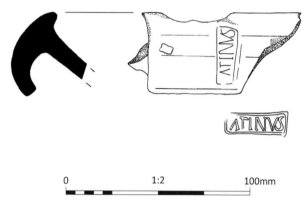

0   1:2   100mm

Figure 9. Stamped mortarium from Settlement 3, illustration by author.

so the distribution pattern may have been influenced by a larger sample, resulting in an increased array of wares, and a shift in distribution patterning. Regardless, a general decrease of the local industries can be seen between Periods 6.2 and 6.3 with no dramatic increase in any other industry, suggesting the changes to the LOV production were unique to this industry (Fig. 8).

3.3.3. Period 6.4

Only Settlement 3 demonstrated occupation during Period 6.4. Here the LOV industry is far less prominent than in previous periods, only accounting for 5% of the full assemblage and 7% of the sample (Fig. 8). In contrast, the Lower Nene Valley colour-coat industry demonstrates a notable increase (16% and 19%), though this was likely a result of change in colour-coat repertoire previously discussed. Furthermore, bucket code fabrics also see an increase, particularly ROB SH (35% and 38%), indicating that a local industry persisted, just not in the form of LOV.

3.4. Sampling Representativeness: Has the sampling strategy missed any forms or fabrics of intrinsic interest to the project that would result in a limitation of our understanding of the landscape block?

Here, a ware was considered of intrinsic interest if any component could alter our understanding of pottery consumption or production within the wider area; or could contribute to a wider corpus of wares. For example, whilst multiple base sherds with deliberate post-firing holes were identified in the non-sampled wares, they were not considered of intrinsic value as similar wares were included in the sample and so did not contribute to our understanding of pottery consumption and use in any way the sample did not.

3.4.1. Mortarium

Two sherds of a bead-and-flange type mortarium were recovered from a ditch in Settlement 3 (located in TEA 14) and the context indicated they were associated with Period 6.2. The vessel is a fine sandy oxidised ware,

though the industry was not identified. One mortarium sherd stamped [...TINVS] is interpreted as possibly being MATINUS (Fig. 9). It is highly likely that this is the stamp of a new potter discovered in the area (Kay Hartley pers. comm.), thus the sherds are of high informational value to the project and potentially, more generally.

3.4.2. Triple vase

Another sherd of intrinsic value came from the fill of a ditch in Settlement 3 (located in TEA 15) associated with Period 6.2. The sherd, thought to be part of a triple vase, is a fragment of a hollow, circular tube, made in a sandy oxidised fabric. The form has a flat base and two pre-firing holes in the top which do not penetrate the base (Fig. 10). Preservation is good, though significant lamination has occurred on the top.

No other examples of this form were identified and evidence of a triple vase is particularly interesting as the assemblage otherwise consists of table and cooking wares (as demonstrated in Section 3.3 and Fig. 8). In addition, this sherd is of interest due to its fabric. One of the research aims for the early Roman period (Period 6.2) was to undergo a detailed analysis of pottery, kiln furniture, and other associated tools to allow for an understanding of the Lower Ouse Valley industry's organisation. As the fabric of this form has been identified as FSOX (fine sandy oxidised ware) there is a possibility that it could be a product of the LOV industry. If this is the case, it would alter our understanding of the industry and its products. Hence, further fabric assessment of this sherd must be done in order to understand the implications it has on the organisation of the LOV industry.

3.4.3. Amphora

Finally, the rim of a possible Gauloise 4 type amphora was identified from a ditch feature in Settlement 3 (TEA 14). The sherd has a thick rounded rim and the remnants of two flat handles with grooves in the centre positioned either side of the neck, though only one of these handle bases remains intact while the other is only evidenced by a joining scar (Fig. 11). The fabric requires further research to identify due to the blackened nature of the vessel walls, making it difficult to identify with any certainty. The vessel acts as an indicator of continental trade, which is otherwise rare on this site.

These three forms were of intrinsic interest and the unique nature of the vessels contributes to the ways in which the pottery industries and their consumption can be understood both in the landscape block and wider area. Thus, by not including these wares, the sample would have limited our understanding of these. Particularly, had the sample consistently failed to include mortarium sherds displaying the stamp of a new potter (as this sherd demonstrates is a possibility) our understanding of the production of these wares would continue to be less than what available evidence allows and thus the sample would greatly hinder projects such as a regional or national corpus of stamps.

Figure 10. Sherd of triple vase from Settlement 3.

However, their potential exclusion does not directly limit the understanding of key research questions regarding industry organisation, continuation of occupations, or other Roman period specific research aims of the project. In addition, these three forms were the only intrinsically interesting vessels missed by the sampling strategy. Generally, the sample was successful in identifying all key vessels which allowed for similar conclusions about the landscape block to be drawn by the full and sampled datasets. As a result, while the significance of these wares must be acknowledged, it cannot be said that through missing them the sample has been limited to such an extent that the broader trends of the landscape block cannot be understood in the same way as the full dataset allows. Furthermore, it must be remembered that owing to the time limitations faced, some of these interpretations are hypothetical. Thus, it is not definitively possible to say how harmful the exclusion of these wares from the sample has been.

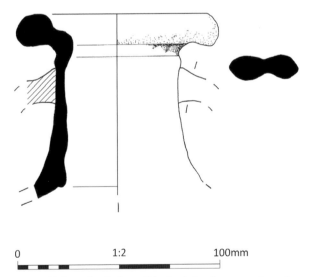

Figure 11. Rim sherd of possible Gauloise 4 type amphora from Settlement 3, illustration by author.

4. Discussion

4.1. The reflectiveness of the sample

The results of these analyses demonstrate that the sample was generally able to reflect the life assemblage to the same extent as the full dataset and give the same broad impressions of the settlement assemblages. The sample was most accurate in its representation of larger fabric categories, particularly well demonstrated by Sections 3.1 and 3.3, allowing for the same conclusions to be drawn regarding the organisation, distribution and eventual decline of the local pottery industry, and the limited quantities of finewares and continental imports as the full dataset did.

Having said this, there were discrepancies in the smaller fabric categories which affected how the distribution of these wares was interpreted. This was illustrated in Section 3.1 where, despite great accuracy in its reflection of a locally driven industry, statistical analysis deemed the sample as illustrating a significantly different distribution of data to the full dataset. This was due to differences in smaller fabric cases such as oxidised wares, finewares and imports. As the quantifiable contribution of these wares to the full dataset was so small, the discrepancies were not immediately apparent in the data visualisations produced and were only flagged by statistical analysis. It is likely that these discrepancies were inflated by the use of statistics, as is usually the case when used on small population groups. As a result, despite being statistically significant, these discrepancies did not have any major impact on the ways in which the data as a whole was interpreted.

However, the variation here does highlight the necessity for methodological transparency should the sampling strategy be utilised. Whilst the implications of the dataset remain the same, data has been influenced in a way deemed statistically significant by the chi-squared goodness-of-fit tests. Therefore, future works concerned with these minor components (i.e., finewares) would benefit from the knowledge that the dataset has been subjected to sampling and that this may impact the distribution of the smaller components of the assemblage. Though notably in this case the variation did not impact the broader interpretation of the site, nor how industry specific questions were answered.

Therefore, the real significance of these discrepancies must be queried – if data discrepancies in the sample did not impact the way in which data was interpreted enough to affect our understanding of the 'life assemblage', can they be considered significant enough reason to call the sample ineffective? In addition, as the data missed by the sample (in this example) has not improved our understanding of the life assemblage, can the full dataset really be considered a more valuable unit of measurement than the sample?

4.2. Interobserver variation

The sample demonstrated a number of discrepancies in smaller fabric cases. These fabrics were predominantly bucket codes and often included variations of very similar fabrics (such as fine sandy oxidised wares, FSOX, or coarse sandy oxidised wares, CSOX). Whilst it is possible that a slight differentiation in the local industry (between fine and coarse products) or a sampling bias (owing to the sample being weighted towards kiln groups) was being observed, it is more likely that interobserver variation was influencing the results. This is due to the fact that differentiating between fine and coarse variations of a fabric is subjective and relies largely on an individual's past experience with materials (Whittaker *et al.* 1998, 143). Thus, where multiple specialists with a range

of experiences and expertise are working on the same materials, it is likely that subjectivity and interobserver variation will affect how the assemblage is interpreted. Interobserver variation is a form of *bias* (Daniels 1972 as cited by Whittaker *et al.* 1998, 135) and is countered by 'quality control', namely the reproduction of results and agreement on these by different observers. On this project, quality control was attempted through constant communication and cross-comparison, but with three observers with a vast range of experiences (the author being new to the field at the time, while Sutton and Hudak each had c. 10 years' experience) and separated geographically, some variation could not be avoided (Rippon 2017, 339). Though, it can be argued that no matter how many years of experience two specialists may have, they are very likely to view assemblages differently. Particularly, divergences in the quantities of LOV industry wares were identified, especially in Section 3.1 where c. 10% discrepancies were noted as well as an unusually high proportion of FSGW in the full dataset of Settlement 3. As the LOV industry is a recent discovery it can be difficult to confidently identify, and the degrees of confidence vary between specialists. As a result, while one observer may confidently identify these wares as LOV, another may assign bucket codes rather than risk misidentification (Rippon 2017, 338; this issue has also been described as 'lumping' by Orton *et al.* 1993, 73), resulting in lower identification rates of LOV and higher rates of FSGW. In sum, some discrepancies between the sample and full dataset are likely the result of interobserver variation rather than that of sample bias. This is a significant methodological issue and that is not often discussed in literature, though should be considered when organising large-scale projects that involve multiple specialists, or indeed multiple commercial units (an argument also made on several occasions by Rippon 2017).

4.3. The nature of the sample

Furthermore, potential issues in representation resulting from sample bias were raised. While the discrepancy identified in Section 3.1 between the LOV wares of the full and sampled datasets may have been the result of interobserver variation, it could also be due to all kiln features being included in the sample. Due to the importance of understanding the LOV industry to the research aim, all production sites of these wares were considered key features. However, this would result in a sample bias meaning that an increased proportion of LOV wares would be included in the sample when compared to any other ware, possibly resulting in the aforementioned discrepancy. While this sample bias was somewhat evident, it did not have any major influence over the interpretation of the landscape block, whilst also being an important aspect of the strategy for the aims of the research.

Moreover, it should be noted that similar selective factors would also affect the interpretation of 'non-sampled' assemblages, and that this issue is not unique to this study. This is due to field teams being selective in their decisions to excavate features, rather than randomly or totally excavating. Thus, the selectivity of the *purposive* method can often already be a factor in excavations and needs to be considered when specialists report on any assemblage. As a result, both specialists and field teams must be explicit in their decisions that could affect the composition of an artefact assemblage, especially when sampling methods are being employed.

4.4. Wares of intrinsic interest

One of the major pitfalls of this method was the accidental exclusion of intrinsically interesting sherds from the sample. As the sherds discussed here came from contexts producing minimal assemblages, it is likely they were not included in the sample due to not meeting the minimum weight requirement (700 g) rather than being deemed unimportant during an initial assessment. One way to counter this exclusion would be for sherds of high informational value to be flagged during the initial assessment of the assemblage before the sample is conducted. This could be during the spot-dating stage, which is often implemented on assemblages of this scale. Through doing so it would be possible to ensure these wares were accounted for and included in the sample without necessarily retaining the entire context they were identified in.

4.5. Theoretical issues

This study has examined the accuracy of the sampling strategy by comparing the results of the sample to those of the full dataset, an opportunity not many other theoretical discussions are granted. However, assessing the representativeness of a sample is not a simple question. One of the primary issues is that the sample very rarely demonstrated absolutely accurate reflections of the full data when results were visualised, despite accurately translating the broader trends. For example, the predominance of a locally driven industry was clearly illustrated by the sample, which was also accurate in demonstrating which industries dominated the assemblage, though exact percentages varied slightly, and smaller fabric categories were not represented entirely accurately. So, what does this say about the effectiveness of the sample? Again, the answer is not clear cut. While it is true that the proportions of the smaller fabric categories were not reflected with absolute accuracy, the sample was able to reflect that they comprised minute parts of the wider assemblage, the proportions of these in relation to one another, and the general trends that they illustrated. Furthermore, we must question how important the absolute accuracy of these categories is. Not only would statistical variation be inflated by the small populations of these groups, but the degree to which these discrepancies hinder interpretation of specific forms and fabrics is questionable. In the greater picture, does it matter that amphorae, for example, form

0.5% of the full assemblage and only 0.1% of the sample when both would be reported at >1% and thus provide the same implications to anyone reading the site report?

Moreover, the sustainability of the data going forward must be considered. The fact that these small categories have been affected by the strategy does raise questions regarding the potential for this data to influence the results of future studies. However, owing to the fact that the influence of the strategy on these wares was so minimal, it is likely there would be no significant implications for the use of this data by other researchers. Regardless, the transparency of this methodological approach – provided within the context of numerical discussion does mean that the potential for bias is explicitly discussed and researchers have the opportunity to determine whether they feel it is suitable for their use on an individual level.

This raises the further issue of how harshly it is possible to critique representativeness when, as archaeologists, we cannot be sure of what the sample represents in the first place. This study has compared the sampled data to that of the full dataset, but when the full dataset is not a complete population and a sample in of itself (Orton 2000, 40), how can we be sure it is an accurate unit of measurement to compare a further sample to? This is an inherent issue with pottery studies. Owing to the natural processes that transform a life assemblage to a death assemblage and eventually an archaeological assemblage, very few vessels will reach the final stage complete and not all vessels will be identified during excavation (Tyers 1996, 24). Thus, the full dataset is not synonymous with a complete population and so the accuracy of the sample to the full dataset does not equate accuracy of reflection of the original life assemblage. This is not to say that it does not matter how the sample presents the data as, as previously discussed, the prime requirement of any sample is to provide an accurate representation of the wider population (Orton 2000, 20; Neyman 1934, 560; Rice 2015, 267). However, as it is impossible to determine whether the full dataset is representative of the wider population, the degree to which the sample must be an accurate representation of the full dataset is not absolute. Thus, while it is important the sample is accurate, or at least to a certain extent, it is not necessary to fixate on minor discrepancies when the general trends are indeed reflected, as to do so is to suggest the full dataset is a pure representation of the life assemblage which cannot be ascertained.

4.6 Financial factors

All research projects have finite resources, and so decisions always need to be made about the efficient use of these resources with the aim to get maximum value of return, in terms of ability to answer research questions. For this reason, it was important that this project considered the cost efficiency of the sampling strategy within the context of pottery assessment by A14 specialists, to best determine the relief of resources it may offer.

To assess the financial benefits of processing a sample compared to the full dataset, a comparison of days spent by specialists on specific tasks relating to the WoO landscape block pottery analysis was made (it has been deemed appropriate to use person days as a proxy for any actual financial details of the project during this section). The A14 pottery specialists operate on an estimated rate of 400 sherds recorded per day. Recording the entire WoO pottery assemblage equates to around 44 days, while recording the 60% sample only equates to around 26.4 days. This demonstrates the potential for greater cost effectiveness and resource relief this strategy can be capable of.

However, sampling does accumulate hidden administrative time that does not accrue when working with a full dataset. In this case, this involved devising a sampling policy (c. 5 days) and undertaking sample selection (c. 4 days), which increased the total sample processing time to 35.4 days (Fig. 12). Though, once a policy is devised, it is likely that the time spent doing so for future projects will decrease. Regardless, even with these hidden administrative costs, the sample was still c. 20% more cost effective to process than the full dataset and saved nearly 9 working days.

It should be noted that while cost effective, the sample is not as efficient as originally thought. Based on person days, the c. 60% sample saved c. 20% of specialist time, meaning that two-fifths of the full data was lost in order to save one-fifth of the time. While this is not as greatly efficient, it is cost effective and as the data is representative of the full assemblage, the dataset was not made poorer as a result. Importantly, the data produced is sustainable,

and the strategy has allowed for a clear methodological approach that may be implemented on future projects at the discretion of individuals when deemed appropriate. While it is still uncertain as to whether admin costs are relative to sample size, the project has demonstrated that through employing this method of sampling, analysis can be more cost effective, relieve a demand on resources, and still provide results that accurately reflect the trends of the assemblage.

5. Conclusion

The experimental sampling strategy proposed has been effective in accurately illustrating the general trends of the full WoO landscape block dataset. Through analysing the results of the sampled dataset several key trends were identified. The results of the full dataset were then assessed to determine whether these same trends were present. This was done primarily through the comparison of data visualisations and statistical significance tests which illustrated similar results across both datasets. While the sample was not absolutely accurate in its representations, especially regarding fabric categories occurring in smaller quantities, these did not influence the results of the data significantly, nor did it change the way in which the landscape block was interpreted. It is important to note that at this time, the discussed sampling technique remains solely appropriate for large scale projects, such as infrastructure schemes, owing to a bias towards larger ware categories, and the fact that the method has only been tested within this context. It would be appropriate for further study

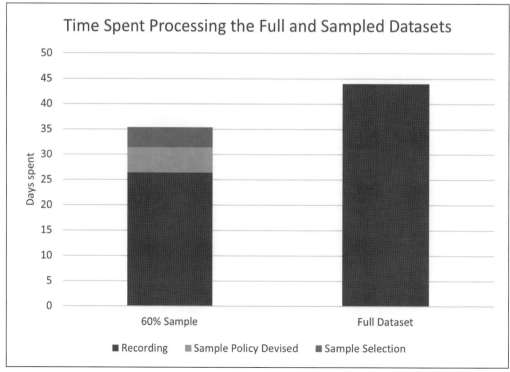

Figure 12. Chart illustrating the time spent processing the sampled and full pottery assemblages.

to include comparisons of this technique with different sample sizes to determine whether accuracy decreases as sample size does.

Sampling was effective despite the effects of interobserver variation, which undoubtedly impacted the study's results, perhaps more so than the research and sampling strategy itself. A further study, using the same (or indeed one experienced) pottery specialists for both the sample and the total dataset, could provide insight into the question about the extent of the impact of interobserver variation. This paper has suggested ways in which pottery specialists can mitigate for the potential loss of information on intrinsically interesting sherds by flagging these during spot-dating which can be common with large scale projects, before the sample selection takes place, but this is not thought to be a major limitation. As the limitations of this approach require further study to combat, it is not possible at this time to recommend the strategy be employed by professional units.

There are clear financial benefits for commercial units in adopting this approach for very large infrastructure projects, as time that would have been spent on the full assemblage could instead be spent on other areas such as C14 dating or answering other research questions with methods that may otherwise have been outside the allocated budget of a project. Having said this, the time and cost saving is not as significant as first thought, given the hidden administrative costs identified in this study.

Though it should be noted that some administrative costs such as the time needed to devise a sampling policy would naturally decrease the more the method is implemented. Nevertheless, the paper has demonstrated the potential of adopting a deliberate sampling strategy for large pottery assemblages, as well as outlining a clear methodology and showing the importance of transparency when utilising and influencing data. The benefits, in terms of both finance and time, have allowed for a unique contribution to the broader discussion of statistics and sampling theory.

Acknowledgements

This article is based on research carried out by the author's MA dissertation project at Reading University as generously supported by National Highways as part of the A14 Cambridge to Huntingdon Road Improvement Scheme, and therefore utilises pottery from these excavations. Special thanks go to all of these institutions for the facilities and support provided.

Notes

The pottery assessments discussed within this article and other digital data and reports will all be available for public access in the A14 digital archive on ADS https://archaeologydataservice.ac.uk/archives/view/a14_he_2020/

Appendix 1. List of fabric names and codes used in the West of Ouse pottery sampling strategy analysis.

Fabric	Code	Full Dataset				Sampled Dataset			
		Ct.	Wt. (g)	EVE	ENV	Ct.	Wt. (g)	EVE	ENV
Iron Age Types	-	**2872**	**26303**	**18.06**	**338**	**1974**	**16029**	**10.43**	**178**
Amphora	**AMPH**	**23**	**801**	**0.73**	**6**	**8**	**60**	**0**	**2**
Black Burnished Wares	**BB**	**224**	**1694**	**1.78**	**40**	**210**	**1444**	**1.49**	**34**
Dorset Type 1	DOR BB 1	30	441	0.63	9	30	441	0.63	9
Horningsea	HOR BB	167	886	0.39	19	159	748	0.33	17
Other		27	367	0.76	12	21	255	0.53	8
Colour Coated Wares	**CC**	**578**	**5624**	**9.65**	**197**	**351**	**4130**	**6.63**	**108**
Lower Nene Valley	LNV CC	363	3669	7.19	153	163	2353	4.24	74
Oxfordshire White Slipped	OXF WS	4	18	0	1				
Oxfordshire Red Slipped	OXF RS	8	246	0.3	6	8	246	0.3	6
Colchester	COL CC	4	17	0	1				
Hadham Red Slipped	HAD RS	1	31	0	1	1	31	0	1
Other		198	1643	2.16	35	179	1500	2.09	27
Fine Reduced Wares	**FNRD**	**40**	**335**	**0.95**	**2**	**40**	**335**	**0.95**	**2**
London Fine Reduced Ware	LON FR	40	335	0.95	2	40	335	0.95	2
Miscellaneous	**MISC**	**2180**	**29821**	**19.93**	**501**	**1244**	**19047**	**11.65**	**246**
Romano-British Shelly Ware	ROB SH	1900	24555	16.64	413	1060	14768	9.46	183
Other		280	5266	3.29	88	184	4279	2.19	63

(Continued)

Appendix 1. List of fabric names and codes used in the West of Ouse pottery sampling strategy analysis. (Continued)

		Full Dataset				Sampled Dataset			
Oxidised Wares	**OXID**	**2699**	**30179**	**24.44**	**641**	**1533**	**20677**	**16.53**	**287**
Lower Ouse Valley Oxidised	LOV OX	929	13475	10.01	132	912	13397	10.01	129
Horningsea Oxidised	HOR OX	303	5469	3.38	81	281	4998	3.15	70
Hadham Oxidised	HAD OX	44	395	0.51	20	6	45	0	6
Other		1423	10840	10.54	408	334	2237	3.37	82
Reduced Wares	**REDU**	**9255**	**84431**	**89.85**	**1694**	**5651**	**53926**	**57.36**	**880**
Fine Sandy Grey Wares	FSGW	2691	23096	28.14	588	216	1375	3.88	45
Lower Ouse Valley Black	LOV BW	1767	14314	12.05	172	1765	14309	12.05	171
Lower Ouse Valley Grey	LOV GW	1740	18083	17.95	245	1691	17647	17.87	237
Lower Nene Valley Grey	LNV GW	54	723	0.91	36	41	521	0.8	25
Horningsea Reduced	HOR RE	315	4697	4.16	73	313	4641	4.16	71
Horningsea Grey	HOR GW	320	5037	4.9	78	309	4955	4.7	74
Other		2368	18481	21.74	502	1316	10478	13.9	257
White Wares	**WW**	**1733**	**24720**	**37.84**	**436**	**1009**	**15608**	**24.34**	**210**
Godmanchester White	GOD WH	141	1934	4.26	44	4	236	0	3
Verulamium White	VER WH	561	10071	16.51	107	424	7572	13.42	59
Lower Nene Valley White	LNV WH	164	1814	2.71	55	5	219	0	5
Lower Nene Valley Self-Coloured	LNV SC	25	209	0	7	18	130	0	6
Oxfordshire White	OXF WH	3	30	0	2	1	4	0	1
Other		839	10662	14.36	221	557	7447	10.92	136
Samian	**SAM**	**267**	**3988**	**10.49**	**194**	**150**	**2924**	**7.3**	**104**
Grand Total		**19871**	**207896**	**213.72**	**4049**	**12170**	**134180**	**136.7**	**2051**

Appendix 2. Data used in Figure 7 excluding that from Settlements 3 and 4.

Site and Phase	County	Site type	Jar	Bowl/ Dish	Mortarium	Other	Total	Quantification method	Reference
Higham Ferrers Phase 3 (E-MC2)	Northamptonshire	Roadside Settlement	27.28	9.35	0.78	0.78	44.94	EVE	Timby 2009
Higham Ferrers Phase 4 (M-LC2-E/MC3)	Northamptonshire	Roadside Settlement	82.54	41.64	2.82	2.82	175.27	EVE	Timby 2009
Brackmills Phase 4a (E-MC1)	Northamptonshire	Rural	10.85	3.38	0	0	14.81	EVE	Sutton forthcoming
Brackmills Phase 4b (LC1-EC2)	Northamptonshire	Rural	9.74	0.91	0	0	11.37	EVE	Sutton forthcoming
Brackmills Phase 5 (MC2-EC3)	Northamptonshire	Rural	17.77	2.52	0.3	0.3	21.26	EVE	Sutton forthcoming
Wellingborough East Phase 4 (LC1-EC2)	Northamptonshire	Rural	41.95	13.74	1.27	1.27	59.53	EVE	Sutton 2020
Wellingborough East Phase 5 (LC2-C3)	Northamptonshire	Rural	11.03	9.05	0.45	0.45	23.25	EVE	Sutton 2020
Pineham Phase 3 (LC1-EC2)	Northamptonshire	Rural	28.26	8.17	0.18	0.18	38.86	EVE	Sutton 2018
Pineham Phase 4 (M-LC2)	Northamptonshire	Rural	48.23	9.94	0.48	0.48	65.17	EVE	Sutton 2018

(Continued)

Appendix 2. (Continued)

Site and Phase	County	Site type	Jar	Bowl/ Dish	Mortarium	Other	Total	Quantification method	Reference
Piddington 'Courtyard' (LC1-C4)	Northamptonshire	Villa	402	272	47	47	817	Vessel Estimate	Powell 2019
Alchester Phase 5	Oxfordshire	Small Town	39.38	8.31	1.22	1.22	62.06	EVE	Evans 2002
Alchester Phase 6	Oxfordshire	Small Town	55.32	25.96	2.1	2.1	118.66	EVE	Evans 2002
Alchester Phase 7	Oxfordshire	Small Town	46.7	30.85	2.45	2.45	105.06	EVE	Evans 2002
Alchester Phase 8	Oxfordshire	Small Town	62.31	51.56	Pp	8.42	151.93	EVE	Evans 2002
Alchester Phase 9	Oxfordshire	Small Town	41.52	32.89	5.36	5.36	101.3	EVE	Evans 2002
Orton Hall Farm Period 1 (MC1-MC2)	Cambridgeshire	Rural	350	67	7	7	472	Vessel Estimate	Perrin 1996
Orton Hall Farm Period 2 (MC2-EC3)	Cambridgeshire	Rural	117	24	9	9	166	Vessel Estimate	Perrin 1996
Warth Park	Northamptonshire	Rural	66.26	33	1.17	1.17	118.27	EVE	Lyons 2019

Bibliography

Anderson, K., with Montiel, G. 2013. Roman Pottery, in C. Evans, with G. Appleby, S. Lucy and R. Regan (eds) *Process and History, Romano-British Communities at Colne Fen, Earith*, CAU Landscape Archives: The Archaeology of the Lower Ouse Valley, Vol. II, Cambridge Archaeological Unit, Cambridge, 299–324.

Barclay, A., Knight, D., Booth, P., Evans, J., Brown, D.H. and Wood, I. 2016. *A Standard for Pottery Studies in Archaeology*. Historic England, the Prehistoric Ceramics Research Group, the Study Group for Roman Pottery, and the Medieval Pottery Research Group.

Booth, P. 1991. Inter-site comparisons between pottery assemblages in Roman Warwickshire: ceramic indicators of site status, *Journal of Roman Pottery Studies* 4(1), 1–10.

Campbell, S., Greenwood, M., Prior, S., Shearer, T., Walkem, K., Young, S., Bywaters, D. and Walker, K. 2020. Purposive sampling: complex or simple? Research case examples, *Journal of Research in Nursing* 25(8), 652–61.

Colley, S. and Evans, J. 2018. Big Data Analyses of Roman Tableware: information standards, digital technologies and research collaboration, *Internet Archaeology* 50. https://doi.org/10.11141/ia.50.19.

Doherty, A. 2015. *Using Archaeological Archives: A case study of finds from Roman Essex*, Spoilheap Publications, Portslade.

Doherty, A., Pitts, M. and Perring, D. 2013. Methodological Approaches, in D. Perring and M. Pitts (eds) *Alien Cities: Consumption and the Origins of Urbanism in Roman Britain*. SpoilHeap Publications, Portslade, 13–22.

Evans, J. 2001. Material approaches to the identification of different Romano-British site types, in S. James and M. Millett (eds) *Britons and Romans: Advancing an Archaeological Agenda*, CBA Research Report 125, York, 26–35.

Evans, J. 2002. Iron Age, Roman, and Anglo-Saxon Pottery, in J.G. Evans, J. Hiller and P. Booth (eds) *Excavations in the Extramural Settlement of Roman Alchester, Oxfordshire, 1991*, Oxford Archaeology Monograph 1, Oxford, 263–384.

Fulford, M. and Brindle, T. 2016. Introduction, in A. Smith, M. Allen, T. Brindle and M. Fulford (eds) *New Visions of the Countryside of Roman Britain, Volume 1, The Rural Settlement of Roman Britain*, Britannia Monograph Series 29, Society for the Promotion of Roman Studies, London, 1–16.

Fulford, M. and Holbrook, N. 2011. Assessing the contribution of commercial archaeology to the study of the Roman period in England, 1990–2004, *The Antiquaries Journal* 91, 323–45.

Lyons, A. 2019. Romano-British Pottery, in L. Moan (ed.) *Multi-period remains at Warth Park Phase 3, Raunds, Northamptonshire. Post-Excavation Assessment and Updated Project Design*, Oxford Archaeology East Report 2225, unpublished report, available at: https://eprints.oxfordarchaeology.com/5895/, 125–62.

Neyman, J. 1934. On the Two Different Aspects of the Representative Method: The Method of Stratified Sampling and the Method of Purposive Selection, *Journal of the Royal Statistical Society* 97(4), 558–625.

Orton, C. 2000. *Sampling in archaeology*. Cambridge University Press, Cambridge.

Orton, C., Tyers, P. and Vince, A. 1993. *Pottery in Archaeology*. Cambridge University Press, Cambridge.

Percival, S. with Williams, D. 2007. Iron Age Pottery, in C. Evans, M. Knight and L. Webley, Iron Age Settlement and Romanisation on the Isle of Ely: the Hurst Lane Reservoir Site, *Proceedings of the Cambridge Antiquarian Society* 96, 41–78.

Perrin, J.R. 1996. The Roman Pottery, in D.F. Mackreth (ed.) *Orton Hall Farm: A Roman and Early Anglo-Saxon Farmstead*, East Anglian Archaeology Report 76, Nene Valley Archaeological Trust, Manchester, 114–204.

Powell, M.A. 2019. *Iron Age and Roman Piddington: A comparative report on the pottery in three deposits from the 1989–92 'Courtyard' excavations at Piddington Roman Villa*, Upper Nene Archaeological Society Fascicule 7, Northampton.

Rice, P. 2015. *Pottery Analysis, A Sourcebook*, 2nd ed., The University of Chicago, Chicago.

Rippon, S. 2017. Romano-British coarse ware industries and socio-economic interaction in eastern England, in M. Allen, L. Lodwick, T. Brindle, M. Fulford and A. Smith (eds) *New Visions of the Countryside of Roman Britain Volume 2: The Rural Economy of Roman Britain*, Britannia Monograph Series 30, Society for the Promotion of Roman Studies, London, 336–52.

Shennan, S. 1997. *Quantifying Archaeology*, 2nd ed., University of Iowa Press, Iowa City.

Smith, A., Bowsher, D., van Wessel, J. and West, D. 2020. *A14 Cambridge to Huntingdon, Cambridgeshire*, Archaeology Data Service, York. https://doi.org/10.5284/1081261.

Sutton, A. 2018. Iron Age and Roman Pottery, in T. Preece (ed.) *Archaeological excavation, recording and analysis on land at Pineham, Upton, Northamptonshire*, MOLA Northampton Report 18/126, unpublished report, available at: https://doi.org/10.5284/1078735, 59–76.

Sutton, A. 2020. The Roman Pottery, in T. Preece (ed.) *Archaeological excavation and analysis on land at Wellingborough East, Area 3, Northamptonshire, April to December 2017*, MOLA Northampton Report 20/009, unpublished report, 97–119.

Sutton, A. forthcoming. Iron Age and Roman Pottery, in C. Chinnock (ed.) *An Iron Age settlement and Roman complex farmstead at Brackmills, Northampton*, Archaeopress, Oxford.

Timby, J. 2000. The Pottery, in M. Fulford and J. Timby (eds) *Late Iron Age and Roman Silchester Excavations on the Site of the Forum-Basilica 1977, 1980–86*, Society for the Promotion of Roman Studies, London, 180–3.

Timby, J. 2009. The Roman Pottery, in S. Lawrence and A. Smith (eds) *Between Villa and Town: Excavations of a Roman roadside settlement and shrine at Higham Ferrers, Northamptonshire*, Oxford Archaeology Monograph No.7, Oxford Archaeological Unit Limited, Oxford, 147–83.

Tyers, P. 1996. *Roman Pottery in Britain*, Routledge, London.

Whittaker, J.C., Caulkins, D. and Kamp, K.A. 1998. Evaluating consistency in typology and classification, *Journal of Archaeological Method and Theory* 5(2), 129–64.

Means to an end: The use of average sherd weights and rim percentages to better understand ceramic fragmentation and deposition patterns

Edward Biddulph

Abstract

The study of pottery fragmentation allows ceramic specialists to assess the relative condition of pottery assemblages and address questions of site preservation, pottery deposition, waste disposal and context formation, among others. The mean sherd weight statistic (MSW), calculated by dividing the number of sherds in a group or assemblage by the weight, is a commonly used measure of fragmentation. The measure, however, depends on methods of quantification that are statistically biased. Consequently, mean sherd weight values are themselves inherently biased. Estimated vessel equivalent (EVE), or more usually rim equivalent (RE), is a quantification method that measures the percentage of the surviving rim. It is less statistically biased and offers an alternative measure of fragmentation: mean rim equivalent (MRE), or Orton's 'completeness' statistic, calculated by dividing the rim equivalent by the number of vessels. This paper presents case studies to demonstrate how the two statistics can provide complementary, and sometimes diverging, pictures of pottery fragmentation. It draws on the case studies to illustrate how pottery fragmentation data has been used to understand site activities. Using the MSW and RE statistics together, the paper presents scattergrams or 'fragmentation plots' that at a glance highlight well- or poorly preserved pottery or pottery that otherwise 'stands out' and aid interpretation of pottery deposition.

Pottery researchers in the United Kingdom are familiar with the quantification methods of sherd count, weight, minimum number of vessels represented and estimated vessel equivalents or EVE (Orton 1989). The first is a simple count of sherds forming any unique group of pottery, the second is the weight of that group, the third is a count of vessels represented, which ideally takes into account all sherds but for practical purposes may be confined to a count based on the most diagnostic elements, typically the rim. The last, EVE, is the measurable fraction remaining of a component part of a vessel, typically the rim circumference. Thus, a vessel with half its rim surviving has a measurement of 50% or 0.5 EVE or, more correctly, RE (rim equivalent), 100% or '1' being the score for a complete rim. The value of each of these measures, particularly rim equivalents, have been subject to much – and continuing – debate (see, for example, Pollard 1990; Evans 1991; or Symonds and Haynes 2007). This paper will not revisit the arguments for and against in detail but will demonstrate the value of taking what could be termed a 'belt-and-braces' approach and adopting a comprehensive methodology to quantification – that is, using all four measures listed above – for all assemblages,

whether large or small, from evaluations or excavations, or deriving from primary or secondary deposits.

Such quantification methods can be used to obtain measures of pottery fragmentation, allowing researchers to investigate pottery condition, waste disposal patterns, redeposition, residuality and so on. The commonest measure is average or mean sherd weight (MSW), calculated by dividing the weight by sherd count. The late Iron Age and Roman pottery assemblage from Leybourne Grange in Kent (Biddulph 2018), consisting of 3812 sherds weighing a total of 50,083 g, has a MSW of 13.14 g. An equivalent measure can be calculated for rims to obtain a mean RE value. At the same site, there were 279 individual vessels based on rims, and a total RE value of 29.86. Dividing the RE value by the number of vessels produces a mean RE value (MRE) of 0.11; in other words, on average, 11% of the rim circumference of each vessel identified by rim was present. This calculation is essentially Clive Orton's 'completeness' statistic, defined as estimated vessel equivalent divided by estimated vessels represented (Orton 1989, 97), but when confining the quantification to rims and to bring it in line with MSW, it is perhaps more convenient to refer to the statistic as MRE.

No form of quantification is without bias or a degree of subjectivity. As Orton shows (1989, 96; see also Orton and Hughes 2013, 206–8), sherd count and weight are biased measures. Sherd weight is affected by a vessel's inherent quality of 'brokenness', with certain types such as thin-walled vessels tending to break up more easily than robust, thick-walled vessels, the result being, that vessels with relatively high 'brokenness' can appear to be over-represented in an assemblage. Conversely, if using weight as a relative measure, heavy, thick-walled vessels such as storage jars may be over-represented in an assemblage. The level of subjectivity involved with vessel count based on one of the most diagnostic elements of the vessel, the rim, is low to negligible when dealing with small groups, but can increase with relatively large groups of identical type, for example, from a kiln assemblage. Rim equivalent (RE) is, in theory, an unbiased measure, the measurement obtained from the rim being unaffected by brokenness or weight. A complete rim will have an RE value of 100% or 1 whether it is a single piece or has been broken into five, ten or twenty pieces. Similarly, complete rims, whether from a robust storage jar or delicate beaker, will have an identical value of 1. However, the rims of some vessel types, particularly constricted neck types, such as flagons and amphorae, tend to survive relatively well, often being found intact, their narrow mouths and relatively thick

walls rims making them quite robust. In this sense, RE is not without bias, although flagons and amphorae tend to form a minor part of many assemblages in Roman Britain and so the impact is limited. Setting apart all these issues, calculating MRE can provide a different picture about the condition of the pottery than that offered by MSW, as can be seen from the following case-study.

Excavations by Oxford Wessex Archaeology in 2001 on the A120 upgrading scheme between Braintree and Stansted Airport in Essex uncovered a Roman-period farmstead at Little Canfield, the site usually being known as Strood Hall (Timby *et al.* 2007). Among the discoveries was a small, early Roman enclosed cemetery of 28 graves, all but one being cremation burials. The earliest burials dated to the mid-1st century AD, the latest dating up to the mid-2nd century AD. Of the pottery, 20 vessels were identified as cremation urns, mainly jars but also large beakers and flagons. Forty-nine accessory vessels were recovered (Biddulph 2007, table 3.2). The heavy, sticky, boulder-clay geology that characterised the soil at the site meant that, while the pottery obviously had been placed whole in the graves, some of the vessels had cracked after deposition, and on recovery fragmented into many small pieces (Fig. 1). This is evident from the MSW of the cemetery pottery of just 6 g. This is only marginally higher than the MSW of 4 g obtained from the pottery

Figure 1. Ceramic grave goods, fragmented after deposition, in cremation 1855 from the early Roman cemetery at Strood Hall, Essex.
© *Oxford Archaeology and Wessex Archaeology.*

recovered from contemporaneous, early Roman pits. Given the blanket effect of the soil on all pottery, there appears to be little to distinguish pottery deposited whole in the ground from pottery deposited through the normal course of domestic pottery use, discard and redeposition using MSW alone. However, the two groups can be separated when MRE is calculated, the values being 0.03 RE for the pottery from the pits and 0.36 RE for the pottery from the graves. While there had been some loss of rim from the cemetery pottery after deposition, most probably caused by the plough slicing off the tops of tall vessels lying close to the ploughsoil, as is so often the case with such pottery, the pottery from the graves is clearly more complete than the pottery from the pits, based on MRE, as one would expect, given that the vessels were deposited whole. While MSW is normally of little relevance to the analysis of funerary pottery, for which the principal method of quantification is typically not RE but a straightforward vessel count (whether the rims have survived or not), as was indeed used for the recording and analysis of the assemblage at Strood Hall, the comparison of values obtained from graves and pits at that site demonstrates that MSW does not necessarily distinguish between groups of pottery with very different depositional histories. The presence of, say, ritual or otherwise 'special' deposits or primary dumps of material therefore may not be fully appreciated where the pottery is not obviously complete or near complete, and that MRE as a statistic is sometimes more appropriate than MSW when calculating the degree of ceramic fragmentation.

Typically, pottery fragmentation is used to provide insight into pottery condition, patterns of waste management, disposal and the level of redeposition, drawing on principles established through both archaeological and ethnographic studies. In several publications, Michael Schiffer made a case for artefact size as a proxy for context formation, for example citing a study of artefact movement in Alyawarre settlements in central Australia. There it was noted how larger debris was removed from occupation areas (huts and hearths) to secondary areas of refuse, leaving tiny fragments only, and listing other factors leading to artefact size reduction and sorting, including ploughing, trampling and natural processes (Schiffer 1983, 679–80). In a study of refuse disposal in the Maya Highlands of Mexico and Guatemala, Hayden and Cannon (1983) identified a pattern of systematic disposal. Waste generated through household activities would first be moved to provisional locations within the household compound, taking the waste away from activity areas. There, the waste might be denuded or become mixed through the removal of useful items, recycling materials or the act of children removing or adding material. When the waste became a hindrance, the larger, harder fragments, including pottery, were removed to convenient dumps – including pits, streams and ravines – outside the compounds, although these tended to remain reasonably close to the compounds, usually within a two-minute walk. Once there, the material was subject to further weathering and destruction. The authors additionally observed that small fragments and micro-waste might always remain within the compound, for instance being in spaces of non-activity, such as corners and under beds (*ibid.*, 134, 157–60). Other studies have pointed to additional factors to account for the distribution of material. For example, Wilkinson (1982), examining the distribution and density of pottery sherds around ancient settlement sites in the Middle East, suggested that the material had been transported with compost or manure and spread onto fields. Following systematic surface collection and the mapping of pottery scatters, Wilkinson observed that scatters occupied zones of some 3–6 km from the settlement centres, scatter density decreasing with increasing distance. Differences in pottery condition were not reported, but Wilkinson (1982, 323, 330) noted that the scatters generally consisted of small, battered sherds, and that, of the featured sherds collected – rims, bases etc. – only 57% could be identified to form and closely dated with any confidence (Wilkinson 1982, 323, 330).

Such studies encompass vast geographical and temporal differences, but there are commonalities: the removal of nuisance material from living spaces, the sorting and mixing of material in secondary waste areas, the continued fragmentation of material by human and natural processes. How these ideas might apply to the context of Romano-British settlement is a matter of discussion, but consideration might be given to the existence of areas of initial discard, pots immediately after breakage being put somewhere temporary before being thrown, along with organic waste, onto household middens or convenient ditches or pits. Middens or ditches might then be cleared, the material being scattered onto fields as manure or dumped in peripheral areas further away from the settlement core. Such processes would lead to further fragmentation, mixing of material from different households and dumping events, and separation of constituent parts of individual vessels – rim, base, handle etc. Mean sherd weight (MSW) is, of course, a standard measure of fragmentation and means of examining distribution and disposal patterns, but as observed above, the results are open to misinterpretation. For a more nuanced picture of fragmentation and the factors responsible for the condition of the pottery, MSW and MRE may be used in combination. What is more, the values can be plotted on a scattergram, providing a useful way of visualising both measures and establishing interpretative principles. As can be seen on the theoretical model (Fig. 2), the most fragmented pottery – that is, pottery displaying low MSW and low MRE – will be concentrated towards the bottom left-hand corner of the scattergram, closest to zero. What might be termed the best-preserved pottery – the complete or near-complete pots with relatively high MSW and high MRE – will be moving towards the top

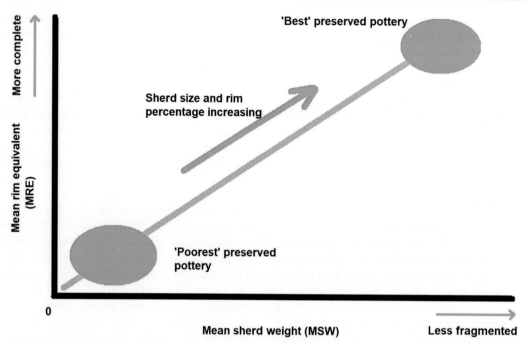

Figure 2. Theoretical model of pottery fragmentation, showing the relationship between mean sherd weight (MSW) and mean rim equivalent (MRE).

right-hand corner of the chart. This assumes a predictable, statistically testable, relationship between the two measures, MRE increasing as MSW increases, but results that do not demonstrate a predictable pattern can still be of considerable interest.

By way of example, let us look at the pottery from Berryfields, part of a Roman nucleated roadside settlement at Fleet Marston outside Aylesbury. The area excavated by Oxford Archaeology between 2007 and 2016 represented the hinterland of the settlement and comprised areas of field systems and areas of settlement that lined Akeman Street and minor roads. During the post-excavation analysis, areas of the site were divided into landscape zones, such as 'early Roman field system', or 'ladder settlement', or 'the surface of Akeman Street'. These provided useful categories when investigating patterns of pottery deposition using the measures of fragmentation (Biddulph 2019, table 3.11; Biddulph *et al.* 2019, table 1.2). For each landscape zone, the MSW and MRE were calculated and displayed on a scattergram (Fig. 3). As can be seen, the pottery that is most fragmented, having low MSW and zero MRE values, is plotted in the bottom left-hand corner, the material coming from agricultural field ditches (group G21) and as intrusive occurrences in a Bronze Age ring-ditch (G20). In contrast, landscape group G10, a pond and pit complex that contained several complete or near-complete vessels, has correspondingly high MSW and high MRE values and is closer to the right-hand corner of the scattergram. Another notable group is G9, which has a high MSW but a low MRE. Based on MSW alone, the pottery from the group would seem to be very well-preserved, but its MRE value suggests otherwise. The MSW value is explained by the presence of a single, large storage jar body sherd in thick-walled, robust pink grogged ware (Tomber and Dore 1998, fabric PNK GT) within a small group. Given that group G9 is a surface of Akeman Street, the pottery was suggested to represent road repair. Apart from these groups, three broad clusters can be detected. Cluster 1, with its fairly middling MSW and MRE values, comprises enclosures and field systems along Akeman Street and reflects deliberate deposition and management of waste from domestic or other activities along the Roman road, potentially representing the relocation from provisional dumps of waste into convenient, nearby spaces, similar to the pattern observed by Hayden and Cannon (1983). Cluster 2 includes field systems and trackways further away from the core areas of settlement or other activities along Akeman Street, the pottery being more fragmented and characteristic of incidental deposition and redeposition related to agricultural activity, such as manuring (cf. Wilkinson 1982); the pottery therefore has relatively low MSW and low MRE values. Cluster 3 comprises further landscape groups along Akeman Street, for example roadside plots or enclosures, but also part of a ladder settlement where domestic activity was attested, again potentially representing the removal of nuisance waste from temporary locations near living areas (cf. Hayden and Cannon 1983; Schiffer 1983). Overall, then, the pottery from areas along roads was better preserved than the pottery from more outlying, sparser, areas, and reflects where activities, whether domestic or industrial, were focused. Accordingly, the pottery has relatively high MSW and high MRE values.

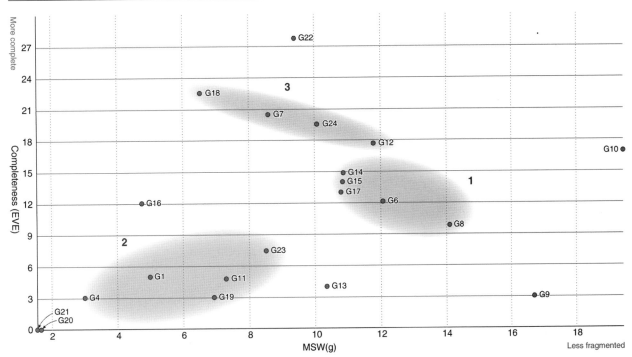

Figure 3. Scattergram showing the relationship between mean sherd weight (MSW) and mean rim equivalent (MRE; here called 'completeness') of the pottery from landscape groups at Berryfields, near Aylesbury. MRE is expressed as a rim percentage (Biddulph 2019, fig. 3.5). © Oxford Archaeology.

It is worth noting that in this analysis, all the pottery was included, from the smallest group (G4 comprising features associated with an earlier, Iron Age settlement), which contained just a single sherd, to the largest group (G14, the ditches of enclosures lining Akeman Street) of 1861 sherds. From a statistical point of view, it might be thought necessary to remove very small groups like G4, but for this type of analysis they are retained, as they do not skew the results – excluding them does not affect the MSW and MRE calculations or the display of the values obtained (the data points of the excluded groups are simply taken off the plot) – and even the smallest groups provide some insight into deposition patterns. The position group G4 occupies on the scattergram reinforces how marginal the area of the Iron Age settlement was for Roman pottery deposition and that the pottery found there is most likely intrusive. Nevertheless, when publishing the results of such analysis, it is recommended that the values themselves are also presented.

A pottery assemblage from Panattoni Park, near Northampton and adjacent to a villa at Harpole, the site forming part of the villa's agricultural landscape (Simmonds and Lawrence 2022), offers another example. One aspect that the analysis of that assemblage addressed was the distribution of pottery in the late Iron Age and early Roman field systems across the excavation areas. Was it, for example, possible to detect different zones of activity, such as areas of domestic occupation and refuse disposal, from the distribution? No part of the landscape appears to have been an area of very concentrated pottery deposition;

pottery was recovered in fairly small quantities across the landscape. However, examination of the relationship between MSW and MRE by ditch and pit group (Fig. 4; Biddulph 2022a, 92–3) provided some clues. As stated, pottery groups with the 'best preserved' pottery tend to have relatively high MSW and MRE values and represent vessels that have retained a good level of integrity, plausibly having been discarded reasonably rapidly after disuse and close to areas of use. A group of pottery from pit 71, largely comprising the substantial part of a globular jar, would appear to fall into this category. Pit 570 was lined with a complete storage vessel, which had become fragmented after deposition, but may have been inserted into the pit used to store foodstuffs and possibly belonged to a single household. The unusual nature of the pottery from that pit is demonstrated by its isolated position on the scattergram. The pottery from pit 1292 is a clear outlier, comprising a single storage jar sherd whose deposition may have been incidental. The remaining groups are not so clearly differentiated, but of these, it is possible to detect a loose cluster of groups (circled on the scattergram), largely from the central part of an area of field system to the south-west of the main villa buildings, which contain reasonably well-preserved pottery, the relatively high MRE of between 0.1 and 0.3 RE per group being particularly notable. The analysis points to occupation across the site, but with a greater focus on deposition within the groups of that highlighted area, representing relatively rapid deposition or middening after initial breakage in nearby households.

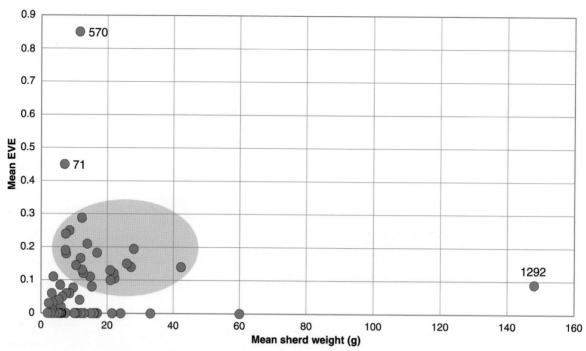

Figure 4. Scattergram showing the relationship between mean sherd weight (MSW) and mean rim equivalent (MRE; here call 'mean EVE') of assemblages from ditches and pits in the late Iron Age and early Roman settlement at Panattoni Park, near Northampton (Biddulph 2022a, fig. 4.6). © Oxford Archaeology.

Such fragmentation analysis is applicable at the inter-site, as well as intra-site, level, and provides a useful way of gauging differences in the cultural usage of pottery across a geographical area or sites of different type. For example, the MSW and MRE values of pottery recovered from pits or ditches could be compared across multiple sites, potentially highlighting similarities or differences in the condition and depositional histories of the pottery and the use of the features. Even at the much broader scale of whole assemblages, an inter-site comparison offers some insight, as suggested by the following example. Archaeological investigations on section 1 of High Speed 1 uncovered a number of late Iron Age and Roman sites along a linear transect between Folkestone and Gravesend in Kent (Foreman 2018). The sites included a villa, a cemetery, farms and industrial settlements. Comparing the MSW and MRE values for the sites (Fig. 5) – categorising the sites by type (according to the Rural Settlement of Roman Britain project (Allen *et al.* 2018)) – it can be seen that the cemetery at Pepper Hill stands out, its assemblage being characterised by the highest MRE value and a relatively low MSW value, as might be expected given the presence in the assemblage of many vessels with complete rims deposited as grave goods and the effects of post-depositional processes (as at Strood Hall). The remaining sites, mainly farms, have fairly similar MRE values, but the range of their MSW values is much wider. There are no doubt site-specific factors to consider here, but it is worth observing that the assemblages with the highest MSW values have the strongest association with jars and bowls, their composition being largely restricted to those classes, as may be predicted from the more basic rural character of

those sites and their chronological emphasis (late Iron Age and early Roman). While their MSW values skew towards the heavy side, their MRE values are not dissimilar from the MRE value of the Thurnham villa assemblage, which is more diverse, vessel classes other than jars and bowls being well represented. Overall, then, apart from Pepper Hill, which is a clear outlier, the condition of the assemblages from sites across HS1 appears to be remarkably similar, as measured by MRE, which allows us to calibrate the values obtained by MSW.

Returning to Buckinghamshire, Fleet Marston, the nucleated roadside settlement or 'small town' of which Berryfields formed a part, lies a little further to the west of Berryfields. The site is on the route of High Speed 2 (HS2) and archaeological investigations were undertaken by COPA, a joint venture between Oxford Archaeology and Cotswold Archaeology, on behalf of Fusion Joint Venture HS2 Enabling Works Contractor. Full-scale excavation in 2021 was preceded by trial trenching in 2019. Some 120 trenches were dug across the site, and inevitably these yielded large amounts of pottery (Biddulph 2020). As with the landscape groups of Berryfields, the relative condition of the pottery by trench can be examined using MSW and MRE. The results not only provide insight into material preservation but also show the potential for informing decision making with regard to targeting subsequent mitigation works. The results are shown on Figure 6, with selected trenches – those that stand out with either relatively high MRE or high MSW or both – labelled. Placing the locations of the trenches onto the geophysical survey of the site (Fig. 7), it can be seen that the high-lighted trenches with both relatively high MSW and MRE

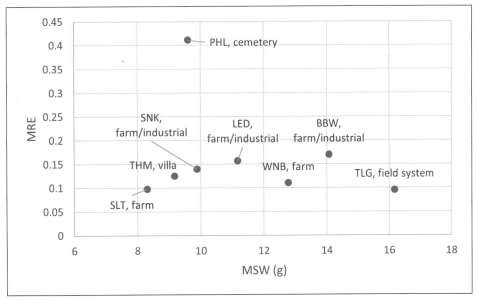

Figure 5. Scattergram showing the relationship between mean sherd weight (MSW) and mean rim equivalent (MRE) of assemblages from High Speed 1, Section 1 (Foreman 2018). Key: BBW Beechbrook Wood, Westwell; LED Leda Cottages, Ashford; PHL Pepper Hill, Northfleet; SNK Snarkhurst Wood, Maidstone; SLT Saltwood Tunnel, Saltwood; THM Thurnham; TLG Tollgate, Cobham; WNB Northumberland Wood, Gravesend.

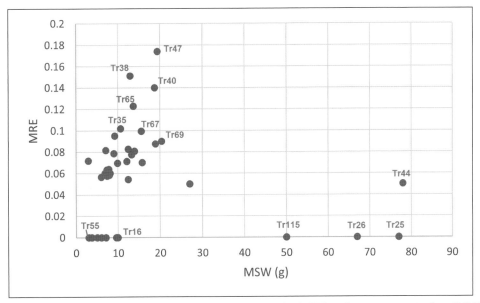

Figure 6. Scattergram showing the relationship between mean sherd weight (MSW) and mean rim equivalent (MRE) of the pottery from evaluation trenches at HS2 site of Fleet Marston, near Aylesbury. MRE is expressed as a decimal fraction of 1. © HS2.

values extend across plots or enclosures that line Akeman Street (trenches 35, 38, 40 and 47) and another road that is tentatively identified as the road connecting Fleet Marston to the Roman town at Dorchester-on-Thames (trenches 65, 67 and 69). Like the data from Berryfields, the results suggest that these roadside locations provided a focus for settlement and other activities, for example commercial and industrial, with pottery deposited close to areas of use and initial discard (if not in primary refuse locations). Trenches containing pottery with very low or zero MRE values (among them trenches 16, 25, 26, 44, 55 and 115)

tend to be located some distance away from the core of the settlement, as indicated by the geophysics, or in 'blank' areas of archaeology in between the denser parts or to the north of Akeman Street. Pottery deposition here may have been incidental, the material having been spread on fields or otherwise undeveloped or marginal land through, say, agricultural activity or the scattering of waste. The very high MSW values of the pottery in trenches 25, 26, 44 and 115 are explained by single body sherds from storage jars, invariably pink grogged ware (PNK GT), which tend to remain heavy even if very fragmented.

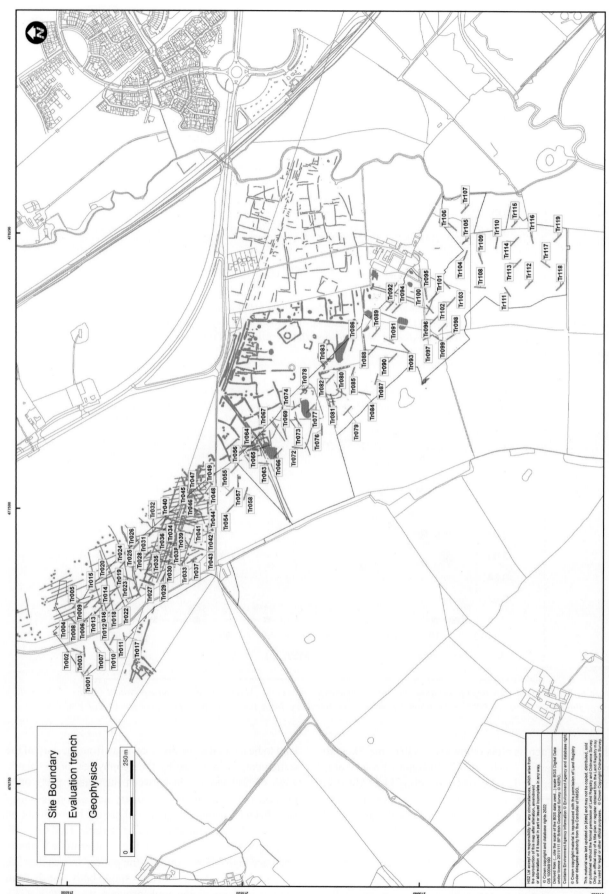

Figure 7. Plan of evaluation trenches and geophysical survey results at HS2 site of Fleet Marston, near Aylesbury © HS2.

The pattern illustrates the advantage of using MRE and MSW together and the need to be cautious about using MSW values alone. The data can also be used as a predictive tool, the areas of site with relatively high MSW and high MRE being likely to provide the densest settlement evidence and the best quality pottery assemblages in terms of quantity and condition. This was indeed borne out in the mitigation phase, the majority of the pottery from the site coming from the areas opened across Akeman Street and the putative Fleet Marston-Dorchester-on-Thames road and having some of the highest MSW values (Biddulph 2022b, table 20).

The combination of MSW and MRE can be used to identify at a glance pottery that potentially has a different depositional history or is otherwise out of place compared with the remaining pottery in the group or feature. By way of example, let us return to landscape group G10 from Berryfields. As seen in Figure 3, pottery from this group, a pond and adjacent pit, was an outlier on account of the suite of complete or near-complete vessels present. The complete or near-complete vessels were in fact recovered from the pit (feature number 3067), which had been dug close to the Roman road of Akeman Street. The pit breached the water-table and had filled with water. Initially, the pit was used in the malting and brewing process, but by the late 3rd century AD, it had been put to another use: as a special place where the inhabitants of the Roman town and passers-by could throw in coins and other items for good luck or as votive offerings. The pit remained waterlogged up to the time of excavation, and this had preserved a remarkable collection of organic objects, including a wooden basket, leather shoes, wooden vessels and tools, and, most extraordinary of all, four complete chickens' eggs. These were in addition

to coins and the complete or near-complete pottery vessels, all of which appear to have been deliberately deposited, although whether the pottery contained food or other offerings or was deposited for its own sake or is unknown. Other pottery was recovered from the feature, but this was much more fragmented, suggesting that not all the pottery shared the same depositional history. This is evident when the respective MSW and MRE values for each fill are plotted on a scattergram and interpreted with reference to the section drawing of the feature (Figs 8 and 9; Biddulph *et al.* 2019, fig. 2.26).

The first, primary, fill (3074) of pit 3067 contained the complete or near-complete vessels and accordingly plots close to the top right-hand corner of the scattergram, having relatively high MSW and high MRE. Twenty-nine sherds were collected from the two second fills (3072 and 3075). The material was fragmentary and represents disturbed or redeposited pottery and consequently the groups plot closer to the bottom left-hand corner. The third fill (3073) contained the complete eggs, as well as a leather shoe and coins, and, like context 3075, represents an episode of deliberate deposition. No complete pottery vessels were found, but the fill contained a relatively large portion of a South Gaulish form 29 decorated bowl, ostensibly residual but which may have been curated, the remains of a samian form 38 copy in a colour-coated fine ware, a fine reduced ware beaker base, and a large body sherd of a Gauloise 4 amphora. While this group is chronologically mixed, it almost entirely comprises relatively well-preserved fine and specialist wares (cf. Booth 2004) and may have been, at least in part, deliberately assembled and deposited because of its attractiveness or unusual appearance and quality. This is supported by the group's position on the scattergram, which demonstrates relatively

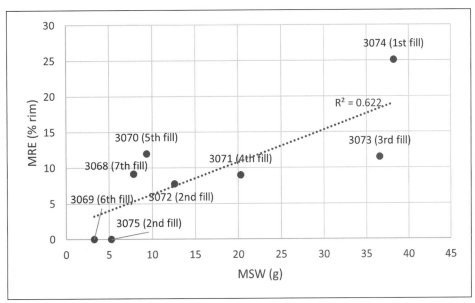

Figure 8. Scattergram showing the relationship between mean sherd weight (MSW) and mean rim equivalent (MRE) of the pottery from the fills of pit 3067 at Berryfields, near Aylesbury. MRE is expressed as a rim percentage.

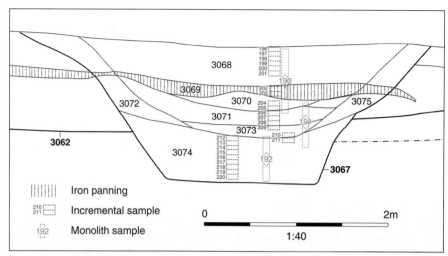

Figure 9. Section of pit 3067, Berryfields, near Aylesbury (after Biddulph et al. 2019, fig. 2.26) © Oxford Archaeology.

high MSW and MRE values. Pottery was collected from the fourth (3071), fifth (3070), sixth (3069) and seventh (3068) fills, but this was more fragmentary, suggesting that deposition higher up in the filling sequence was of a more accidental nature, the pottery perhaps having been deposited incidentally as waste in a conveniently open feature, although coins continued to be deposited until the pit had fill entirely, suggesting that the still wet feature continued to attract votive offerings. Indeed, it is not implausible that the fragmented pottery from the upper fills was deliberately thrown into the pit as token offerings; there is otherwise little material to suggest the routine deposition of household waste.

Whatever the exact nature of deposition through pit 3067, the scattergram indicates that the character of the material changed over time as the pit filled up. If deliberate deposition for ritual or other special purpose continued throughout its use, then this appears to have changed from having something of a formal character to something of a more casual, tokenistic character. Staying with Figure 8, it is worth considering another aspect of the theoretical model (Fig. 2) showing the relationship between the variables of MSW and MRE. Assuming a perfect relationship between the two variables – that is, as MSW weight increases, MRE increases in proportion – then regression analysis, which measures the strength of the relationship between two variables, would show a positive trendline and a coefficient of determination or r squared of +1, representing a strong positive correlation. Conversely, −1 represents a strong negative correlation and 0 equals no correlation (Shennan 1997, 141). Applying regression analysis to the scattergram of the pottery from Berryfields pit 3067 (Fig. 8), gives us a positive trendline and coefficient of determination of 0.62, which suggests that 62% of the variation in MRE is determined by MSW. For the pottery from pit 3067, this is a reasonably strong and predictable relationship, although it is

acknowledged that the sample size here is statistically too small for the results to be entirely reliable; recent research recommends a minimum sample size of 25 observations (cf. Jenkins and Quintana-Ascencio 2020). Carrying out the analysis on larger datasets, the relationship is often shown to be a weak one. Regression analysis applied to the landscape groups shown in Figure 3 gives us a coefficient of determination of just 13%. As high mean sherd weight increases, we do not necessarily – and indeed rarely – see MRE increase in proportion. The strength of the relationship between the variables is improved by removing outliers but doing this risks losing insight into the nature of pottery deposition. A weak relationship, which potentially demonstrates a low level of assemblage integrity resulting from, say, a high level of residuality, the mixing of pottery from different sources, separation of rims and other component parts of vessels, and diverse discard processes and depositional histories, can be just as informative as a strong one, which potentially demonstrates the opposite pattern.

This paper has sought to demonstrate that mean sherd weight (MSW), while a useful measure of pottery fragmentation, can potentially be misleading, being subject to the biases inherent in the quantification methods of sherd count and weight. For a more reliable picture of fragmentation, it is proposed that MSW be used in conjunction with mean rim equivalent (MRE), which is based on a measure that is statistically less biased, to provide a more rigorous means of examining fragmentation. For convenience, MSW and MRE values obtained for an assemblage or group of pottery can be displayed on a scattergram. The resulting plot (what might usefully be termed 'fragmentation plot') is a powerful tool that shows at a glance groups of pottery, in whatever way they are organised (context, feature type, site zone or area, stratigraphic grouping, evaluation trench, fabric, phase and so on), that are relatively well-preserved or otherwise stand out. The patterns offer clues to the interpretation of the pottery, potentially revealing, for example, variable depositional histories, foci of pottery use and activity areas, groups deposited more incidentally or in more marginal areas of site, and deposition that is in some way out of the ordinary. The analysis potentially gives us an objective means of separating the ritual from the mundane, helping identify, for example, feasting or propitiatory deposits, as well as household waste. In addition, applying regression analysis to the data can help measure the level of integrity of an assemblage. What is more, the analysis provides a systematic means of identifying the type of context formation and depositional processes outlined by Schiffer, Hayden and Cannon and others. Clusters or separation of groups on the plot can reveal where the pottery is similar or dissimilar, and by considering the level of pottery fragmentation with context or feature type, the plots can potentially reveal waste disposal patterns and areas of primary, secondary and tertiary deposition. More ambitiously, the technique can be applied to datasets comprising pottery from multiple sites, providing a useful means of inter-site comparison. Large-scale infrastructure projects encompassing transects through the landscape, such as High Speed 1, where uniform recording protocols tend to be applied, are obvious candidates for such an approach.

The fragmentation plots and regression analysis are straightforward to produce in any spreadsheet programme, but naturally, the analysis requires rims of all the pottery of an assemblage to be measured, not just large, well-dated 'key groups'. Routine recording of rims from evaluations is also recommended. As well as recently recorded material, the analysis can of course be applied to 'legacy' data from past excavations, provided that the required information is available and can be extracted. It is additionally recommended, then, that datasets, not just synthesised pottery reports or summary data, be routinely published, for example through the Archaeology Data Service. It must be acknowledged that the fragmentation analysis outlined here cannot currently be applied to most Continental assemblages, which are typically quantified by sherd count and minimum number of individuals (NMI; Symonds and Haynes 2007, 69). This not only limits the scope of analysis on context formation processes, waste disposal patterns, site organisation and so on using assemblages from, say, France or Belgium, but also prevents comparison between British and Continental assemblages. It is perhaps a forlorn hope that one day pottery quantification methods will be compatible across Europe – and it is worth remembering that approaches to quantification are far from consistent even in Britain – but if this paper manages to persuade its readers that, while no single quantification method is perfect, we get the most out of our assemblages by bringing those methods together, even if it means adopting certain methods reluctantly, then it will have fulfilled a purpose.

Acknowledgements

The author is indebted to Leo Webley, Head of Post-excavation at the Oxford office of Oxford Archaeology, and John Halsted, Senior Historic Environment Manager at HS2, for permission to use images and data from Oxford Archaeology and HS2 projects. The author would also like to thank the anonymous reviewers for their encouraging and insightful comments. Needless to say, any errors are the author's alone.

Bibliography

Allen, M., Blick, N., Brindle, T., Evans, T., Fulford, M., Holbrook, N., Lodwick, L., Richards, J.D. and Smith, A. 2018. *The Rural Settlement of Roman Britain: an online resource*, Archaeology Data Service, York, https://doi.org/10.5284/1030449.

Biddulph, E. 2007. Conquest and change? The Roman period, in Timby *et al.* 2007, 81–147.

Biddulph, E. 2018. A late Iron Age and early Roman pottery assemblage from Leybourne Grange, West Malling, Kent, *Journal of Roman Pottery Studies* 17, 74–91.

Biddulph, E. 2019. Late Iron Age and Roman pottery, in Biddulph *et al.* 2019, 55–80.

Biddulph, E. 2020. Pottery, in AWHh Fieldwork Report for Trial Trench Evaluation at Fleet Marston Cottages and Putlowes, Aylesbury, Buckinghamshire (Site Code: 1C19FLMTT), AC240/2, doc. no.: 1EW03-FUS_COP-EV-REP-CS04_CL19-000003, unpublished document for Fusion Joint Venture HS2 Enabling Works Contractor, 45–49.

Biddulph, E. 2022a. Late Iron Age and Roman pottery, in Simmonds and Lawrence 2022, 79–99.

Biddulph, E. 2022b. Pottery, in AWHi – Post-excavation assessment report for archaeological recording at Fleet Marston Cottages and Putlowes, Aylesbury, Buckinghamshire (Site Code: 1C20FLMAR) AC240/2, doc. no.: 1EW03-FUS_COP-EV-REP-CS04_CL20-000013, unpublished document for Fusion Joint Venture HS2 Enabling Works Contractor, 88–117.

Biddulph, E., Brady, K., Simmonds, A. and Foreman, S. 2019. *Berryfields. Iron Age Settlement and a Roman Bridge, Field System and Settlement along Akeman Street near Fleet Marston, Buckinghamshire*, Oxford Archaeology Monograph, 30, Oxford.

Booth, P. 2004. Quantifying status: some pottery data from the Upper Thames Valley, *Journal of Roman Pottery Studies* 11, 39–52.

Evans, J. 1991. Not more pot, *Journal of Roman Pottery Studies* 4, 69–76.

Foreman, S. 2018. *Channel Tunnel Rail Link Section 1*, Archaeology Data Service, York, https://doi.org/10.5284/1000230.

Hayden, B. and Cannon, A. 1983. Where the garbage goes: refuse disposal in the Maya Highlands, *Journal of Anthropological Archaeology* 2, 117–63.

Jenkins, D.G. and Quintana-Ascencio, P.F. 2020. A solution to minimum sample size for regressions, *PLoS ONE* 15(2), e0229345, https://doi.org/10.1371/journal.pone.0229345.

Orton, C. 1989. An introduction to the quantification of assemblages of pottery, *Journal of Roman Pottery Studies* 2, 94–7.

Orton, C. and Hughes, M. 2013. *Pottery in Archaeology*, 2 ed., Cambridge University Press, Cambridge.

Pollard, R. 1990. Quantification: towards a standard practice, *Journal of Roman Pottery Studies* 3, 75–9.

Schiffer, M.B. 1983. Toward the identification of formation processes, *American Antiquity* 48(4), 675–706.

Shennan, S. 1997. *Quantifying Archaeology*, University of Iowa Press, Iowa City.

Simmonds, A. and Lawrence, S. 2022. *Harpole: The landscape of a Roman villa at Panattoni Park, Northamptonshire*, Oxford Archaeology Monograph, 34, Oxford.

Symonds, R.P. and Haynes, I. 2007. Developing methodology for inter-provincial comparison of pottery assemblages, in R. Hingley and S. Willis (eds), *Roman finds: context and theory*, Oxbow Books, Oxford, 67–76.

Timby, J., Brown, R., Biddulph, E., Hardy. A. and Powell, A. 2007. *A Slice of Rural Essex: Archaeological Discoveries from the A120 Between Stansted Airport and Braintree*, Oxford Wessex Archaeology Monograph, 1, Oxford.

Tomber, R. and Dore, J. 1998. *The National Roman Fabric Reference Collection: a Handbook*, Museum of London Archaeology Service Monograph, 2, London.

Wilkinson, T.J. 1982. The definition of ancient manured zones by means of extensive sherd-sampling techniques, *Journal of Field Archaeology* 9(3), 323–33.

Communities of practice in 2nd–5th century AD pottery production: A case study from south-western *Noricum*, Austria

Barbara Borgers and Martin Auer

Abstract

Grey ware pottery circulated widely in 2nd–5th centuries AD Noricum, covering most of present-day Austria, south-western Germany, as well as northern Italy and Slovenia. This article examined two types of grey ware bowls from Aguntum and Lavant in south-western Noricum, combining macroscopic observation with thin section petrography. The aims of this paper were two-fold: first, to reconstruct the composition and production technology of the bowls studied, and second, to consider potters' social interactions during their practice, which permits to define the existence of communities of practice, who were fundamental for the participation, regulation and transmission of technological knowledge.

The results suggest that the grey ware bowls from Aguntum and Lavant were produced with a similar clay source, tempered with crushed calcite fragments, and hand-built with slabs. The surface seems to have been smoothed and decorated with various motifs, and the bowls were fired in a reducing atmosphere. Three differences were recorded among the bowls, including 1) paste recipe: for instance, one bowl from Aguntum has been tempered with additional grog; 2) rim diameter: more specifically, bowls from Lavant tend to display a wider rim, in comparison with the bowls from Aguntum) and 3) decorative pattern: for instance, one bowl type from Lavant is defined by a unique motif.

The results have further indicated that the two bowl types from Aguntum and Lavant were produced with a standard production sequence between the 2nd and the 5th centuries AD. This has been taken to indicate the existence of one overarching community of practice, where potters shared a technological tradition, and learning patterns and knowledge transmission remained continual through time. The subtle differences observed in paste recipe, rim diameter and decorative motif appear to have been within the acceptable range of variation in technological choices of the production sequence and have been interpreted as individual expression of identity.

1. Introduction

The Roman province of *Noricum* covered present-day Austria, parts of Germany (Bavaria), northern Italy and Slovenia. The area was incorporated in the Roman Empire during the reign of Claudius between AD 41 and AD 54 (Gassner *et al.* 2002). During that time, the capital was created at *Virunum* (Zollfeld), and several chief towns (*municipia*) developed, including *Aguntum* (Dölsach), *Teurnia* (St Peter in Holz) and *Iuvavum* (Salzburg). Several other settlements are known, including road stations such as *Immurium* (Moosham), and hilltop settlements, such as Lavant (Fig. 1).

Grey ware is very common on 1st to 5th centuries AD Roman sites in western (and wider) *Noricum*. This pottery comprises a range of jars, tripods and bowls (Fig. 2), and is characterised by a dark grey to black colour with large white inclusions. Several workshops at *Iuvavum* in north-western *Noricum*, dated to between the 1st and 3rd centuries AD, have produced this ware, as indicated by the presence of various kiln structures and pottery waste (Lang *et al.* 2012). However, no workshops have been found in the south-western part of the province. Consequently, little is known about the communities that produced grey ware in this area.

This study examined two types of grey ware bowls from the sites at *Aguntum* and Lavant in south-western *Noricum* in more detail. Type III bowls are defined by a slightly everted rim and narrow base, while type IV bowls display an inverted rim and broad base. The occurrence and distribution patterns of the two bowl types appear to have been slightly different. More specifically, type III bowls circulated mainly in the northern area between the second half of the 2nd and early 3rd centuries AD, while type IV bowls occurred exclusively in the southern part and beyond the borders of the province between the late 3rd and 5th centuries AD (Auer 2019; Fig. 1). Research has further indicated that the grey ware bowls from *Aguntum* have been tempered with coarse calcite (Auer and Daszkiewicz 2016) and were fired in a reducing atmosphere of an open fire (Auer 2017; 2019; Borgers *et al.* 2022). The functionality (or use) of the bowls is ambiguous: they may have served as cooking ware, as suggested by their coarse paste; however, very few bases, that would confirm this hypothesis, have been found. Alternatively, they may have been used as tableware, as suggested by their various decorative motifs (Auer 2019).

Building upon this, the current paper has two aims. The first is to gain insight in the composition and production technology of the two types of grey ware bowls that were found in *Aguntum* and Lavant. Macroscopic observation was combined with ceramic thin section petrography, to reconstruct the production sequence of the bowls studied. The second aim is to consider the social agency and the *habitus* of potters (Dietler and Herbich 1998), by adopting a framework, based on practice theories (Wenger 1998; Wendrich 2012). This will permit to identify the existence of broader potters' groups or 'communities of practice', who were responsible for the access, the regulation, and – most importantly – the reproduction of technological knowledge through time.

2. Background to the sites

The sites at *Aguntum* and Lavant were located in the mountainous area of south-western *Noricum*. They were situated 6 km apart, and on the left and right banks of the Drau River respectively (Fig. 1). The two settlements had different histories during the Roman era (1st–3rd centuries AD) and Late Antiquity (4th–6th centuries AD).

The town of *Aguntum* was founded in the early 1st century AD and received *municipal* rights during Emperor Claudius' reign. The town expanded in the 1st–2nd centuries AD, when several public buildings were constructed, including a bathhouse (*thermae*), marketplaces (*forum* and *macellum*) and city walls, in addition to numerous private houses and villas (known as the *Atrium* house) (Fig. 3). Around the mid-3rd century AD, a fire destroyed large parts of the town. Nevertheless, numerous small finds and several burials near an Early Christian church suggest that the town continued to be inhabited until the early 5th century AD, albeit with a gradual decline and final abandonment. Indeed, reconstructions carried out at the *forum* and *macellum* have been taken to suggest that the administrative and economic role of the town changed after the 3rd century AD fire. More specifically, a large area of the *forum* was levelled, and some buildings appear to have been partly abandoned, while others were reused as dwellings and workshops. Similarly, the *macellum* appears to have been reused for domestic purposes (e.g., dwellings) and crafts (e.g., workshops) (Auer 2016; 2018). After its abandonment, the town appears to have

been buried under several layers of alluvium (Auer *et al.* 2014). Acid groundwater has percolated in the archaeological remains and artefacts, including mortar walls (Auer and Tschurtschenthaler 2016) and grey ware (Auer and Daszkiewicz 2016), leading to the dissolution of calcite, which had been used to produce these artefacts.

The oldest finds of Lavant, which was located on a hilltop on the right bank of the Drau River, date to the Neolithic, while the first settlement remains date to the Bronze Age and Iron Age. However, only a few finds date to the 1st–2nd centuries AD, suggesting that the hill was used sporadically at that time. The settlement seems to have mainly developed between the 3rd and 6th centuries AD, as witnessed by several building activities (Fig. 4) and imported pottery, including African Red Slip Ware and amphorae (Grabherr and Kainrath 2011). Excavations of an Early Christian church nearby (known as the Episcopal Church) have indicated that it comprised several building phases dated to between the late 4th and 6th centuries AD. From this evidence it has been inferred that the settlement at Lavant prospered at that time. The ancient remains and artefacts from the site do not appear to have been affected by acid groundwater, given that they have been well preserved.

3. Ceramic samples and method

A total of 44 sherds of type III and type IV bowls have been selected from the sites at *Aguntum* and Lavant and were examined in both macroscopic and microscopic analysis (Table 1). The aim was to reconstruct all the steps of the production sequence, including raw materials, paste recipe, forming, finishing and firing. Attention has also been paid to the existence of divergent technological choices and shared manufacturing traditions, which were used to produce these two types of bowls.

In the first step, the rim diameter, wall thickness, and decorative motifs of all (44) ceramic bowls were recorded at the University of Innsbruck (Table 1). In the second step, all 44 samples were cut perpendicular to the wall surface in the plane parallel to the vessel wall as proposed by Whitbread (1996), prepared as ceramic thin sections, and analysed with an Olympus BX 51 polarised light microscope at the Paris-Lodron University of Salzburg. The ceramic thin sections were classified in petrographic groups, based upon the nature of the inclusions, clayey matrix, and voids (Quinn 2013, 73–9). The texture of the thin sections was also examined to detect the presence of specific technological practices, such as added temper (Quinn 2013, 156–71).

In the third step, the observation of compression marks and fracture patterns on the sherds in hand specimen (Courty and Roux 1995) was combined with the analysis of fractures, voids and particle orientation in thin section (Quinn 2013, 174–80; Rückl and Jacobs 2016; Thér *et al.* 2019), to identify which forming techniques might have been used by ancient potters. Further to this, the isotropic

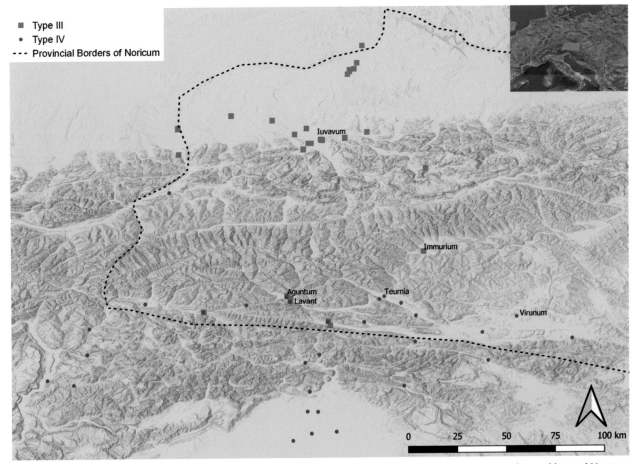

Iuvavum

Immurium

Aguntum
Lavant

Teurnia

Virunum

0   25   50   75   100 km

Figure 1. Grey coarse ware type III (red squares) and type IV (blue circles) bowls and their distribution within and beyond Noricum (marked with dashed line). Image reproduced from Auer (2019).

Figure 2. Different shapes of grey coarse ware displayed at the Archaeological Park of Aguntum in Dölsach. Photo: Martin Auer.

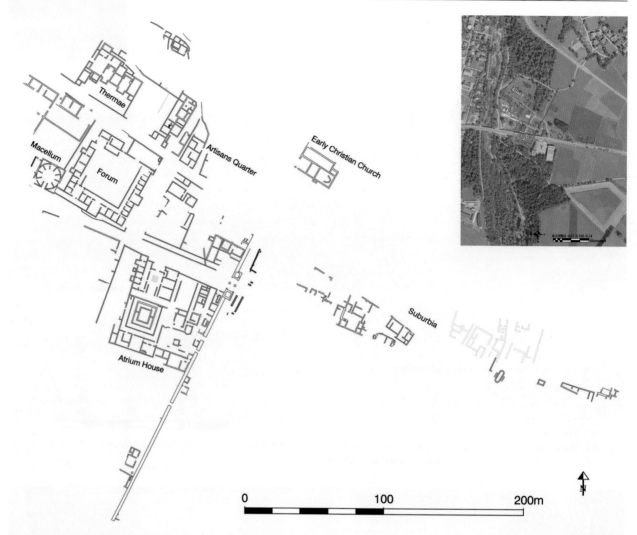

Figure 3. Plan of the settlement at Aguntum with its bathhouse (thermae), marketplaces (forum and macellum), city walls and Early Christian Church.

or anisotropic nature of the clayey matrix (in thin section analysis), as well as the colour of the samples (in hand specimen observation) were useful criteria to reconstruct aspects of firing technology, including temperature and atmosphere (Orton *et al.* 1993, 136–8).

4. Results

4.1 Macroscopic analysis

Most bowls from *Aguntum* display a dark yellowish brown or black surface colour (Munsell (1994) hue 10YR, with values 3/4-3/6, 2/1) and a black core (Munsell (1994) hue 10YR, with value 2/1). In comparison, the colour of the pottery from Lavant tends to be uniformly very dark grey (Munsell (1994) hue 10YR, with value 3/1).

The wall thickness of the type III and type IV bowls from *Aguntum* and Lavant was examined and combined with evidence seen in compression and breakage pattern with the aim to identify the forming technique. The wall thickness of the type III and type IV bowls from *Aguntum* varies between 0.5 and 0.9 cm (Table 1). In comparison,

the wall of the type III bowls from Lavant appears to be slightly thinner, ranging between 0.5 and 0.6 cm, while the wall thickness of the type IV bowls varies between 0.5 and 1 cm (Table 1).

No coils or seams between individual coils were visible neither on the outside nor on the interior of the vessels studied, but several fragments display an irregular surface topography. More specifically, on the exterior walls of some bowls, irregularities in the form of compression undulations have been noticed (Fig. 5a). It has further been found that pottery from *Aguntum* tends to show a preferential breakage, oblique to the external surface of the vessel wall (Fig. 5b). Although it has been argued that fracture patterns are influenced by several factors (Courty and Roux 1995), oblique oriented breaks seem to be a good indication of slab-building (Rückl and Jacobs 2016). In this technique, palm pressure is exerted on both the internal and external vessel wall, pushing two slabs both inward and upward or downward. The undulation then is the feature where two slabs might have been slightly displaced during compression.

Figure 4. Plan of the hilltop settlement at Lavant with its Early Christian Church (Complex H on the plan).

Several vessels from Lavant display a smoothed rim, as witnessed by fine horizontal parallel striations (Fig. 5a). This might have been achieved by (slowly) rotating the bowl(s) on a rotating device (as a secondary forming technique); a technique, which would have obliterated any indication of the primary forming technique used.

In comparison, it is more difficult to identify any kind of surface finish, such as smoothing, on the sherds from *Aguntum*, because the pottery has become fragile due to soil acidity. Despite this, decorative motifs on the bowls permit to identify similarities and differences between the two sites. More specifically, six different decorative

Table 1. *Macroscopic and mineralogical characteristics of grey ware bowls from Aguntum and Lavant, as determined in hand specimen observation and thin section analysis. Abbreviations: Qz – Quartz; Fsp – Feldspar; Ms – Muscovite; Cal – Calcite; Fe aggr – Iron-rich aggregates; ARF – Argillaceous rock fragment.*

Crt. No.	Sample No.	Site	Type/ Variant	Decorative Motif	Wall Thickness (cm)	Rim Diameter (cm)	OM Group	Mx	Qz	Fsp	Ms	Cal	Fe aggr	ARF
1.	AG1	*Aguntum*	III/1	Curvilinear lines	0.5	15	2	Isotropic	●	●	●	●	●	
2.	AG2				0.6	18	1	Isotropic	●	●	●	●	●	
3.	AG3				0.8	22	1	Isotropic	●	●	●	Ghost	●	●
4.	AG4				0.7	25	1	Isotropic	●	●	●	Ghost		●
5.	AG5				0.8	17	1	Isotropic	●	●	●	●	●	
6.	AG6				0.6	n.d.	2	Isotropic	●	●	●	●	●	
7.	AG8		III/2	Multiple linear punctuations	0.8	23	1	Isotropic	●	●	●	Ghost	●	
8.	AG9				0.6	16	1	Isotropic	●	●	●	Ghost	●	
9.	AG10				0.8	18	1	Isotropic	●	●	●	Ghost	●	
10.	AG11				0.9	n.d.	Loner	≈Δ to Δ	●	●	●	Ghost	●	
11.	AG12		III/4	Horizontal and curvilinear lines	0.6	18	1	Isotropic	●	●	●	Ghost	●	
12.	AG13				0.6	22	1	≈Δ to ‾Δ	●	●	●	Ghost	●	
13.	AG16		III/5	Single and curvilinear lines	0.5	17	1	Isotropic	●	●	●	Ghost	●	
14.	AG21		IV/1	Single row of impressed punctuations	0.5	25	1	≈Δ to ‾Δ	●	●	●	●	●	●
15.	AG22				0.5	19	1	Isotropic	●	●	●	Ghost	●	●
16.	AG23				0.9	23	1	Isotropic	●	●	●	Ghost	●	
17.	AG26		IV/2	Linear punctuations	0.8	n.d.	2	Isotropic	●	●	●	●	●	
18.	AG27				0.8	25	1	Isotropic	●	●	●	Ghost	●	
19.	AG28				0.8	19	2	Isotropic	●	●	●	●	●	
20.	AG29				0.6	19	2	Isotropic	●	●	●	●	●	
21.	AG30				0.5	17	2	Isotropic	●	●	●	●	●	
22.	AG31				0.8	n.d.	2	Isotropic	●	●	●	●	●	●
23.	AG32				0.7	15	1	Isotropic	●	●	●	Ghost	●	
24.	AG33				0.8	20	1	Isotropic	●	●	●	Ghost	●	
25.	AG34				0.5	20	2	Isotropic	●	●	●	●	●	●
26.	AG43		IV/3	Punctuation row and single curvilinear line	0.5	16	1	‾Δ to Isotropic	●	●	●	Ghost	●	
27.	AG45				0.6	20	1	‾Δ to Isotropic	●	●	●	●	●	

(Continued)

Table 1. (Continued)

Crt. No.	Sample No.	Site	Type/ Variant	Decorative Motif	Wall Thickness (cm)	Rim Diameter (cm)	OM Group	Mx	Qz	Fsp	Ms	Cal	Fe aggr	ARF
28.	LA7	Lavant	III/1	Equidistant curvilinear lines	0.6	24	2	Isotropic	●	●	●	●	●	●
29.	LA14		III/4	Horizontal and curvilinear lines	0.5	19	2	Isotropic	●	●	●	●	●	
30.	LA15				0.5	17	2	Isotropic	●	●	●	●	●	
31.	LA18		III/5	Single and curvilinear lines	0.5	26	2	Isotropic	●	●	●	●	●	
32.	LA20		III/6	Single curvilinear line with punctuation above	0.6	27	2	Isotropic	●	●	●	●	●	
33.	LA24		IV/1	Single row of impressed punctuations	0.6	14	2	Isotropic	●	●	●	●	●	
34.	LA25				0.8	27	2	Isotropic	●	●	●	●	●	
35.	LA35		IV/2	Linear punctuations	0.5	17	2	Isotropic	●	●	●	●	●	
36.	LA36				1	22	2	Isotropic	●	●	●	●	●	
37.	LA37				0.5	24	2	Isotropic	●	●	●	●	●	
38.	LA38				1	20	2	Isotropic	●	●	●	●	●	
39.	LA39				0.7	30	2	Isotropic	●	●	●	●	●	
40.	LA40				1	24	2	Isotropic	●	●	●	●	●	
41.	LA41				0.6	27.5	2	Isotropic	●	●	●	●	●	
42.	LA46		IV/3	Punctuation row and single curvilinear line	0.6	14	2	Isotropic	●	●	●	●	●	
43.	LA47				0.5	22	2	Δ	●	●	●	●	●	
44.	LA48				0.8	23	2	Isotropic	●	●	●	●	●	

motifs have been identified on type III bowls. More specifically, five motifs have been recorded on bowls from both *Aguntum* and Lavant, while one decorative pattern has been found on bowls from Lavant alone (Table 1). Three decorative motifs have been recorded on type IV bowls, and they occur on both sites (Auer 2019). The various decorative motifs have been described as 'variants' (Auer 2019) and will be described accordingly.

Type III variant 1 bowls (n = 7) are defined by impressed curvilinear lines. Some vessels display a repeated pattern of unitary motifs (Fig. 6a; Fig. 7a), while other vessels show continuous thin, parallel (or equidistant) striations (Fig. 6b; Figs 7b and 7c; Table 1).

The decorative motif of most **type III variant 2** bowls (n = 4) comprises multiple linear punctations with a square- and wedge-shaped tool (Fig. 6c). The rows tend to be regular, parallel and continuous. It should be noted that one vessel differs from the others because of its irregularly incised round punctations (e.g., AG11 in Table 1;

Fig. 7d), suggesting that a pointed tool might have been used. While this variant has been recorded on bowls from both *Aguntum* and Lavant (Auer 2019), this study has examined bowls from *Aguntum* only (Table 1).

Type III variant 4 bowls (n = 4) are defined by multiple parallel incisions of horizontal and curvilinear lines (Fig. 6d). This indicates that the tool was held stationary for the horizontal lines, and moved up and down for the curvilinear lines, while the vessel was revolving on a device (Table 1).

The decorative motif of **type III variant 5** bowls (n = 2) consists of a single curvilinear line combined with multiple curvilinear lines (Fig. 6e). The pattern indicates that the tool was moved up and down while the vessel was turned slowly on a wheel or turntable. The width, depth and frequency of the lines vary on the different bowls studied, indicating that a pointed implement might have been used. This decorative pattern has been found on bowls from both *Aguntum* and Lavant (Table 1).

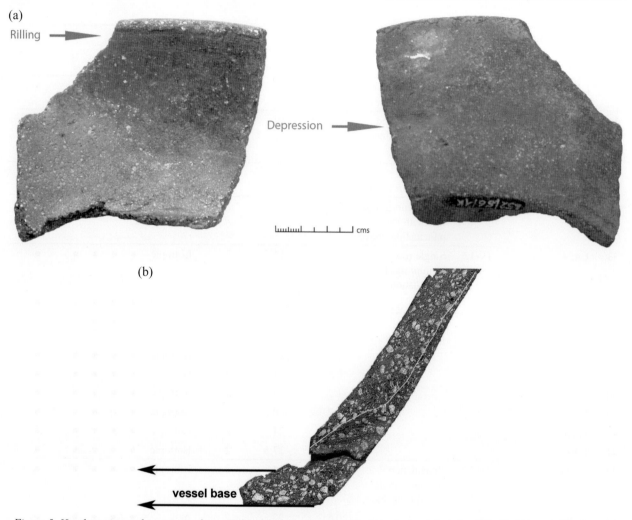

(a)

Rilling →

Depression →

⊢ᴜᴜᴜᴜᴜᴜᴜᴜᴵ   ⊥   ⊥   ⊥   ⊥ cms

(b)

vessel base ←

Figure 5. Hand specimen observation of type IV bowl from Lavant (LA41): frontal view (a) and profile (b). Photos: Martin Auer.

The motif of **type III variant 6** bowls (n = 1) is characterised by a single curvilinear line with one or two punctations above (Fig. 6f). It is likely that this motif was applied with a pointed tool, given that the depth, frequency, and width of the curve and punctation vary. This variant has been found exclusively at Lavant (Table 1).

Type IV variant 1 bowls (n = 5) are defined by a single row of incised punctations (Fig. 6g). Both the depth and frequency of the impressions vary on the vessels, indicating that a fingernail or a pointed instrument might have been used. Bowls decorated with supposed fingernails or pointed tools have been found at both *Aguntum* and Lavant (Table 1).

Type IV variant 2 bowls (n = 16) are characterised by a pronounced bead with linear punctations (Fig. 6h). The irregular placement and varying depth and shape (e.g., elongated, rounded) of the punctations are tentatively taken to suggest that a pointed instrument or a fingernail might have been used (Fig. 7e). This decorative motif has been identified on bowls from both *Aguntum* and *Lavant* (Table 1).

The decorative pattern of **type IV variant 3** bowls (n = 5) consists of a punctation row and a single curvilinear line (Fig. 6i). For this motif, a pointed instrument or a fingernail would have been held stationary for the punctation row and moved up and down for the curvilinear line, while the vessel revolved on a device. Bowls at both *Aguntum* and Lavant display this variant (Table 1).

4.2 Microscopic analysis

Thin section petrographic analysis of the 44 samples indicates the presence of two main fabrics, including the 'Very Coarse Calcite and Mica', and the 'Coarse Calcite' groups. One sample contains additional grog inclusions and has been separated in the 'Calcite, Quartzite and Grog' fabric (e.g., AG11). This sample has a unique composition in the assemblage and is consequently defined as a 'loner' (Table 1).

The samples of the **'Very Coarse Calcite and Mica'** group (n = 18) are defined by very coarse calcite fragments and large mica flakes (Fig. 8a). The calcite

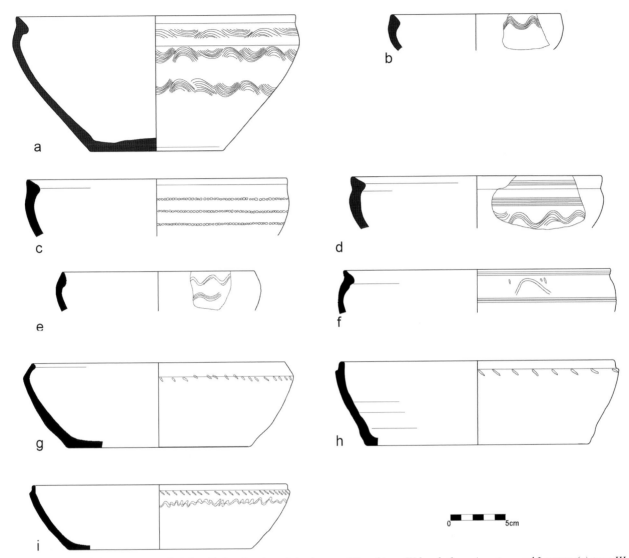

Figure 6. Several decorative motifs (identified as 'variants') in the type III and type IV bowls from Aguntum and Lavant: (a) type III variant 1 bowl with a repeated pattern of curvilinear striations, (b) type III variant 1 bowl with continuous equidistant striations, (c) type III variant 2 bowl with multiple linear punctations, (d) type III variant 4 bowl with multiple parallel incised horizontal and curvilinear lines, (e) type III variant 5 bowl with a single curvilinear line combined with multiple curvilinear lines, (f) type III variant 6 bowl with a single curvilinear line with one or two punctations, (g) type IV variant 1 bowl with a single row of impressed punctations, (h) type IV variant 2 bowl with a pronounced bead with linear punctations, (i) Type IV variant 3 bowl with punctation row and a single curvilinear line (after Auer 2019).

fragments are euhedral sparry crystals and are dominant in the matrix, comprising between 30 to 35%. They are sub-angular and sub-rounded in shape, and their size varies between 0.5–1.5 mm, suggesting that they have been deliberately added. In 15 samples of this group (Table 1), all calcite inclusions have disappeared, leaving voids behind. Given that the shape of these voids is suggestive of the former presence of calcite, they have been defined as 'calcite ghosts (Fabbri *et al.* 2014; Fig. 8a). The mica inclusions measure between 0.25 and 0.5 mm. Other coarse inclusions consist of rare, rounded quartz grains. The clayey matrix contains small quartz grains and mica and is isotropic in most samples, except

for four (AG13, AG21, AG43, AG45) where it displays moderate or low birefringence (Table 1). All ceramic samples in this group comprise type III and type IV bowls from *Aguntum*.

One sample (AG11) is defined as '**Very Coarse Calcite, Quartzite and Grog**', given that it has the same composition as the 'Very Coarse Calcite and Mica' group, as well as further coarse fragments of quartzite (0.5–2 mm) and grog (0.5–0.7 mm). The grog fragments are isotropic, while the clayey matrix of the (host) sample contains small quartz and mica inclusions and is moderately to highly birefringent (Fig. 8b). The sample comprises a type III bowl from *Aguntum* (Table 1).

Figure 7. Images of various decorative motifs in the type III and type IV bowls from Aguntum and Lavant: (a) type III variant 1 bowl with a repeated pattern of curvilinear striations, (b) and (c) type III variant 1 bowl with multiple continuous equidistant striations, (d) type III variant 2 bowl with multiple linear punctations, (e) type IV variant 2 bowl with a pronounced bead with linear punctations, (f) and (g) bowls with multiple parallel horizontal lines.

The **'Coarse Calcite'** group (n = 25) is characterised by coarse calcite fragments. They are well-preserved, and seem to comprise deliberately added temper, as suggested by their shape (sub-angular and sub-rounded) and size (0.3–0.5 mm). The clayey matrix is defined by small quartz and rare mica inclusions and is isotropic in most samples (Fig. 8c), except for one (LA47). One sample in this group contains additional large quartzite inclusions (0.5–2 mm; Fig. 8d). This group includes type III and type IV bowls from Lavant and *Aguntum* (Table 1).

As soon as it was recognised that the bowls from *Aguntum* and Lavant could have been slab-built, special attention was paid to microstructural evidence – i.e., particular orientation of voids and inclusions in the ceramic thin sections. During the analysis, it was assumed that if slabs had been slightly displaced, their interfaces would be visible in the cross-sections of oblique fractures.

In the left vessel wall of two ceramic thin sections (AG29, AG28), it was found that thin irregularly and long channel-shaped voids on the left-hand side of the section run oblique to the left (i.e., the external surface of the vessel wall), while inclusions and voids on the right-hand side of the section (i.e., the internal surface of the vessel wall) tend to run straight from the top to the bottom (Figs 9a and 9b).

Similarly, in the right vessel wall of two other ceramic thin sections (AG34, LA41), inclusions and voids on the right-hand side of the section tend to run oblique to the right (i.e., the external surface of the vessel), whereas they run straight from the top to the bottom on the left-hand side of the section (i.e., the internal vessel wall) (Figs 9c and 9d). This microstructural evidence is in agreement with the macrostructural evidence and is thus tentatively taken to suggest that two slabs were compressed inward (i.e., the internal vessel wall) and downward or upward (i.e., on the external surface of the vessel).

5. Manufacturing technology

The macroscopic observations and thin section petrography analysis of the 44 samples have indicated that the grey ware bowls from *Aguntum* and Lavant share broad aspects of their production technology, including paste preparation, forming, finishing and firing. Nevertheless, there appear to be subtle differences in the different steps of the production sequence and decorative motifs applied.

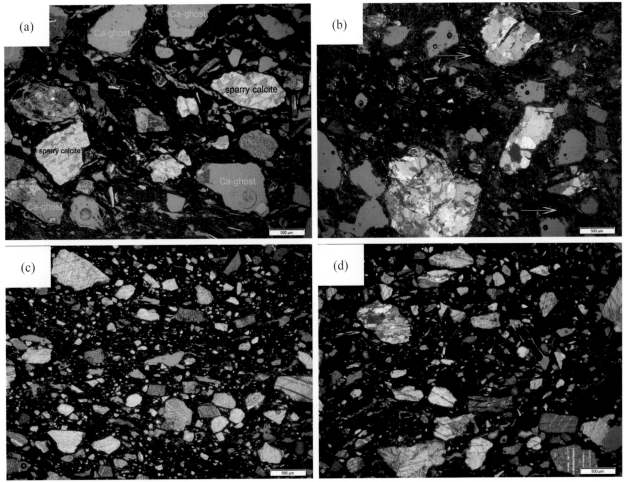

Figure 8. Thin section petrography analysis. (a) Very Coarse Calcite and Mica in AG45, (b) Very Coarse Calcite, Quartzite and Chamotte (marked with yellow arrow) in AG11 (c) Coarse Calcite in LA15, (d) Coarse Calcite and Quartzite in LA7.

5.1 Raw materials

The type III and type IV bowls from *Aguntum* and Lavant tend to be grey in hand specimen and isotropic in thin section analysis (Table 1), making it difficult to determine the nature of the clay confidently. The dominant presence of mica flakes in the clayey matrix of the 'Very Coarse Calcite and Mica' group (Fig. 8a) and the 'Coarse Calcite, Quartzite and Grog' sample (Fig. 8b), and the comparatively few and small mica inclusions in the matrix of the 'Coarse Calcite' group (Figs 8c and 8d) suggests that minor differences exist in the type of clay used for manufacture. Despite this difference, detailed compositional analyses that have been conducted elsewhere (Borgers *et al.* 2022) confirm that the bowls from both *Aguntum* and Lavant were produced with a similar alluvial clay source that was extracted on the left and right banks of the Drau River respectively.

5.2 Paste preparation

All three petrographic classifications in the studied assemblage display evidence for having been tempered with large fragments of sparry calcite crystals. More specifically, the bowls of the 'Very Coarse Calcite and Mica' (Fig. 8a) and the 'Coarse Calcite' groups (Fig. 8c) seem to have been tempered with coarse, crushed calcite only, while the 'Coarse Calcite, Quartzite and Grog' fabric displays additional temper in the form of crushed grog (Fig. 8b).

The origin of calcite inclusions (with residual presence of quartzite) is in agreement with the geological setting of the sites at *Aguntum* and Lavant and is thought to have been sourced locally by the potters (Borgers *et al.* 2022).

5.3 Forming

No bases of type III and type IV bowls from *Aguntum* and Lavant have been preserved, which might have permitted to identify their forming technique confidently. However, there are some indications which suggest that the bowls were hand-built and finished on a slowly rotating device, such as a turntable or wheel device.

Evidence for hand-building in macroscopic observation of the bowls is suggested in three ways: (1) the variation

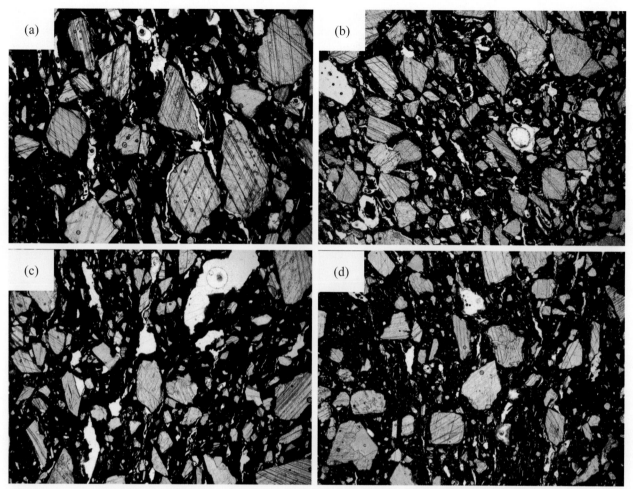

Figure 9. Ceramic Thin sections cut perpendicular to the wall surface in the plane parallel to the (a) left vessel wall in AG29 (a) and AG28 (b), as well as to the right vessel wall in LA41 (c) and AG34 (d), showing fractures, voids, and orientation of coarse calcite inclusions running oblique through the core of the vessel wall section.

in wall thickness, which is due to discontinuous pressure application during manufacture (Table 1), (2) the compression that is often witnessed on the vessel body (Fig. 5a), and (3) the particular breakage or fracture of the sherds. Combined with the microstructural evidence in thin section (i.e., orientation analysis, see Fig. 9), it seems that the bowls were slab-built. More specifically, the oblique orientation of the large calcite inclusions and voids suggests that two slabs were thinned and joined with overlapping margins in the vessel wall. This is taken to suggest that the upper slabs join the lower slabs on the interior of the vessel. The junction between the slabs seems to have been obliterated by spreading the clay, leaving compressions all around the body of the vessel (Fig. 5a). This primary technique was obliterated by secondary wheel-finishing, as suggested by the grooves (e.g., rilling marks), which are visible on the internal rim on the bowls from Lavant (Fig. 5a).

The wall thickness of type III and type IV bowls from *Aguntum*, varying between 0.5 and 0.9 cm, is similar

to the wall thickness of type IV bowls from Lavant. In comparison, the wall of type III bowls from Lavant is thinner, measuring between 0.5 and 0.6 cm, but it should be noted that fewer samples of this type and site have been analysed (Table 1).

The rim diameter of the type III and type IV bowls from *Aguntum* ranges between 15 and 25 cm (Table 1), whereas the rim diameter of the bowls from Lavant is slightly wider. More specifically, the diameter of type III bowls varies between 19 and 27 cm, and the diameter of type IV bowls varies between 14 and 30 cm (Table 1).

5.4 Finishing

Except for type III variant 6, all the bowls from *Aguntum* and Lavant are characterised by impressed or incised decorative motifs – i.e., textured patterns, which render it difficult to comprehend the shared or divergent practices of this visual aspect of pottery manufacture. No potters' tools have been found in south-western *Noricum*, which would help to interpret the evidence seen on the ancient pottery confidently. For instance, for some decorative motifs, it seems that a fine pointed tool (e.g., Fig. 7d) or a fingernail (e.g., Fig. 7e) may have been used, while for other motifs, consisting of multiple parallel horizontal lines (Figs 7f and 7g), it is unclear which tool might have been used.

The decorative motifs observed on the bowls have also been noted on other types of grey ware pottery, including jars (*e.g.*, Auer 2019, type IX variant 3, type X and type XVII) that circulated in south-western *Noricum*. Following on from this, experimental research, using diverse tools, would have to be carried out to confidently interpret the techniques (and tools) used for decorating the surface of the ancient pottery.

5.5 Firing

The birefringence of the clayey matrix in thin section analysis has been used to infer firing temperature. Most type III and type IV bowls from *Aguntum* are defined by an isotropic clay matrix, indicating a high firing temperature. Only few samples from the site are characterised by a moderately birefringent matrix, indicating a comparatively low firing temperature. Some ceramic thin sections from *Aguntum* further display an isotropic core, while the surface displays a low birefringence (Fig. 8a). This suggests a variable firing temperature within the same vessel. In comparison, the clayey matrix of the samples from Lavant is uniformly opaque (Table 1).

The hand specimen sherds from *Aguntum* tend to display a black core and brown surface, while the fragments from Lavant have a uniformly grey colour. The reasons for thinking that the grey ware bowls may have been fired in a reducing atmosphere of an open fire are twofold: (1) in the region of Lavant and *Aguntum*, no evidence for workshops (i.e., in the form of kiln structures or pottery waste deposits) has been found; and (2) experimental an ethnoarchaeological research have shown that firing of calcite-tempered pottery can be achieved in a reducing atmosphere of an open fire (Maggetti *et al.* 2011; Carlton 2019).

6. Discussion

The macroscopic and microscopic analysis of type III and type IV grey ware bowls from *Aguntum* and Lavant in south-western Austria, known as *Noricum*, has permitted to gain insight in the technology used by Roman potters between the 2nd–5th centuries AD. More specifically, the results have indicated that the production sequence of the grey ware bowls remains broadly the same between the 2nd and the 5th centuries AD. Potters used similar raw materials (e.g., similar clay deposits with more, or less, mica flakes, depending on the place of exploitation), paste recipes (e.g., crushed calcite with residual quartzite), forming techniques (e.g., slab-building),

firing strategies (e.g., high firing temperature and a predominantly reducing atmosphere) and visual appearance (e.g., decorative motifs).

Ethnographic research has shown that technological choices are the result of a learning process: potters tend to produce pottery in the way that they have been taught – a process that is determined by the *habitus* and the agency of a pottery-making group (van der Leeuw 1993; Dietler and Herbich 1998; Wendrich 2012). More specifically, it has been shown that some stages of the production process, including paste recipe (such as temper), firing, decorative motifs and post-firing techniques, might vary within a single potter community. Forming technique, on the other hand, usually constitutes a very stable stage of the production sequence, and differences noted therein reflect a clear social boundary, and consequently, the presence of different communities of practice (Herbich 1987; Dietler and Herbich 1989; Gosselain 1992; 1998).

Following on from the observations in present-day potter communities (Herbich 1987; Dietler and Herbich 1989; Gosselain 1992; 1998), it might be tentatively suggested that the Roman potters, who produced type III and type IV bowls between the 2nd and 5th centuries AD and supplied them to *Aguntum* and Lavant, worked within the same broad technological tradition of one overarching community of practice; this community appears to have shared learning networks, and transmitted this knowledge continually through time.

Despite the overall standard production sequence, subtle differences have been noted in the type III and type IV bowls studied. These include: (i) paste recipes (such as temper), (ii) aspects of form (such as rim diameter), and (iii) decorative motifs. This permits to infer that within the overarching craft community that was defined by a continuous knowledge transmission, there was room for the construction and expression of individual identity (Herbich 1987; David *et al.* 1988; Dietler and Herbich 1989; Gosselain 1992; 2000; Albero *et al.* 2016). More specifically, regarding (i) paste recipes, while all bowls have been tempered with crushed calcite (some of which has been dissolved in the bowls from *Aguntum*, because of soil acidity), one sample (AG11) is defined by additional large grog fragments. This bowl further displays a decorative motif with multiple incised linear punctuations (e.g., type III variant 2) that differs slightly from other bowls with this variant, because the punctuations are irregular (in comparison with the parallel and continuous punctuations on the other bowls). The two technological particularities of this bowl (AG11), i.e., paste recipe and decorative motif, suggest that individual expression was allowed within the craft community.

Ad (ii), there appears to be a difference in the rim diameter of the bowls from *Aguntum* on the one hand, and those from Lavant, on the other. More specifically, the rim diameter of the bowls from *Aguntum* varies between

15 and 25 cm, while the bowls from Lavant tend to be comparatively wide, with a rim diameter ranging between 14 and 30 cm (Table 1). This width difference observed on the bowls seems to have been within the acceptable limits of variation set by the community.

Ad (iii), not only did acid soil at *Aguntum* dissolve the calcite (temper) in the bowls, it also corroded the decorative motifs, making it difficult to identify them confidently. Despite this, it seems that most types III and IV bowls from *Aguntum* and Lavant display the same decorative motifs. The bowls from Lavant tend to be comparatively better preserved and display a well-smoothed surface (Fig. 7a), obliterating traces of the primary forming technique. This indicates great care and skill on behalf of the potters. One decorative motif (variant 6) on type III bowls occurs exclusively at Lavant. This decorative pattern might be taken to indicate an expression of individual creativity as well.

7. Conclusions and further research

Grey ware pottery circulated widely in ancient *Noricum*, covering present-day Austria, south-western Germany, and northern Italy and Slovenia between the 2nd and 5th centuries AD. This article examined two types of grey ware bowls from *Aguntum* and Lavant in south-western *Noricum*, combining macroscopic (i.e., hand specimen) and microscopic (i.e., thin section petrography) observation, with the aims to (i) reconstruct the production technology, and (ii) infer the existence of pottery communities, who were fundamental for the access, regulation and, above all, the maintenance of technological knowledge.

The results indicated that the grey ware bowls were produced with a similar clay source (whose composition varies slightly, depending on the extraction location), tempered with coarse crushed calcite fragments, and formed with slabs. The surface of the vessels was smoothed and decorated with various motifs, and the bowls were fired in a reducing atmosphere, possibly in an open fire. Three divergent technological choices were recorded in the broadly shared tradition, including 1) the width of the rim, for instance, bowls from Lavant are defined by a slightly wider diameter, 2) one paste recipe, such as one bowl from *Aguntum*, comprises additional grog, and 3) one decorative motif, comprising a pattern that occurs exclusively on bowls from Lavant.

Against a broader framework based on practice theories (Wenger 1998; Wendrich 2012), the results have been taken to indicate the existence of one overarching craft community, who was responsible for the continuous transmission of the technological knowledge of the bowls that were found in *Aguntum* and Lavant. As for the (three) divergent technological choices observed on the bowls, they are seen as a matter of personal expression, which was permitted by the potter community.

The ideas that have been put forward in this paper can be verified in two ways. First, if Roman workshops with pottery waste, tools and kilns were to be found in south-western *Noricum*, insight could be gained in the location, production sequence, tools, and organisation of the ancient potters. Second, the combined method of orientation analysis (in thin section petrography) with fracture of sherds (in hand specimen) does not permit to confidently identify the hand-building technique, which has been used to produce grey ware bowls from Lavant and *Aguntum*. Other techniques, such as recent developments in CT scanning technology (Kozatsas *et al.* 2018) and scanning of ceramic thin sections (Ross *et al.* 2018) might yield more robust results and will be applied in the next stage of research.

Acknowledgements

This paper is dedicated to Roberta Tomber, who kindly encouraged the first author of this manuscript to write a paper on 'communities of practice'. Sadly, she passed away before the manuscript was finalised. The authors would like to thank Katrin Winkler for her assistance to select the grey ware bowls that have been analysed in this study. They are also grateful to the two anonymous referees for their thorough engagement with the manuscript, as this has helped to improve it. The research in this paper was financially supported by the Austrian Science Fund (FWF project T-1085G), and by the University of Innsbruck.

Bibliography

Albero. D., Calvo, M. and García Rosselló, J. 2016. Formal Analysis and Typological Classification in the Study of Ancient Pottery, in A. Hunt (ed.) *The Oxford Handbook of Archaeological Ceramic Analysis*, Oxford University Press, Oxford, 1–25.

Auer, M. 2017. Zur Organisation des Töpferhandwerks in Noricum – Familienunternehmen oder Großbetrieb?, *Ethnographisch-Archäologische Zeitschrift* 55(1/2), 119–56.

Auer, M. 2018. Municipium Claudium Aguntum. Excavations in the city centre (2006–2015), in M. Janežič, B. Nadbath, T. Mulh and I. Žižek (eds) *New Discoveries between the Alps and the Black Sea. Results from Roman Sites in the period between 2005 and 2015*, Proceedings of the 1st International Archaeological Conference, Ptuj 2015, Institute for the Protection of Cultural Heritage Slovenia, Ljubljana, 93–113.

Auer, M. 2019. Municipium Claudium Aguntum. Keramikregionen als Interaktionsräume. Eine westnorische Perspektive, Ager Aguntinus, *Historisch-Archäologische Forschungen* 2, 417.

Auer, M. and Daszkiewicz, M. 2016. Archaeological expectations and archaeometric results. Some considerations on imported coarse wares and local pottery production in Aguntum, Austria, in A. Konestra and G. Lipovac Vrkljan (eds) *Roman Pottery and Glass Manufacture. Production and Trade in the Adriatic Region*, Proceedings of the 3rd

International Archaeological Colloquium, Croatia, Crikvenica Municipal Museum, Zagreb, 97–126.

Auer, M. and Tschurtschenthaler, M. 2016. Zum Stand der archäologischen Forschung in Aguntum, in B. Hebert and N. Hofer (eds) Alte Mauern – Neue Konzepte. Aguntum – Konservierung und Entwicklung, *FÖ Tagungsband* 3, 9–25.

Auer, M., Bleibinhaus, F., Tschurtschenthaler, M. and Unterwurzacher, M. 2014. Municipium Claudium Aguntum. Geophysikalische Prospektion auf geologisch schwierigem Terrain, *Jahreshefte des Österreichischen Archäologischen Instituts* 82, 7–21.

Borgers, B., Ionescu, C. Auer, M., Gál, A., Barbu-Tudoran, L., Kasztovszky, Zs., Gméling, K., Szilagyi, V., Harsányi, I., Neubauer, F., Von Hagke, C. 2022. Production Technology and Knowledge Transfer of Calcite-Tempered Grey Ware Bowls from 2nd–5th centuries AD Noricum, Austria, *Archaeometry*, 1–18.

Carlton, R. 2019. Tempering Expectations: What Do West Balkan Potters Think They Are Doing?, in S. Amicone, P.S. Quinn, M. Marić, N. Mirković-Marić and M. Radivojević (eds) *Tracing Pottery-Making Recipes in the Prehistoric Balkans 6th-4th Millenia BC*, Archaeopress, Oxford, 8–24.

Courty, M.A. and Roux, V. 1995. Identification of Wheel Throwing on the basis of Ceramic Surface Features and Microfabrics, *Journal of Archaeological Science* 22, 17–50.

David, N., Sterner, J. and Gavua, K. 1988. Why pots are decorated, *Current Anthropology* 29(3), 365–89.

Dietler, M. and Herbich, I. 1989. Tich Matek: the technology of Luo pottery production and the definition of ceramic style. *World Archaeology* 21(1), 148–64.

Dietler, M. and Herbich, I. 1998. Habitus, techniques, style: an integrated approach to the social understanding of material culture and boundaries, in M. Stark (ed.) *The Archaeology of Social Boundaries*, Washington Smithsonian, 232–63.

Fabbri, B., Gualtieri, S. and Shoval, S. 2014. The presence of calcite in archeological ceramics, *Journal of the European Ceramic Society* 34(7), 1899–911.

Gassner, V., Jilek, S. and Ladstätter, S. 2002. Am Rande des Reiches. Die Römer in Österreich. Österreichische Geschichte 15 v. Chr.-378 n. Chr., in H. Wolfram (ed.), *Ergänzungsband 2*. Verlag Carl Ueberreuter, Wien, 488.

Gosselain, O.P. 1992. Technology and Style: Potters and Pottery among Bafia of Cameroon, *Man* (New Series) 27, 559–86.

Gosselain, O.P. 1998. Social and Technical Identity in a Clay Crystal Ball, in M.T. Stark (ed.) *The Archaeology of Social Boundaries*, Washington Smithsonian, 78–106.

Gosselain, O.P. 2000. Materializing Identities: An African Perspective, *Journal of Archaeological Method and Theory* 7, 187–217.

Grabherr, G. and Kainrath, B. 2011. *Die spätantike Höhensiedlung auf dem Kirchbichl von Lavant* Ikarus, 5, Innsbruck University Press, Innsbruck.

Herbich, I. 1987. Learning Patterns, Potter Interaction and Ceramic Style among the Luo of Kenya, *The African Archaeological Review 5 Papers in Honour of J. Desmond Clark*, 193–204.

Kozatsas, J., Kotsakis, K., Sagris, D. and David, K. 2018. Inside out: assessing pottery forming techniques with micro-CT scanning. An example from Middle Neolithic Thessaly, *Journal of Archaeological Science* 100, 102–19.

Lang, F., Knauseder, D. and Kovacsovics, W.K. 2012. Handwerk im Municipium Claudium Iuvavum – Salzburg. Keramik-, Metall- und Beinverarbeitung, in F. Lang, S. Traxler and W. Wohlmayr (eds) Stadt, Land, Fluss/Weg. Aspekte zur römischen Wirtschaft im nördlichen Noricum, *Archaeoplus* 3, 95–117.

Maggetti, M., Neururer, Ch. and Ramseyer, D. 2011. Temperature evolution inside a pot during experimental surface (bonfire) firing, *Applied Clay Science* 53, 500–8.

Munsell Colour Co. Inc. 1994. *Munsell soil colour charts* (revised edition), Munsell Colour Co. Inc., Baltimore.

Orton, C., Tyers, P. and Vince, A. 1993. *Pottery in Archaeology*. Cambridge Manuals in Archaeology, London.

Quinn, P.S. 2013. *Ceramic Petrography: the interpretation of archaeological pottery and related artefacts in thin section*, Archaeopress, Oxford.

Ross, J., Fowler, K.D., Shai, I., Greenfield, H.J., Maeir, A.M. 2018. A scanning method for the identification of pottery forming techniques at the mesoscopic scale: A pilot study in the manufacture of Early Bronze Age III holemouth jars and platters from Tell es-Safi/Gath, *Journal of Archaeological Science Reports* 18, 551–61.

Rückl, S. and Jacobs, L. 2016. With a Little Help from my Wheel. Wheel-Coiled Pottery in Protogeometric Greece. *Hesperia* 85, 297–321.

Van der Leeuw, S.E. 1993. Giving the Potter a Choice: Conceptual Aspects of Pottery Techniques, in P. Lemonnier (ed.) *Technological Choices: Transformation in Material Cultures since the Neolithic*, Routledge, London, 238–88.

Thér, R., Květina, P. and Neumannová K. 2019. Coiling or slab building: Potential of orientation analysis for identification of forming techniques used by Early Neolithic potters, *Journal of Archaeological Science: Reports* 26, 101877.

Wendrich, W. 2012. Archaeology and Apprenticeship: Body Knowledge, Identity, and Communities of Practice, in W. Wendrich (ed.) *Archaeology and Apprenticeship: Body Knowledge, Identity, and Communities of Practice*, The University of Arizona Press, Tucson, 1–20.

Wenger, E. 1998. *Communities of practice: learning, meaning, and identity*, Cambridge University Press, Cambridge.

Whitbread, I.K. 1996. Detection and interpretation of preferred orientation in ceramic thin sections, in T. Higgins, P. Main and J. Lang (eds) *Imaging the Past: Electronic Imaging and Computer Graphics in Museums and Archaeology*, British Museum Occasional Paper, British Museum, London, 173–81.

A late Roman 'Nene Valley colour-coated ware' kiln site beside the River Witham at Lincoln in 2009

*Hugh G. Fiske and Ian M. Rowlandson, with Dr G. Monteil,
pottery drawings by Charlotte Bentley*

Abstract

This excavation beside the River Witham in Lincoln confirmed the presence of a predominantly late 3rd to 4th century AD pottery production site which has been previously noted in The Pottery Kilns of Roman Britain *(Swan 1984, LINCOLN (1)) and more fully online at www.romankilns.net. Large quantities of kiln waste clearly show it was producing a range of colour-coated wares along with utilitarian grey wares; the range of products mostly consisted of bowls of various sizes and forms, beakers and jars, along with a few more specialised vessels such as Castor boxes and lids. Many of the colour-coated vessels present were similar in both form and fabric to those produced in the Lower Nene Valley industry near modern Peterborough. Pottery production on the site appears to have ended by the late 4th century AD. The presence of a range of colour-coated pottery wasters in forms and fabric hitherto considered to have been produced in the Lower Nene Valley has wide reaching implications for our understanding of the significance and distribution of pottery produced at Lincoln. The site raises questions about wares that have traditionally been attributed to the Nene Valley: which valley were the colour-coated pots from Lincoln produced in? How much did the potters move or were moved around (Buckland 2004)? Can we be sure we are provenancing the work of potters working in one specific area? Or are we sometimes seeing the work of a school of potters and their apprentices working at a variety of different sites?*

1. Archaeological and historical background

Roman activity at Lincoln has been extensively discussed by Jones and others as part of the City of Lincoln Archaeological Unit's publication series (Jones 2002; 2003a; 2003b; Steane 2001; 2005; 2016) including the settlements stretching to the south of the city in the Brayford suburb. A number of excavations in the Brayford suburb have found evidence for pottery production as far north as Tentercroft Street (Chavasse and Clay 2008; Rowlandson 2010; Anchor Street: Mike Jarvis pers. com; Fiske and Rowlandson 2017).

It has been postulated that the Fosse Way originally crossed the River Witham south of the present Brace Bridge. A watching brief was carried out in 2003 during work on land between Newark Road and Beech Street, close to the modern river crossing of Brace Bridge (Bradley-Lovekin 2004; 2010). Pottery was recovered dating to the early Roman period (AD 40–125) including some Iron Age tradition wares; the forms were of types recovered from legionary deposits in the City suggesting a military connection. The Hykeham Road site (Fig. 1) is located near to pottery kilns working in the 2nd century AD at North Hykeham (Fig. 2; Swan 1984; Thompson 1958) and a late Roman kiln at Rookery Lane, approximately 700 m north-west of the site (Webster 1960). The site is also close to the late Roman Swanpool industry (Webster and Booth 1947; Darling 1977; Darling and Precious 2014).

2. Project background

The site is situated within the Lincoln suburb of Bracebridge, 4.5 km south-west of the centre of Lincoln. It lay immediately to the west of the River Witham, centred on SK 9640 6794. Land to the south was occupied by allotment gardens; the north was bounded by commercial buildings, and housing/gardens were located to the west. The scheme was undertaken as part of a planning application for housing. Eight evaluation trenches were investigated in May 2008 (Fig. 3; Williams 2008), which revealed evidence of Roman industrial use comprising a large area of black occupation deposits, a series of short drainage ditches and a pottery kiln. There was a concentration of features towards the north of the site

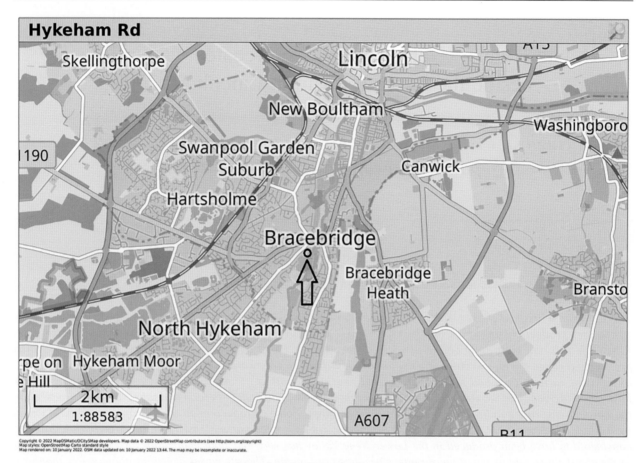

Figure 1. Map of south of Lincoln showing site location.

and artefacts were in a good state of preservation. The earliest feature was a possibly 2nd century AD boundary or drainage ditch seen in Ditch 8, at the northernmost extent of the site, the remaining dated features were all from the late Roman period. The evaluation confirmed that extensive well-preserved archaeological remains survived, including a previously unknown 'Swanpool' type pottery production site complete with a large assemblage of 3rd to 4th century AD grey ware pottery including complete and freshly broken vessels, along with an unusually large 'Nene Valley Colour Coated' assemblage.

A restricted scheme of works by PCA Lincoln (now PCAS Ltd) was approved by the city archaeologist, which investigated a limited portion of the site. The main access road strip and house plots were recorded under watching brief conditions and a full description of this part of the work is presented in the client report (Fig. 3; Fiske and Rowlandson 2021). It was clear that some significant archaeology including kilns had been uncovered during the course of the main excavation, particularly in Areas A–C. The pottery work was commissioned in late 2013 and recording was completed by December 2013 with draft illustrations completed at the same time. Due to unforeseen circumstances work was stopped on the pottery report and all other sections of the site report by early 2014. The importance of the site had however been recognised and when it became clear that the project site

report would not proceed to completion it was requested that the authors might use the excavation archive to complete a partial report to enable dissemination of the results of the pottery work. A basic developer funded report was put together using the archive and the ceramic reports that were available (Fiske and Rowlandson 2021), which will be made available online via the Archaeology Data Service. The description of the site presented here is a *precis* of the information contained in the developer funded report designed to support the pottery contribution. No detailed scientific fabric analysis was undertaken due to the lack of funding although the material has been deposited at The Collection, Lincoln.

3. The site

3.1. Geology and topography

The underlying geology of the locale is mapped as Charmouth Mudstone Formation of the Lower Lias, consisting of clay, shales and sands (BGS Map viewer; BGS 1973, sheet 114). Alluvium from the River Witham was observed across part of the site. It is likely that iron-rich potting clays for the manufacture of orange and grey wares could be easily procured in close proximity to the site. Outcrops of light-firing iron poor clays amongst the Jurassic deposits found to the east of the modern River Witham channel would have provided raw materials for production of the white bodied colour-coated wares (see Rowlandson *et al.* 2022; Sumbler pers. comm.).

3.2. Site phases and their associated pottery

All features from excavation Areas A–C were sealed by a grey layer of sandy soil beneath the topsoil that included occupation deposits and kiln rake out material including significant quantities of Roman pottery sherds. Alluvial deposits within a paleochannel of the River Witham were recorded from the eastern edge of excavation area A.

Phase 1: early to mid-Roman activity

A range of early Roman pottery on the site was recognised within a number of the areas. A proportion of the early Roman period was stratified in Phase 1 features whilst other material was stratified with later pottery. Group **A1** from Area A included gullies, pits and ditches at the north end of the site (Fig. 4). The majority of the pottery dated to the mid-1st to perhaps earlier 2nd century AD including fresh sherds from a Dressel 20 amphora, a sherd from a Lincoln Legionary grey ware dish (No. **109**), a Lincoln hook-rimmed mortarium (No. **1**), a native tradition sand-gritted transitional ware vessel (No. **106**), a native tradition jar with a wedge-shaped rim (No. **104**) and a large necked storage jar.

From Area B a small number ditches (**118**, **124** and **130**), beam slot **134** and gully **106** had evidence for early Roman activity (Fig. 5). Significant vessels included a Hofheim type flagon (No. **54**) and the pedestal base from a beaker in a fine Parisian type fabric (No. **10**). Ditch group **B7** (**108** and **114**) also contained an early assemblage including a flat bottomed Gauloise amphora, a handle from a Dressel 2–4 amphora, a samian cup form Drag. 24/25, a Lincolnshire mortarium, a jar in legionary type fabric with thick applied vertical strips, and sherds from a native tradition cooking pot. Also present was a large proportion of a jar with an out-curved rim in Black Burnished ware 1 fabric which made up almost half of the total sherd count. Grey wares included a sherd from a carinated bowl with roller-stamped decoration (No. **88**) and a rim sherd from a butt beaker (No. **58**). The majority of the pottery was dated late 2nd to 3rd century AD but some 1st and also 4th century fabrics and forms were also present. The triple vase type vessel found within Area B phase 3 deposits may also be of early to mid-Roman date (No. **57**).

Phase 1 activity in Area C was restricted to a sequence of overlapping north–south aligned ditches (Fig. 6; Groups **C1–3**) that included a range of pottery dating to the later 1st to 2nd century AD. Ditch Group **C2** included a closed vessel in the local white ware fabric, Dressel 20 amphora sherds, a large proportion of a 'Roxby A' type lid seated jar with stab decoration on the shoulder (No. **60**, probably not produced here but perhaps locally, e.g. Thompson 1958), and native tradition ware including grog-gritted sherds and fragments from a single native tradition sand-gritted jar with a bead rim (No. **105**). Group 3 included a single sherd from a grey ware necked jar

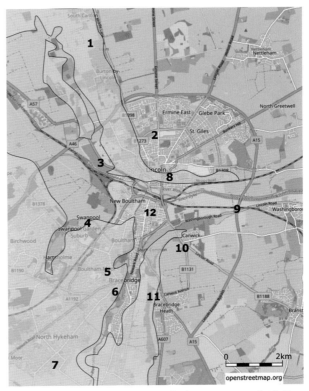

Figure 2. Key Lincoln kiln sites with clay sources overlaid. Key: 1: South Carlton – White ware (Webster 1944); 2: Newport suburb – White ware, light-fired colour-coated wares, fabric as South Carlton products (Rowlandson et al. *2022); 3: Lincoln Racecourse – Grey ware (Corder 1950); 4: Swanpool – Mixed, including white ware (Webster and Booth 1947); 5: Rookery Lane – Grey ware (Webster 1960); 6: Hykeham Road – Light-fired colour-coated wares, grey ware; 7: North Hykeham – Grey ware (Thompson 1958); 8: Lincoln Technical College – White wares, in a coarser, more granular white fabric than South Carlton (Baker 1937a; 1937b); 9: Washingborough Road (Lincoln Eastern Bypass) – Grey ware (Rowlandson and Fiske 2021); 10: Bomber Command Museum – Grey ware (Allen Archaeology, unpublished); 11: Bracebridge Heath – Grey ware (Donel 1992; Darling 2006); 12: Monson St – White ware flagons, colour-coated wares and Black Burnished ware 1 copies (Rowlandson 2010; Allen* et al. *2010).*

or bowl (No. **86**) which was dated mid- to late 1st century AD to 2nd century.

Further early Roman pottery was retrieved from Area D/Trench 9 including transitional wares, a Hofheim type flagon and a Gauloise amphora. The most intriguing find from the archaeological monitoring phase was a group of three small almost identical globular flagons (Nos. **51–3**, Fig. 23a) and a small cup (No. **50**) from the Trench 10 extension, these did not appear to the excavators to have been associated with a feature and may have been a structured deposit perhaps associated with a burial situated beside the Fosse Way. In general, however, the waterlogged ground conditions and the adopted methodology meant that much of the site outside of the main excavations (Fig. 3; Areas A–D, Trench 10 extension) was not recorded in detail.

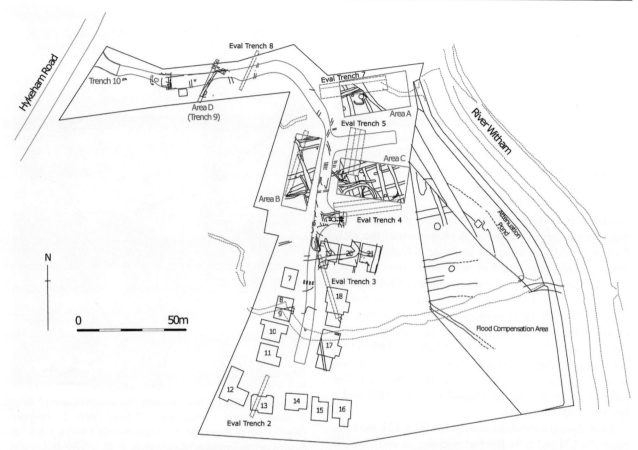

Figure 3. Overall Site Plan including evaluation trenches and identified features.

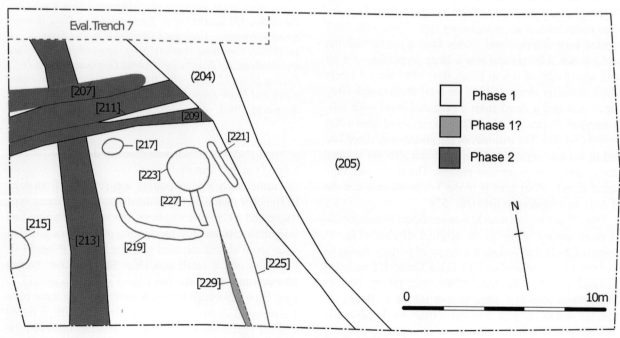

Figure 4. Area A detailed plan.

It would appear from the range of early Roman pottery found from across the site that there was occupation on the site prior to the commencement of pottery production in the late Roman period. If the Brace Bridge crossing was established in the early Roman period, the site would have been a significant nodal point and contemporary activity was recognised to the north-west of the site across the river (Bradley-Lovekin 2004; 2010). The watching brief undertaken along Hykeham Road along with the evidence from Area D/Trench 9 it was evident that there was a focus of early to mid-Roman activity in the area investigated to the south-east of Hykeham Road. The limited archaeological recording undertaken produced interesting finds, but the keyhole nature of the interventions prevented a more detailed understanding of the nature of Roman activity. It is possible that the construction of the housing along Hykeham Road in the 20th century may have largely destroyed buildings facing the road similar to those recorded on the site between Newark Road and Beech Street (Bradley-Lovekin 2004; 2010) but this was largely untested due to the scope of the excavations.

Phase 2: field system features

Much of the excavated area appears to have been covered by a 'lattice' of criss-crossing east–west and north–south aligned ditches, it seems likely that the former were for drainage as they were oriented towards the river. The features contained a range of pottery dating from the later 2nd to 4th century AD. It is possible that these features were in part established in the 2nd century AD as the excavations in Area C appeared to show repeated phases of ditch digging along the same axes probably beginning in the second century AD (e.g., Phase 1 ditch groups **C1** and **C2**). The stratigraphically earlier features only contained limited quantities of domestic pottery. The later ditch system features included a proportion of pottery production waste suggesting that some of these features must have remained at least partially open after the commencement of pottery production on the site. The full site report (Fiske and Rowlandson 2021) presents a more detailed discussion of these features and the account offered here is intended to support the discussion of the pottery and present the evidence for the kilns. It appears likely that the site on the riverbank was used for cultivation, pasture or other functions possibly to the rear of roadside settlements prior to the commencement of pottery production on the site.

Phase 3: Features with significant dumps of pottery waste

Curving gullies were recorded from Areas B and C that appear likely to have been contemporary with pottery production on the site. It is possible that these ditches helped to drain the area around the kilns or may have also served

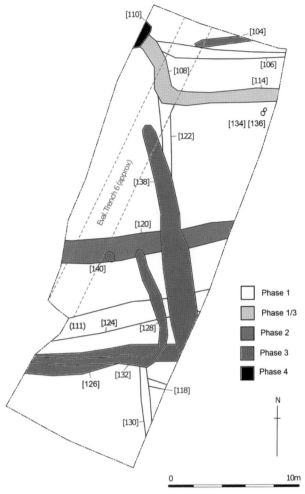

Figure 5. Area B detailed plan.

a clay preparation function (Peacock 1982, 52–5). It was noticeable that a considerable proportion of the pottery waste was backfilled into these features. The main groups are described in detail below.

Group **B11** comprised a single ditch **125** aligned east–west (Fig. 5). Sixty-four sherds were retrieved including grey ware flanged bowls and jars, one jar having an everted rim (No. **65**); colour-coated flanged bowls (e.g. No. **28**), plain-rimmed bowls (e.g. No. **34**), a flagon or jug neck (No. **14**) and a beaker; over-fired grey ware, a light-fired Nene Valley type mortarium with slag trituration grits, a horizontal reeded rim and dunting cracks caused by uneven or too rapid cooling in the kiln. The group was dated to the 4th century AD.

Group **B12** comprises two late ditches, **128/132** and **138**, both were cut through a series of earlier features towards the southern end of Area B (Fig. 5). Ditch deposit **128** also contained abundant Roman pottery including misfired vessels presumably due to its close proximity (c. 2 m at closest point) to Kiln **142**. Ditch **138** on the other hand appears more likely to be akin to Ditch **213** from Area A,

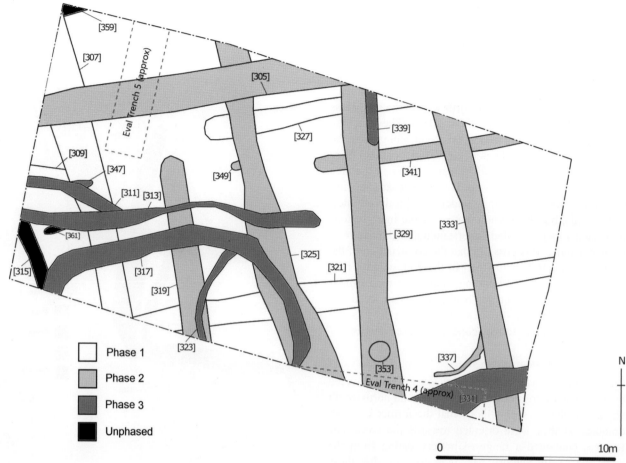

Figure 6. Area C detailed plan.

which was on a similar broadly north–south alignment. Ditch **138** also contained abundant Roman pottery though at least some of the earlier material may have been residual. Seventy-eight sherds were recovered from Group **B12**, they included a heavily abraded decorated samian fragment, cream ware, a fragment from a Dressel 20 amphora, grey ware including a jar with a frilled collar, another with an everted rim, a single narrow necked jar with rouletted and burnished decoration and a wide mouth bowl. Many of the grey ware sherds showed signs of dunting cracking; one jar with a string cut base was high fired with a spalled surface. Native tradition ware sherds were also present. The assemblage as a whole was dated 3rd to late 4th century AD, along with the native tradition ware of the 2nd century AD.

Group **C7** consisted of late Roman ditches: **311**, **313**, **317**, **323**, **339** and **347**, which were narrow and mean-dering or curvilinear and thus quite unlike the earlier, relatively straight grid-like pattern into which they cut (Fig. 6). These features contained pottery production waste and represent a change from ditches performing a boundary and drainage function to features contemporary with pottery production. Pottery from the group comprised a large group of 689 sherds, mostly grey ware of which a proportion were misfired or over-fired, it included frag-ments from a disc-necked flagon, Dales ware type jars, a jar with a cavetto rim, wide mouthed bowls, a bowl with

an in-turned bead and flange and a bowl with a high bead and flange. Colour-coated forms present included a beaker with almond shaped rim, a Castor box and lid, bowls with bead and flange rims and plain rims. Also present were a burnt base possibly from a local mortarium, oxidised ware and shell-gritted ware. The date range was 3rd century to very late 4th century AD.

Group **C8** comprised the wide curvilinear Ditch **331** (Fig. 6). It is the most noteworthy feature in Area C due to the large quantities of pottery wasters, near complete spalled vessels and kiln furniture that were recovered from it. These included a large proportion of colour-coated wasters whose presence clearly demonstrates that vessels in this fabric were being produced here. The material found may have come from Kiln **414** discovered during the evaluation phase adjacent to Trench 4, but as this was approximately 30 m away it seems more likely that the source was another unidentified kiln closer by (Fig. 13). The pottery comprised a large fresh group of 210 grey ware and colour-coated sherds, most heavily misfired, including a single nearly complete colour-coated bead and flange bowl which had suffered a catastrophic spalling blowing away the whole of the base and cracking the vessel down the wall and rim (No. **30**, also Fig. 20c), fragments from a Castor box and lid (No. **45**), bowls with bead and flange rims, two nearly complete colour-coated

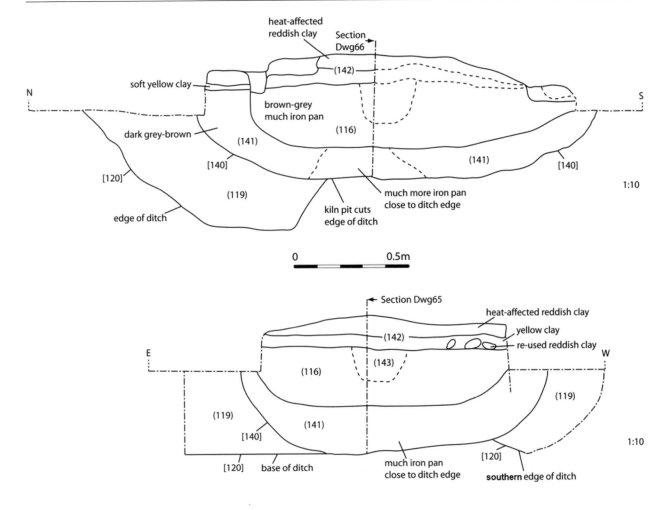

Figure 7. Sections of Kiln 142, Pit 140 and Ditch 120.

beakers, one squat with long neck and almond rim (No. **15**), the other with rouletted decoration and pentice moulding (No. **17**), a closed vessel and a large flagon or jar. Grey ware forms present included a jar with an everted rim (No. **64**), a bowl with in-turned bead and flange rim (No. **97**), wide mouthed bowls (No. **82**) and a large bowl with an everted rim. The assemblage is dated 4th and very late 4th century AD.

Phase 3: The pottery kilns

Phase 3 Group **B9** comprised an *in-situ* Roman kiln structure **142** contained within Pit **140**, which itself was cut into Ditch **120** of Group B6 (Figs 5 and 7–10). Kiln **142** comprised an ovoid pit **140**, which contained the kiln remains **142**, cut into existing Ditch **120** from Group B6 (pottery from which was dated late 2nd century AD or after), which dates the construction of the kiln. The upper central fill **143** was a small cup-shaped deposit possibly indicating the position of the flue. On top of the pit fills was the clay kiln base **142**, comprising light reddish-yellow clay with occasional fragments of re-used heat affected clay and small stones, it was 1.6 m × 1.2 m × <0.15 m thick. The reason that the structure is standing

proud of the ground surface in the photographs is because the surrounding material has been over-cut during excavation. Forty-three sherds that were dated to the 3rd to 4th century AD were recovered from Group B9. They included colour-coated bowls and a plain rim dish, coarse grey ware Dales ware type jars (Nos. 100, 101); other grey wares including abraded bowls, and an unusual white ware triple or quadruple vase base (No. **57**; Fig. 23b).

Kiln **414** was identified and half-sectioned, possibly inadvertently, by Evaluation Trench 4 (the Evaluation report states that only part of the kiln was recovered and recorded). It was comprised of a fired clay floor **416**, wall structure **413** with a red-orange fired clay lining, a fired clay kiln bar **415** within oval construction cut **414** which was 1.5m in diameter (Figs 11–13). Pottery sherds dated 4th century AD were recovered. Unfortunately, the kiln did not survive to be fully recorded during the main excavation.

3.3. Discussion of the pottery kilns

Both identified kilns are typical of the Swanpool, or evolved Linwood type, which Swan (1984, 123–4) states probably came into use in the first half of the

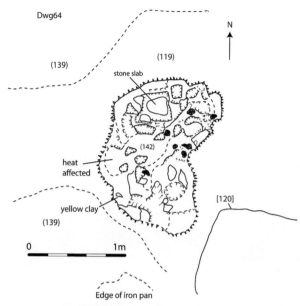

Figure 8. Kiln 142 setting in Ditch 120.

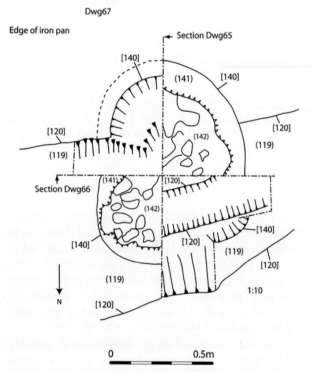

Figure 9. Quartered plan of Kiln 142, Pit 140 and Ditch 120.

4th century AD and continued until the end of the Roman period at Swanpool itself (Webster and Booth 1947). Swanpool type kilns are typified by having two integral 'D' shaped pedestals occupying most of the firing chamber, and most unusually were constructed by first digging a large oval pit (or in the case of Kiln 142 apparently making use of a pre-existing ditch), dumping raw clay into it then sculpting the kiln *in situ*. It was noticeable that the surviving clay superstructure of both kilns appeared fairly well oxidised, with Kiln **142** showing a

yellow/light-fired colour and Kiln **414** an orange iron-rich oxidised colour. The almost complete lack of reduction of the clay superstructure would support the theory that these kilns, at least for their last few firings, had been used to fire oxidised wares, most probably the colour-coated fabric found on the site. Although a fired clay report was not available at the time of the production of this report it was noteworthy that Young (in Williams 2008, 35) wrote of the HYRL08 evaluation trenching:

> All of the Roman tile, fired clay and kiln furniture appears to have utilised the same, probably local, clay source. The fabric contains fine to medium-sized round to subround quartz (0.2–0.6mm), common iron-rich grains, clay pellets (cream and red), and occasional small pebbles in an often marbled (cream and orange) fine clay. The presence of light firing streaks in the clay indicates that the clay was not well mixed and may suggest that light firing clay is available in the locality.

The firing chamber of Swanpool-type kilns was typically above ground and thus very few have survived intact. Other kilns of Swanpool type, however, have been excavated in and around Lincoln, including at Rookery Lane very close to this site (Webster 1960); at Swanpool itself (Webster and Booth 1947); in the Trent Valley at Knaith (Swan 1984, 123–4), further afield at Holme-on-Spalding-Moor (Corder 1930) and it is very likely that more will be discovered in future. The products of these kilns were mostly grey wares although the Swanpool industry also produced oxidised wares such as mortaria and colour-coated wares using the same kilns, as happened here. For example, Kiln 107003 at Swanpool (excavated in 2014) was of typical Swanpool form with double-D pedestals from which approximately 3,000 mixed misfired sherds of grey ware, white ware, late Roman spiral-grooved ware (SPIR) and similarly late coarse quartz-gritted grey ware (LCOA) were recovered, the latest diagnostic sherds being dated to the late 4th to early 5th century AD (site code SWA14, Rowlandson and Fiske 2018).

The Rookery Lane kiln site on the other hand produced only grey wares:

> The kiln at Rookery Lane produced a very restricted range of forms in only one fabric, in contrast with the known Swanpool repertoire, which included a great variety of vessels in several different fabrics, ranging from iron-free clay fired with a colour-coating to coarse gritty and vesicular wares. Webster suggested that the Rookery Lane kiln was earlier than Swanpool, and there is no reason to doubt him. (Darling 1977, 33)

If the Rookery Lane kilns did indeed pre-date the Swanpool industry then it seems entirely likely that our site at Hykeham Road did so too. Also, the potters who produced

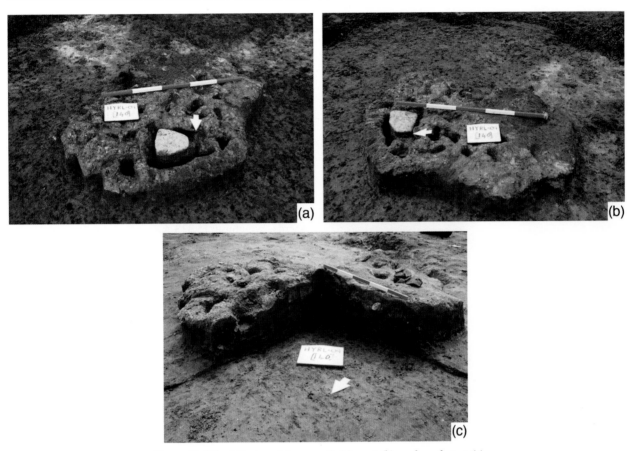

Figure 10. Kiln 142 viewed from south (a), east (b), and south-east (c).

the colour-coated wares here may have migrated to continue production at Swanpool, perhaps once the light firing clay on this comparatively small production site started to become more difficult to obtain, and/or following repeated flooding of the site.

4. The pottery

4.1. Samian ware (Gwladys Monteil)

A total of six sherds of samian ware were recovered from excavations at Hykeham Road, Lincoln and submitted for this report. The fabric of each sherd was examined, after taking a small fresh break, under a x20 binocular microscope and was catalogued by context number. Each archive entry consists of a context number, fabric, form and decoration identification, condition, sherd count, rim EVEs (Estimated Vessel Equivalents), rim diameter, weight, notes and a date range. The presence of wear, repair and graffiti was also systematically recorded. Rubbings of the decorated fragments were undertaken during analysis. They were mounted, scanned and submitted as illustrations. A catalogue of the decorated ware and the stamp (Fig. 14; Cat. nos. 1–2) was compiled and is provided at the end of this report.

The assemblage is small with six sherds representing a maximum of five vessels for a total weight of 79 g and a rim EVE figure of 0.53. The material is relatively fresh particularly in context (102) with large fragments and no abrasion on the slip.

With the exception of an abraded decorated fragment from context (127) which is Central Gaulish and late 2nd century AD (see Cat. No. 2), this group is South Gaulish and probably pre-Flavian: a Dr.15/17 and a Dr.30 (see Cat. No. 10) in context 102, the rim of cup form Dr.24/25 in context (107) and a flake in context (332).

Decorated samian catalogue

The following catalogue lists and identifies the decorated pieces recovered from the site that could be attributed to individual potters or groups of potters. The catalogue is organised in context order; each entry gives a catalogue number, the excavation context number with details of the decoration.

The letter and number codes used for the non-figured types on the Central Gaulish material – such as B223, C281, etc. are the ones created by Rogers (1974). The figured types referred to as Os. *** are the ones illustrated by Felix Oswald in his *Index of figure-types on terra sigillata* (1936–7).

The Inventory Numbers (Inv. No.) quoted are taken from *European intake of Roman Samian ceramics* (http://www1.rgzm.de/samian/home/frames.htm).

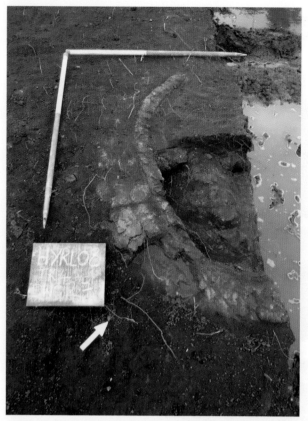

Figure 11. Kiln 414 showing construction cut, fired clay lining, internal kiln bar and backfill. Looking north-west.

1. (102), two non-joining rim sherds, Dr.30, La Graufesenque. Both fragments are large and fresh and show a panelled decoration alternating a large simple medallion with poppy-heads, swirls and leaf inside and a saltire. The ovolo is close to the one on Dr.30s from Colchester illustrated in Dannell 1999 (nos. 391 to 393) as the ovolo used by Martialis and Masclinus. The long leaf with serrated edge in the saltire is close to the one found on a Dr.30 with a Masclus signature (Inv. No. 0005011); the larger leaf also with serrated edge in the medallion is close to the one on a Dr.30 with a Masclinus signature (Inv. No. 1001757). AD 50–75.
2. (127), one body sherd, Dr.37, Lezoux. Abraded. A little decoration remains, possibly the leg and staff of Os.12 near a vertical beaded border and partial medallion. Late Antonine potter Banuus used all these motifs (Inv. No. 0010376). AD 160–200.

4.2. The other Roman pottery

4.2.1. Methodology

The pottery has been archived using count and weight as measures according to the guidelines laid down for the minimum archive by the Study Group for Roman Pottery by Darling (2004), the most up-to-date guideline at the time of recording, and using the codes developed by the City of Lincoln Archaeological Unit (CLAU, see

Darling and Precious 2014, 6, appendices I and II). Rim equivalents (RE) have been recorded and an attempt at a 'maximum' vessel estimate has been made following Pollard (1990). Following the Lincolnshire Archaeological Handbook (Jennings 2019) and current museum deposition practices the pottery has been sub-bagged within each context by fabric (Table 1). Samian, mortaria and amphorae have all been bagged separately. The pottery suitable for illustration has been bagged separately with a 'D' number for ease of further study.

4.2.2. The assemblage

The pottery assemblage as recorded consisted of 2,499 sherds, weighing 75.313 kg, with a total of 49.21 rim equivalents (RE). A maximum of 1,819 vessels were recorded but due to the similarity of many of the vessels made on the site it is quite likely that this is an over estimation. The assemblage as a whole was very fresh with an average sherd weight of 30.13g. Some degree of abrasion or excoriation was evident on 618 sherds (18.075 kg, average weight 29 g), while 582 sherds (22.175 kg, average weight 38 g) were burnt and/or misfired. Many of the colour-coated vessels appeared to have lost much of their surfaces but this may be due to a proportion being poorly fired and the sandy soil conditions on site. It was noticeable that there were many complete or nearly complete vessels.

4.2.3. Firing faults

As is to be expected on a kiln site, dumps containing considerable numbers of misfired, over-fired, warped, dunted and spalled vessels were uncovered, containing mainly grey and colour-coated wares, leaving no doubt that both fabrics were produced here in quantity. Further information is included in the Fine ware and Reduced ware sections below.

4.2.4. Evidence for the use and re-use of vessels

There was only limited evidence for how vessels were used and re-used on site. No evidence of sooting or cooking residue was noted on any vessels from the assemblage. Internal use wear was noted on two mortaria and a large grey ware bowl, and internal attrition on a native tradition storage jar. Five grey ware and one native tradition base were trimmed down to make discs, possibly for re-use as lids, with diameters of 10 cm or just below. Two further grey ware bases had holes pierced through them post firing, presumably to make strainers, and a disc-necked flagon neck was trimmed down possibly to make a spindle whorl.

4.2.5. Amphorae

Thirty-one amphora sherds were recovered (2.748 kg, 0 RE) from a mixture of Spanish and Gaulish vessels. Dressel 20 olive oil transporting types (DR20) were the most numerous of the Spanish examples, with 11 sherds from a maximum of 8 vessels (2.214 kg, 0 RE), and

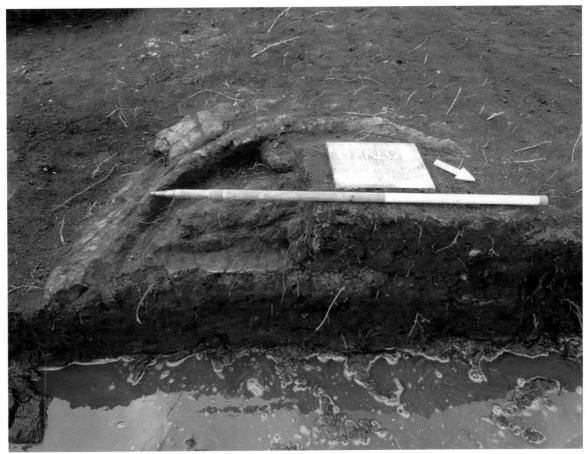

Figure 12. Kiln 414 looking south-west.

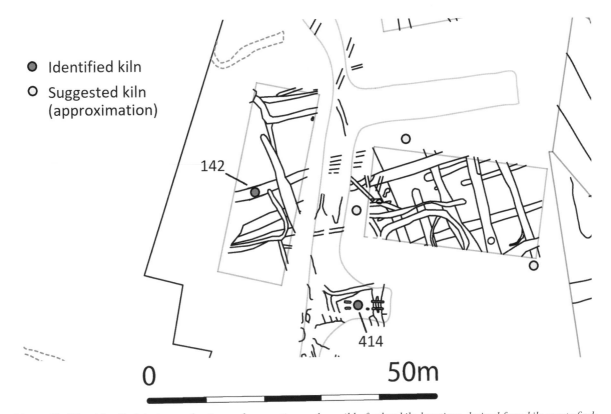

Figure 13. Kilns identified during evaluation and excavation and possible further kiln locations derived from kiln waste finds.

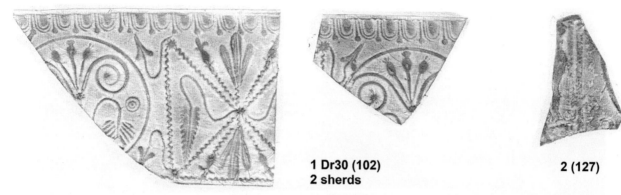

1 Dr30 (102)   **2 (127)**
2 sherds

Figure 14. Decorated samian sherds.

a further handle sherd (116 g) from a Catalan Dressel type 2–4, which most likely held wine. Gaulish wine vessels (GAU, undifferentiated) added 17 sherds (0.389 kg) from a maximum of 4 vessels to the total. Find spots were not focused in any particular part of the site, sherds being found in areas A, B and C, Plot 18 and the Road Strip, mostly from Phases 1 and 2. The range and number of amphora sherds present was far higher than one might expect from a typical rural site or rural pottery production site so it appears likely that the proximity to some form of roadside settlement, probably close to the posited bridging point of Fosse Way across the River Witham immediately to the north of our site, could explain the high proportion of amphora amongst this assemblage.

4.2.6. Mortaria (Figs 15–17)

There were few mortaria from the site; one of these could be considered as typical of the local 1st to 2nd century AD Lincoln or South Carlton products (MOLIN, equates to Darling and Precious 2014, MOLO). A further vessel may have been a Mancetter-Hartshill product of the 2nd century AD (MORT). The majority of the mortaria from the site were of Swanpool type, known to have been produced locally, and Nene Valley type with light-fired fabrics and slag triturationgrits. The origin of these vessels is discussed further below.

FABRICS

> **MOLIN: No. 1, Fig. 15a** Mortaria broadly of Lincoln origin, undifferentiated. Two sherds were recovered from two different hook-rimmed mortaria, one of which was from a Phase 1 deposit in Area A spot-dated late 1st to early 2nd century AD.
>
> **MORT: No. 2, Fig. 16a** Undifferentiated mortarium fabric. No. **2** has a form similar to Gillam 1970 Type 242 (1970), it shows similarities in form to the work of the Mancetter-Hartshill potter *G. Attius Marinus*, probably AD 100–130.
>
> **MONVT: Nos. 3–7, Fig. 16c** Nene Valley type mortaria, with light-fired fabric and slag trituration grits (as Darling and Precious 2014, MONV, 190–204). Sherds from a maximum of 12 vessels were recovered from across the site with four (including Nos. **5**

and **7**) coming from Area C, Group C8, Ditch **331**, which accounted for a large proportion (557 sherds, 21.334 kg) of the total pottery found from across the site, much of which was misfired. Another four sherds came from Area B, Layer 102. Both these deposits were Phase 3. Un-phased contexts that yielded MONVT bead and flange rimmed sherds included House Plots 19 and 21 (Nos. **3** and **4**).

With the production of white bodied Nene Valley colour-coated type wares demonstrated on this site the production of slag-gritted white bodied mortaria in the same style as those manufactured in the Nene Valley would appear entirely possible. Further scientific fabric analysis would need to be conducted on the mortaria from this site to establish whether a few 'Nene Valley type' mortaria were produced here alongside the colour-coated wares. At present this assertion would not be outlandish as material for trituration grits could have easily been procured from metalworkers in the area in the same way as the potters making mortaria at Swanpool. Two sherds in this fabric showed signs of dunting cracking: No. **3** from House Plot 19, and No. **6** from Area B, Group B11, Ditch **125**, which showed signs of both attrition and dunting.

> **MOSP: Nos. 8–9, Figs 15b and 16b** Swanpool mortaria (as Darling and Precious 2014, 172). Six sherds from a maximum of three vessels were recovered; two were bead and flange rimmed, including No. **8**. Most were from un-phased areas but were spot dated either late 3rd to 4th century or 4th century AD.

ILLUSTRATED MORTARIA CATALOGUE (FIG. 17)

> **1. MOLIN:** Hooked rim mortarium, abraded: *Area A, Group A1, Phase 1, Ditch 225, Fill 224, D24*
>
> **2. MOLIN:** Hooked rim mortarium: *Road Strip, Layer 1099, D98*
>
> **3. MONVT:** Bead and flange rim mortarium with dunting cracks: *Plot 19, Feature 1915, Fill 1911, D81*
>
> **4. MONVT:** Bead and flange rim mortarium: *Plot 21, Linear 2107, Fill 2108, D12*
>
> **5. MONVT:** Hammerhead rim mortarium: *Area C, Group C2, Phase 3, Ditch 331, Fill 330, D58*

Table 1. Overall fabric summary.

Fabric code	Fabric group	Fabric details	Sherd	Sherd count %	Weight (g)	Weight %	Total RE %
SAM	Samian	Undifferentiated	3	0.10%	10	0.01%	0
SAMSG	Samian	South Gaulish	5	0.17%	73	0.08%	47
AMPH	Amphora	Miscellaneous amphorae	1	0.03%	20	0.02%	0
AMPH?	Amphora	Miscellaneous amphorae	1	0.03%	9	0.01%	0
CAT24	Amphora	Catalan DR 2–4	1	0.03%	116	0.12%	0
DR20	Amphora	DR 20 amphorae	10	0.34%	2158	2.29%	0
DR20?	Amphora	DR 20 amphorae	1	0.03%	56	0.06%	0
GAU	Amphora	Undifferentiated Gaulish amphorae	17	0.57%	389	0.41%	0
MOLIN	Mortaria	Lincoln mortaria	2	0.07%	489	0.52%	217
MONVT	Mortarium	Nene Valley type – light fabric, slag trits	15	0.50%	1474	1.56%	66
MORT	Mortaria	Mortaria; undifferentiated	1	0.03%	20	0.02%	0
MORT?	Mortaria	Mortaria; undifferentiated	1	0.03%	25	0.03%	0
MOSP	Mortaria	Swanpool mortaria	6	0.20%	274	0.29%	37
GFIN	Fine	Miscellaneous fine grey wares	3	0.10%	35	0.04%	0
LCC1	Fine	Lincoln Nene Valley type colour coat – light firing	560	18.83%	22665	24.01%	2800
LCC1?	Fine	Lincoln Nene Valley type colour coat – light firing	4	0.13%	27	0.03%	0
LCC2	Fine	Lincoln Nene Valley type colour coat – fabric oxidised red	1	0.03%	105	0.11%	0
SCCC?	Fine	South Carlton colour-coated	1	0.03%	78	0.08%	100
CR	Oxidised	Roman cream wares (various)	55	1.85%	1825	1.93%	105
CR?	Oxidised	Roman cream wares	6	0.20%	292	0.31%	52
CR2	Oxidised	Cream ware: Site fabric 2	3	0.10%	875	0.93%	300
OX	Oxidised	Misc. oxidised wares	24	0.81%	371	0.39%	12
OX?	Oxidised	Misc. oxidised wares	9	0.30%	161	0.17%	0
SPOX	Oxidised	Swanpool oxidised wares	3	0.10%	24	0.03%	17
BB1	Reduced	Black burnished 1, unspecified	73	2.45%	587	0.62%	34
GREY	Reduced	Miscellaneous grey wares	2028	68.19%	58027	61.47%	3180
GREY?	Reduced	Miscellaneous grey wares	4	0.13%	150	0.16%	0
GREYC	Reduced	Coarse grey ware	12	0.40%	434	0.46%	54
GREYC?	Reduced	Coarse grey ware	6	0.20%	442	0.47%	29
GREYS	Reduced	Misc grey ware fabrics with rare shell	2	0.07%	94	0.10%	6
IAGR	Reduced	Native tradition/transitional gritty wares	26	0.87%	1237	1.31%	28
IASA	Reduced	IA type sandy wares	25	0.84%	436	0.46%	62
LCOA	Reduced	Late coarse pebbly fabric; double lid-seated jars	3	0.10%	110	0.12%	15
LCOA?	Reduced	Late coarse Lincoln fabric?	2	0.07%	67	0.07%	16
LEG	Reduced	Lincoln 'Legionary' type cream/ light grey	4	0.13%	138	0.15%	21
LEG?	Reduced	Lincoln 'Legionary' type cream/ light grey	1	0.03%	7	0.01%	5
DWSHT	Calcareous	Dales ware type	13	0.44%	152	0.16%	27
IASH	Calcareous	Native tradition shell-tempered	2	0.07%	168	0.18%	14
SHEL	Calcareous	Miscellaneous undifferentiated shell-tempered	40	1.34%	784	0.83%	47

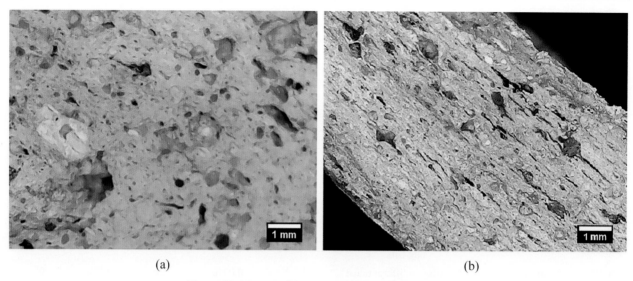

(a) (b)

Figure 15. Mortaria fabrics (a) MOLIN and (b) MOSP.

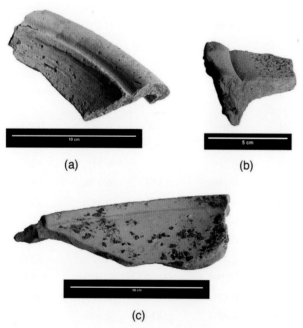

(a) (b)

(c)

Figure 16. Mortaria fabrics (a) MORT, (b) MOSP and (c) MONVT.

6. **MONVT:** Reeded rim mortarium with dunting cracks, abraded: *Area B, Group B11, Phase 3, Ditch 126, Fill 125, D10*
7. **MONVT:** Reeded rim mortarium: *Area C, Group C8, Phase 3, Ditch 331, Fill 330, D59*
8. **MOSP:** Bead and flange rim mortarium, burnt: *Area C, Group C8, Phase 3, Ditch 331, Fill 330, D57*
9. **MOSP:** Hammerhead rim mortarium: *Plot 19, Linear 1913, Fill 1909, D6*

4.2.7. Fine wares (Figs 18–24)

The majority of the fine wares other than samian found on site appear to have been produced here or perhaps

within the wider Lincolnshire area. All the colour-coated wares present may have been produced in the area of Lincoln itself (see discussion below). The fine grey ware from the site was also most probably a Lincoln or wider Lincolnshire product.

Fabrics

Following the example of the Lincoln Newport report (Rowlandson *et al.* 2022) the fabrics have been split into LCC1 (light firing cream fabric with colour coat) and LCC2 (fine red/orange fabric with dark colour coat) although only a single sherd of the latter was recovered from a form B38 bowl. The LCC1 fabric appears similar to the description of the South Carlton fabric (Figs 18–20; cf. Tomber and Dore 1998, SOC CC and LNV CC) but with a greater number of vessels evident with a dull brown or grey blue colour-coat similar to contemporary vessels from the Nene Valley. Although mica can be present amongst the Lincoln/South Carlton wares it is not ubiquitous, and it is the opinion of the authors that the products of the two regions cannot be reliably split or perhaps only with recourse to scientific analysis. Indeed, the authors believe that the distribution of the more noticeably different Lincoln/South Carlton beakers of the 2nd century AD have also often passed unrecognised and have been attributed to other industries (Rowlandson *et al.* 2022, 231–2).

GFIN: No. 10 Miscellaneous fine grey wares (as Darling and Precious 2014, 27–8). Three sherds were recovered including a pedestal base (No. **10**) in PART 'Parisian' type fabric similar to that made at Market Rasen though a more local production source would also be possible.

LCC1: Nos. 11–49 Lincoln colour-coated wares. As already observed (Rowlandson *et al.* 2022) the kiln site at Newport, Lincoln and others in the vicinity were producing colour-coated wares in

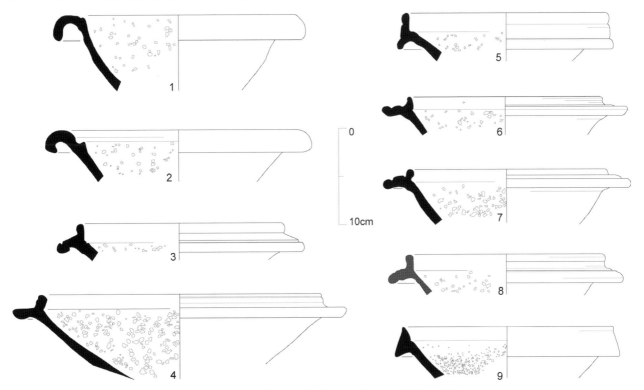

Figure 17. Hykeham Road illustrated mortaria, Nos. 1–9.

the mid-2nd to 4th century AD. As suggested in the Lincoln Roman pottery corpus (Darling and Precious 2014, 20), many local colour-coated products have not been recognised in the past and were believed instead to have come from the substantial Lower Nene Valley pottery industry in the vicinity of modern Peterborough. This is discussed further below. The majority of the assemblage came from Phase 3 features.

A total of 103 sherds in the LCC1 fabric were recorded with serious firing faults (Table 2). These were mostly found in Area C Ditches 331 and 354, which were clearly kiln waste dumps, a handful of others came from Occupation Layer 102 and Ditch 126 in Area B.

SCCC?: No. 50 South Carlton colour-coated wares (as Darling and Precious 2014, 22; Tomber and Dore 1998, code SOC CC), which are considered to be Antonine in date. A small complete cornice-rimmed beaker was found in a structured deposition outside the pottery production area with three locally made cream ware flagons, which were also dated to the mid- to late 2nd century AD.

FORMS

Table 3 shows the Lincoln colour-coated forms (LCC1) within the assemblage; this is sorted by total Rim Equivalents (RE) as an indication of which forms were produced most by the kilns on this site.

A useful comparison for colour-coated form types in particular is the 4th-century site at Stibbington in

Table 2. LCC1 waster find spots.

Area B	5 sherds
Area C	91 sherds
House Plots	7 sherds

the Lower Nene Valley (Upex *et al.* 2008), which was producing both grey wares and colour-coated vessels possibly as late as the early 5th century. Of the two main kilns, Kiln G was used almost exclusively for grey ware production (Upex *et al.* 2008, 328) while Kiln W was of a different, more ramshackle and less airtight construction (Upex *et al.* 2008, 275) and was used for light-fired colour-coated wares.

The most obvious difference between the sites in terms of products is the much higher proportion of colour-coated jars from Stibbington (Table 4). In the 4th century AD, the Nene Valley light-firing clays were used to produce colour-coated vessels in a notably broader suite of forms than at the Hykeham Road site where it is evident that utilitarian jars and large bowls were produced in the iron-rich grey ware fabrics instead. This pattern appears similar to the excavated pottery from Lincoln and Navenby where, in deposits dating to the 4th century AD, colour-coated jars and wide-mouthed bowls are seldom present (e.g., Precious and Rowlandson 2009; Darling and Precious 2014; Rowlandson *et al.* 2015b; Fiske and Rowlandson 2021). Pottery recovered from the south of Lincolnshire exhibits a range of forms more like that seen from the Lower Nene Valley area itself (e.g. Atkins *et al.* 2020).

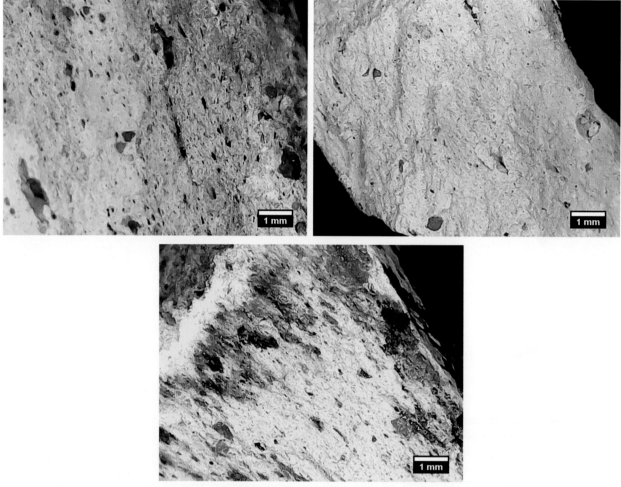

Figure 18. LCC1 fabric from three different vessels.

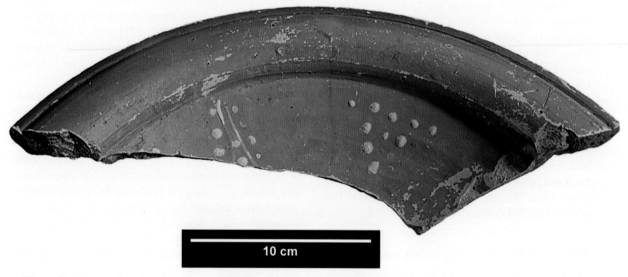

Figure 19. A copy of samian form 38 bowl with internal painted dot decoration in LCC1 fabric, No. 21 (broken non-waster).

(a)

(b)

(c)

Figure 20. Misfired colour-coated plain-rimmed bowls and dishes, including a bead and flange colour-coated bowl with extensive dunting (Fig. 20b, No. 31) and another (Fig. 20c, No. 30) with a spalled off base.

Table 3. Fine ware form types sorted by Rim Equivalents.

Form code	Description	Sherd Count	Max Vessels	Weight (g)	Rim Equivalent (RE)	Illustration nos.
BFB	Bowl, bead and flange rim	84	65	5441	9.56	27–33
DPR	Dish, plain rim	31	26	3309	6.97	36–42
BPR	Bowl, plain rim	25	22	1957	2.61	34, 35
B38	Bowl, copy of samian form 38	38	28	2030	1.54	22–25
JUG	Flagon or jug, pinched neck	1	1	57	1	14
BK	Beaker, unclassified	19	16	230	0.9	
B36	Bowl, copy of samian form 36	9	6	971	0.67	20, 21
F	Flagon, unclassified	11	5	226	0.64	11, 12
LBX	Lid, Castor box	4	4	229	0.57	47–49
BX	Castor box	70	? (fused together)	709	0.5	45, 46
JRR	Jar, rounded rim	4	3	55	0.49	19
FDN	Flagon, disk neck	1	1	97	0.45	13
BKFG	Beaker, funnel-necked, grooved rim	1	1	212	0.35	15
JNK	Jar, necked	2	2	33	0.23	18
BEV	Bowl, everted rim	1	1	45	0.21	26
B	Bowl, unclassified	23	22	1479	0.17	
BKEV	Beaker, everted rim	1	1	17	0.17	
BIBF	Bowl, in-turned bead and flange rim	2	2	30	0.13	
BKPM	Beaker, pentice-moulded	13	5	397	0.11	16, 17
LD	Lid or dish, unclassified	2	2	16	0.08	
J	Jar, unclassified	2	2	127	0.06	
DTR	Dish, triangular rim	1	1	45	0.06	43
JB	Jar or bowl, unclassified	4	4	94	0.04	
L	Lid, unclassified	1	1	19	0.02	44
BD	Bowl or dish, unclassified	50	47	1424	0	
BL	Bowl, large	1	1	84	0	
CLSD	Closed form, unclassified	22	21	469	0	
D	Dish, unclassified	1	1	123	0	
FJ	Flagon or jar, unclassified	44	25	1835	0	
JBL	Jar or bowl large, unclassified	1	1	55	0	
OPEN	Open form, unclassified	13	12	146	0	
Totals:		**482**	**329**	**21961**	**27.53**	

Table 4. Comparison of colour-coated forms with Stibbington kiln site, by percentage of sherd weight.

Form	Lincoln Form types	Stibbington Kiln W	HYRL09
Flanged bowls	BFB and BIBF	21%	36%
Imitation samian bowls	B36, B37 and B38	27%	20%
Bead rim bowls	BPR	5%	13%
Dishes	DPR and DTR	23%	22%
Jars	JRR, JNK and J	17%	1.50%
Castor boxes	BX and LBX	4.50%	6%
Flagons	JUG, FDN and F	2%	2.50%

Note also that beaker sherds represented 5% by weight of the HYRL09 colour-coated assemblage, although present in small numbers no count or weight for beakers was included in the Stibbington Kiln W assemblage for comparison.

ILLUSTRATED FINE WARE CATALOGUE (FIGS 18–22)

10. GFIN: Beaker pedestal base, abraded: *Area B, Group B4, Phase 1, Gully 106, Fill 105, D26*

11. LCC1: Flagon rim, possible trefoil form: *Area C, Group C8, Phase 3, Ditch 331, Fill 330, D46*

12. LCC1: Flagon rim: *Area C, Group C8, Phase 3, Ditch 331, Fill 330, D47*

13. LCC1: Disc-necked flagon, abraded: *Area C, Group C8, Phase 3, Ditch 331, Fill 330, D45*

14. LCC1: Jug neck, abraded: *Area B, Group B11, Phase 3, Ditch 126, Fill 125, D8*

15. LCC1: Beaker with grooved funnel neck: *Area C, Group C8, Phase 3, Ditch 331, Fill 354, D85*

16. LCC1: Pentice moulded beaker, abraded: *Area C, Group C8, Phase 3, Ditch 331, Fill 330, D54*

17. LCC1: Pentice moulded beaker, dunting cracks: *Area C, Group C8, Phase 3, Ditch 331, Fill 354, D84*

18. LCC1: Necked jar, abraded: *Area C, Group C8, Phase 3, Ditch 331, Fill 330, D79*

19. LCC1: Reeded-rim jar, very abraded: *Area C, Group C8, Phase 3, Ditch 331, Fill 330, D56*

20. LCC1: B36 bowl, painted, abraded: *Plot 21, Layer 2113, D33*

21. LCC1: B36 bowl, painted dots: *Road Strip, Ditch/Pit 1056, Fill 1057, D93*

22. LCC1: B38 bowl, misfired: *Area B, Phase 3, Layer 102, D15*

23. LCC1: B38 bowl, misfired, burnt: *Area B, Phase 3, Layer 102, D16*

24. LCC1: B38 bowl, abraded: *Area C, Group C8, Phase 3, Ditch 331, Fill 330, D52*

25. LCC1: B38 bowl: *Plot 21, Pit 2109, Fill 2110, D91*

26. LCC1: Everted rim bowl: *Area C, Group C8, Phase 3, Ditch 331, Fill 330, D55*

27. LCC1: Bead and flange bowl, small example: *Area C, Group C7, Phase 3, Ditch 339, Fill 338, D50*

28. LCC1: Bead and flange bowl, abraded: *Area B, Group B11, Phase 3, Ditch 126, Fill 125, D9*

29. LCC1: Bead and flange bowl, abraded: *Road Strip, Ditch/Pit 1056, Fill 1057, D94*

30. LCC1: Bead and flange bowl, dunting cracks, spalled: *Area C, Group C8, Phase 3, Ditch 331, Fill 354, D114*

31. LCC1: Bead and flange bowl, dunting cracks, abraded: *Area C, Group C8, Phase 3, Ditch 331, Fill 330, D51*

32. LCC1: Bead and flange bowl: *Area B, Phase 3, Layer 102, D18*

33. LCC1: Bead and flange bowl, dunting cracks, spalled, abraded: *Plot 21, Layer 2113, D32*

34. LCC1: Plain rim bowl, misfired: *Plot B, Group B11, Phase 3, Ditch 126, Fill 125, D11*

35. LCC1: Plain rim bowl, misfired, abraded: *Area B, Phase 3, Layer 102, D17*

36. LCC1: Plain rim dish, abraded: *Area C, Group C8, Phase 3, Ditch 331, Fill 330, D38*

37. LCC1: Plain rim dish, dunting cracks, misfired, burnt, found fused to No. 39: *Area C, Group C8, Phase 3, Ditch 331, Fill 330, D43*

38. LCC1: Plain rim dish, dunting cracks, misfired, burnt: *Area C, Group C8, Phase 3, Ditch 331, Fill 330, D42*

39. LCC1: Plain rim dish, dunting cracks, misfired, burnt, found fused to No. 37: *Area C, Group C8, Phase 3, Ditch 331, Fill 330, D44*

40. LCC1: Plain rim dish, warped, dunting cracks, burnt, abraded: *Area C, Group C8, Phase 3, Ditch 331, Fill 330, D39*

41. LCC1: Plain rim dish, sagged base with drips of fused colour coat: *Area C, Group C8, Phase 3, Ditch 331, Fill 330, D40*

42. LCC1: Plain rim dish, spalling, abraded: *Area C, Group C8, Phase 3, Ditch 331, Fill 330, D41*

43. LCC1: Dish with triangular rim: *Area C, Group C8, Phase 3, Ditch 331, Fill 330, D78*

44. LCC1: Lid, abraded: *Road Strip, Curvilinear R21, D31*

45. LCC1: Castor box, spalled: *Area C, Group C8, Phase 3, Ditch 331, Fill 354, D108*

46. LCC1: Castor box: *Area C, Group C7, Phase 3, Ditch 311, Fill 310, D105*

47. LCC1: Castor box lid, misfired, burnt: *Area C, Group C8, Phase 3, Ditch 331, Fill 330, D53*

48. LCC1: Castor box lid: *Area B, Phase 3, Layer 102, D13*

49. LCC1: Castor box lid: *Area C, Group C7, Phase 3, Ditch 339, Fill 338, D80*

50. SCCC?: Cornice rimmed beaker, from structured deposition: *Road Strip, Natural 1002, D4*

4.2.8. Oxidised wares (Figs 23–24)

It would appear that the majority of the oxidised wares within this category were not manufactured on the site. A small number of the oxidised sherds from this group may represent misfired grey wares produced on the site.

CR2: Nos. 51–3 Standard Lincoln white ware fabric, the most common fabric encountered amongst groups from the city and would match well with samples of the South Carlton kiln (Tomber and Dore 1998, SOC WH; Darling and Precious 2014, 52, K23A). The only vessels in this fabric were three very nearly identical flagons (Fig. 23a) found in an un-phased structured deposit in the vicinity of Trench 10 at the northern edge of the site (see Fig. 3), along with the South Carlton colour-coated beaker mentioned above (No. **50**). There is no evidence that they were produced here. Flagons of this type were however produced at the Monson Street kiln site (Rowlandson 2010, form FTR11), the Lincoln Newport suburb production site (Rowlandson *et al.* 2022, No. 31) and South Carlton (Webster 1944, fig. 7.2c).

CR: Nos. 54–7 Early Lincoln white ware fabric with more mica (as Darling and Precious 2014, 52, LRF234). Two possible lids (Nos. **55** and **56**) and the base from a triple/quadruple vase (No. **57**) were found in this fabric, along with the rim and handle from a Hofheim flagon (No. **54**), the handle from a large flagon copying an amphora form, and a Campanulate bowl sherd (as Darling and Precious 2014, No. 384, mid-1st century AD). There is no evidence that any of these vessels were produced here.

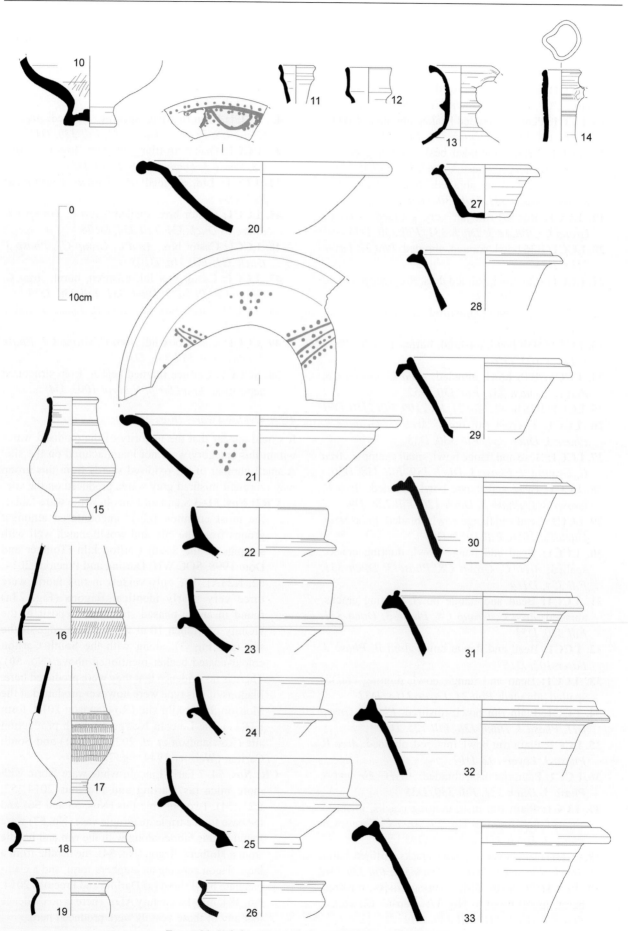

Figure 21. Hykeham Road illustrated fine wares, Nos. 10–33.

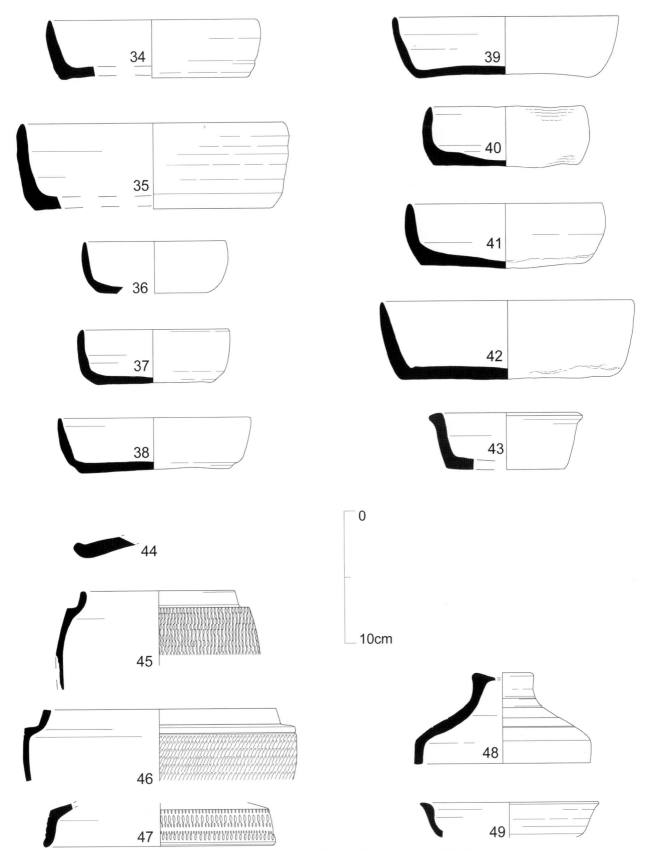

Figure 22. Hykeham Road illustrated fine wares, Nos. 34–50.

(a)   (b)

Figure 23. Three CR flagons from structured deposit (Nos. 51–3), and a triple or quadruple vase base (No. 57).

OX Undifferentiated oxidised wares, it is possible that some were grey ware vessels produced here and oxidised during firing, intentionally or otherwise. Vessels included a bowl with an in-turned bead and flange rim (BIBF), a possibly Gallo-Belgic influenced platter or dish, bowls including samian copies, and jars including a large example with dunting cracks.

SPOX Oxidised wares from the Swanpool kilns near Lincoln, which were operational in the late 3rd and 4th centuries AD (Darling and Precious 2014, 62). A single rim sherd from a plain-rimmed dish was recorded. It was noteworthy that oxidised wares of this type were rare finds here, which contrasts with the assemblages from the Swanpool site itself (Webster and Booth 1947; Rowlandson and Fiske 2017; 2018).

ILLUSTRATED OXIDISED WARE CATALOGUE

51. CR2: Complete ring-necked flagon with expanded top ring, from structured deposit: *Road Strip, Natural 1002, D1*

52. CR2: Complete ring-necked flagon with expanded top ring, from structured deposit: *Road Strip, Natural 1002, D2*

53. CR2: Complete ring-necked flagon with expanded top ring, from structured deposit: *Road Strip, Natural 1002, D3*

54. CR: Hofheim type flagon: *Area B, Group B4, Phase 1, Gully 106, Fill 105, D25*

55. CR?: Lid with finial, abraded: *Area C, Group C8, Phase 3, Ditch 331, Fill 330, D48*

56. CR?: Lid with painted lines under rim, abraded: *Area C, Group C8, Phase 3, Ditch 331, Fill 330, D49*

57. CR: Ring from triple/quadruple vase with attachment points for 3/4 missing cups: *Area B, Group B9, Phase 3, Kiln Base 142, D34*

4.2.9. Reduced wares: Roman and Iron Age transitional (Figs 25–31)

The majority, if not all, of the reduced wares were produced on site or in the Lincoln area.

FABRICS

BB1 A single jar with cavetto rim and acute lattice in Black Burnished ware 1 (as Darling and Precious 2014, 112) was recovered. It may be from Dorset or a more local copy from perhaps the Rossington Bridge (Buckland *et al.* 2001) or Lincoln Racecourse kilns (Corder 1950), although examples from the Racecourse appear to be more consistently wheel-thrown.

GREY: Nos. 58–97 The standard grey ware fabric (Figs 25 and 27; as Darling and Precious 2014, 121–59). Hykeham Road was a production site for mainly utilitarian grey ware, with a considerable quantity of kiln wasters coming from the excavated area. As discussed by Darling (1989; Darling and Precious 2014), there is a great deal of similarity in what was produced in both fabrics and forms at many of the Lincolnshire industries. Samuels drew together much of the extant information about Lincolnshire kilns (1983) and many subsequent excavations have been undertaken although few have been published; it is hoped that this situation will be rectified in the coming years (Field and Palmer-Brown 1991; Field and Williams 1998; Rowlandson 2005; Darling 2007; Cleary *et al.* 2020; Rowlandson and Fiske 2021; Rowlandson *et al.* 2022). The problem faced by the researcher concerns the similarities of many of what might be termed 'medium sandy grey wares' from this area, for example the products of kilns from the Market Rasen area: Barnetby Top, Caistor, Claxby, multiple kilns at Market Rasen

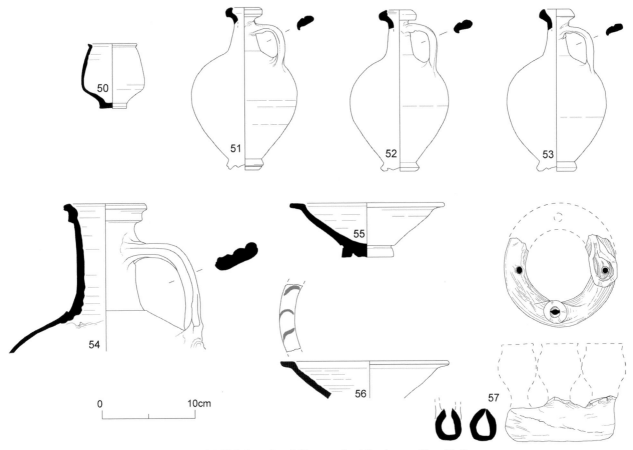

Figure 24. Hykeham Road illustrated oxidised ware, Nos. 51–7.

itself, Legsby, Walesby, Owersby, Linwood Warren and Tealby have very similar fabrics. The 'Trentside kilns' have further sandy grey ware variants, from sites including Widsworth, Lea, Knaith, Fenton/Little London, Newton on Trent, Meering, Newark on Trent, Norton Disney and perhaps an outlier at Worksop (Swan 1984; Field and Palmer-Brown 1991; Swan Roman kilns resource romankilns.net; Darling 2005a). Subdivisions of this ware type have been proposed but at present there has been little scientific work to investigate them further (Vince 2005; Leary 2009; 2013).

GREYC: Nos. 98–102 Coarse grey wares typically with coarse quartz inclusions, similar to the coarse grey ware fabric from Rookery Lane (Webster 1960). Forms include Dales type jars (Nos. **100**, **101**), a large handmade jar with dunting cracks and featuring large quartz inclusions, silver mica, calcareous material and white flint (No. **102**), a necked bowl (No. **99**) and a bead and flange rimmed bowl (No. **98**).

GREYS: No. 103 (Fig. 26) Grey ware with rare shell inclusions; although true shell-gritted fabrics do not seem to have been produced on site some of the clay used was partially fossiliferous and may have been obtained from the Jurassic scarp slope to the east of the River Witham. Two misfired vessels in this fabric were recovered including a large bowl with a conical club rim (No. **103**, as Buckland *et al.* 1980, fig. 4.31), and a further closed vessel with dunting cracks. This fabric may be the result of adding a proportion of fossiliferous Jurassic clay to one or more of the batches of GREY pots produced on site. Such clays were available locally and used by potters working in the area from prehistoric to medieval times (Darling and Precious 2014; Young and Vince 2005).

IAGR: No. 104 An Iron Age tradition fabric which continued in use into the Roman period (as Darling and Precious 2014, 104). It is coarse tempered, often pimply with grog and other inclusions including occasional shell. Vessel forms were almost all jars, mostly large storage vessels, although a single native tradition cooking pot (No. **104**) was recovered from Pit 223 in Area A. This fabric is likely to pre-date the pottery production phase on this site.

IASA: Nos. 105, 106 An Iron Age/transitional sand tempered ware, handmade or wheel finished, may be a finer variant of IAGR (as Darling and Precious 2014, 106). Forms present included a wheel made or wheel-finished jar with a moulded rim (No. **106**) from Pit 217 in Area A, and a handmade bead-rimmed cooking pot burnished over the rim

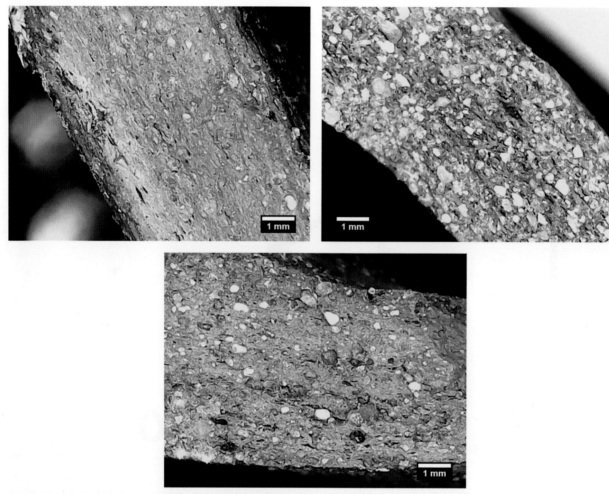

Figure 25. GREY fabric from three different vessels found on site.

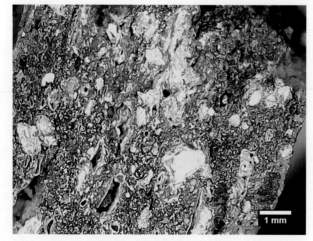

Figure 26. GREYS fabric.

and shoulder (No. **105**) from Ditch 307 in Area C. As with IAGR this fabric is likely to pre-date the pottery production phase on this site.

LCOA: Nos. 107, 108 Late or very late Roman coarse pebbly fabric (as Darling and Precious 2014, 107). Forms represented included two examples of double lid-seated jars (Nos. **107, 108**). Vessels in this fabric

Table 5. Grey ware waster find spots.

Area A	1 sherd
Area B	87 sherds
Area C	135 sherds
Road strip	65 sherds
House Plots, Attenuation Pond etc	42 sherds

are known to have been produced locally at Swanpool (Webster and Booth 1947; Rowlandson and Fiske 2018) and Lincoln Tentercroft Street (Fiske and Rowlandson 2017).

LEG: No.109 Early Roman (1st century AD) 'Legionary' type light-fired grey ware, (as Darling and Precious 2014, 100). Forms included a dish (No. **109**), a jar with applied vertical strip decoration (as Darling and Precious 2014 no. 769), and a jar or beaker with a high shoulder and everted rim.

FIRING FAULTS

A total of 350 grey ware sherds (GREY) showed serious firing faults. These were more widespread across the site than LCC1 with a greater number coming from the southern half of the site (Table 5).

(a)

(b)

Figure 27. Heavily warped grey ware jar No. 76 (Fig. 27a) and a large grey ware bowl (Fig. 27b) with dunting cracks.

FORMS

Table 6 shows the grey ware forms (in fabrics GREY, GREYC, GREYS) within the assemblage, sorted by total Rim Equivalents (RE). Jars, particularly necked jar variants were the most common type from the site followed by wide-mouthed bowls, with smaller numbers of straight sided bead and flanged bowls, bowls with rounded rims, hemispherical flanged bowls, plain rimmed dishes and large bowls with everted rims. In comparison to other contemporary grey ware groups from Lincolnshire there were relatively few grey ware straight sided bead and flanged bowls or plain rimmed dish/bowls; it would appear that the potters on this site produced these key late Roman forms using colour-coated fabric LCC1 instead.

ILLUSTRATED REDUCED WARE CATALOGUE (FIGS 28–31)

58. GREY: Butt beaker: *Area B, Group B7, Phase 1/2, Ditch 108, Fill 107, D95*

59. GREY: Jar, warped, dunting cracks: *Road Strip, Curvilinear R9, Fill R10, D22*

60. GREY: Jar (J105), patchy firing: *Area C, Group C2, Phase 1, Ditch 321, Fill 320, D27*

61. GREY: Large jar or bowl: *Area C, Group C7, Phase 3, Ditch 339, Fill 338, D64*

62. GREY: Collared rim jar: *Area C, Group C8, Phase 3, Ditch 331, Fill 330, D72*

63. GREY: Double lid-seated jar, overfired, dunting cracks: *Area C, Group C7, Phase 3, Ditch 339, Fill 338, D77*

64. GREY: Everted rim jar, warped rim: *Area C, Group C8, Phase 3, Ditch 331, Fill 354, D112*

65. GREY: Everted rim jar: *Area B, Group B11, Phase 3, Ditch 126, Fill 125, D7*

66. GREY: Everted rim jar: *Area C, Group C8, Phase 3, Ditch 331, Fill 330, D70*

67. GREY: Handled jar (JH33): *Plot 20, Linear 2002, Fill 2001, D113*

68. GREY: Large jar, burnished scrolls, over-fired: *Area B, Phase 3, Layer 102, D97*

69. GREY: Large jar, cordon decoration: *Area C, Group C8, Phase 3, Ditch 331, Fill 330, D63*

70. GREY: Large jar, cordon decoration: *Road Strip, Curvilinear R21, Fill R22, D89*

71. GREY: Necked jar, warped: *Road Strip, Curvilinear R9, Fill R10, D21*

72. GREY: Narrow-necked jar, cordon decoration: *Area C, Group C8, Phase 3, Ditch 331, Fill 330, D76*

73. GREY: Narrow-necked jar, cordon/rouletting decoration: *Area B, Group B12, Phase 3, Ditch 128, Fill 127, D83*

74. GREY: Round-necked jar, spalled: *Area C, Group C8, Phase 3, Ditch 331, Fill 330, D61*

75. GREY: Storage jar: *Area C, Group C8, Phase 3, Ditch 331, Fill 330, D71*

76. GREY: Storage jar, heavily warped, dunting cracks: *Unstratified, D100*

77. GREY: Large bowl, dunting cracks: *Area C, Group C8, Phase 3, Ditch 331, Fill 330, D60*

78. GREY: Large bowl with conical bifid rim: *Area B, Phase 3, Layer 102, D14*

79. GREY: Wide mouthed bowl (BWM2), warped: *Area B, Group B1, Phase 2, Ditch 124, Fill 123, D36*

Table 6. Reduced ware forms sorted by Rim Equivalents.

Form code	Description	Sherd Count	Max Vessels	Weight (g)	Rim Equivalents (RE)	Illustration nos.
JL	Jar, large	229	107	9823	4.19	68–70, 102
BFB	Bowl, bead and flange rim	42	38	2025	2.75	92, 93, 98
JEV	Jar, everted rim	32	20	645	2.52	64–66
JNN	Jar, narrow-necked	19	9	1187	2.45	72, 73
BWM3	Bowl, wide mouth, as Darling and Precious 2014 nos. 1229–30	32	29	3015	2.13	83–85
BWM2	Bowl, wide mouth, as Darling and Precious 2014 no. 1228	32	9	2340	2	79–82
DPR	Dish, plain rim	23	22	469	1.42	
BIBF	Bowl, inturned bead and flange rim, as Darling and Precious 2014 nos. 1283–7	13	13	644	1.15	97
JCR	Jar, collared rim, as Darling and Precious 2014 nos. 1022–23	15	11	539	1.1	62
BEV	Bowl, everted rim	9	8	429	0.84	90, 91
BWM	Bowl, wide mouth, as Darling and Precious 2014 nos. 1225–30	34	16	678	0.75	
BFL	Bowl, flanged rim, as Gillam 1970 nos. 218–220	10	10	310	0.7	
J	Jar, unclassified	92	60	2488	0.66	59
BWM1	Bowl, wide mouth, as Darling and Precious 2014 nos. 1225–7	10	4	281	0.61	
JDW	Jar, Dales type	9	8	199	0.61	100, 101
JB	Jar or bowl, unclassified	43	43	1138	0.56	
JS	Jar, storage	42	33	4193	0.56	75. 76
JBK	Small jar or beaker	7	6	121	0.55	
BG225	Bowl, rounded, as Gillam 1970 no. 225	6	3	4	0.43	95, 96
BFBH	Bowl, bead and flange rim with high bead	6	6	264	0.4	94
J168	Jar, storage, as Darling and Precious 2014 no. 1027	2	2	235	0.4	
BCAR	Bowl, carinated	5	5	569	0.38	86–89
BL	Bowl, large	69	46	4102	0.37	77
BPR	Bowl, plain rim	5	5	143	0.32	
JRR	Jar, rounded rim	1	1	75	0.27	74
JBKEV	Small jar or beaker, everted rim	2	2	15	0.26	
JBL	Jar or bowl, large	84	68	4104	0.24	61
JCUR	Jar, curved, as Darling and Precious 2014 nos. 985–9	2	2	67	0.24	
BNNK	Bowl, large, no neck	2	2	57	0.23	
JL148	Jar, large, as Darling 1999 fig. 37.383	6	1	455	0.21	
JDLS	Jar, double lid-seated	4	3	256	0.21	63
B	Bowl, unclassified	14	10	292	0.18	
B38	Bowl, copy of samian form 38	3	2	136	0.18	
BNK	Bowl, necked	3	1	81	0.16	99
JH33	Jar, handled, narrow neck, as Darling 1999 fig. 32.198	1	1	110	0.16	67
JNK	Jar, necked	1	1	33	0.11	71
BKBB	Butt beaker	1	1	6	0.1	58
BLBIF	Bowl, large, conical bifid rim, as Buckland *et al.* 1980 fig. 4.32	1	1	266	0.09	78

(Continued)

Table 6. (Continued)

Form code	Description	Sherd Count	Max Vessels	Weight (g)	Rim Equivalents (RE)	Illustration nos.
JEVS	Jar, stubby everted rim	1	1	28	0.08	
B36	Bowl, copy of samian form 36	1	1	56	0.07	
BGR	Bowl, grooved rim	1	1	8	0.07	
DGR	Dish, grooved rim	1	1	14	0.07	
BLD3	Bowl, large, conical club rim, as Buckland *et al.* 1980 fig. 4.31	1	1	63	0.06	103
BKEV	Beaker, everted rim	1	1	7	0.05	
BLD1	Bowl, large, conical flared lip, as Buckland *et al.* 2001 fig. 49.277	1	1	93	0.05	
OPEN	Open forms, unclassified	5	5	85	0.04	
BDTR	Bowl or dish, triangular rim, as Gillam 1970 nos. 222–3	1	1	10	0.03	
LD	Lid or dish	1	1	9	0.02	
BD	Bowl or dish	20	16	952	0	
CLSD	Closed form, unclassified	244	211	5172	0	
COL	Colander	1	1	5	0	
FDN	Flagon, disc neck	2	2	49	0	
FJ	Flagon or jar	3	3	48	0	
JBEV	Jar or bowl, everted rim	4	4	93	0	
JBNK	Jar or bowl, necked	1	1	14	0	
JEVC	Jar, curved everted rim, as Gillam 1970 no. 135	2	2	28	0	
JFO	Jar, folded, as Darling and Precious 2014 no. 995	1	1	27	0	
Totals:		**1203**	**864**	**48555**	**31.03**	

80. **GREY:** Wide mouthed bowl (BWM2), burnished lines: *Area B, Group B12, Phase 3, Ditch 128, Fill 127, D28*

81. **GREY:** Wide mouthed bowl (BWM2), burnished lines: *Area C, Group C8, Phase 3, Ditch 331, Fill 330, D75*

82. **GREY:** Wide mouthed bowl (BWM2): *Area C, Group C8, Phase 3, Ditch 331, Fill 355, D90*

83. **GREY:** Wide mouthed bowl (BWM3): *Area C, Group C8, Phase 3, Ditch 331, Fill 330, D74*

84. **GREY:** Wide mouthed bowl (BWM3), dunting cracks, patchy surfaces: *Road Strip, Curvilinear R21, Fill R22, D88*

85. **GREY:** Wide mouthed bowl (BWM3): *Unstratified, D23*

86. **GREY:** Carinated bowl: *Area C, Group C3, Phase 1, Ditch 327, Fill 326, D102*

87. **GREY:** Carinated bowl: *Plot 19, Pit 1914, Fill 1910, D110*

88. **GREY:** Carinated bowl, roller-stamped decoration: *Area B, Group B7, Phase 1/3, Ditch 114, Fill 113, D5*

89. **GREY:** Carinated bowl, warped waster: *Road Strip, Curvilinear R9, Fill R10, D20*

90. **GREY:** Everted rim bowl: *Area C, Group C8, Phase 3, Ditch 331, Fill 330, D62*

91. **GREY:** Everted rim bowl: *Area C, Group C8, Phase 3, Ditch 331, Fill 330, D65*

92. **GREY:** Bead and flange bowl: *Area C, Group C8, Phase 3, Ditch 331, Fill 330, D66*

93. **GREY:** Bead and flange bowl: *Plot 21, Linear 2105, Fill 2106, D37*

94. **GREY:** Bead and flange bowl with high bead, dunting cracks: *Plot 20, Linear 2002, Fill 2001, D92*

95. **GREY:** Bowl (BG225), spalled: *Road Strip, Linear 1103, Fill 1102, D82*

96. **GREY:** Bowl (BG225): *Area C, Group C8, Phase 3, Ditch 331, Fill 330, D73*

97. **GREY:** Bowl with in-turned bead and flange rim and notched decoration: *Area C, Group C8, Phase 3, Ditch 331, Fill 355, D86*

98. **GREYC:** Bead and flange bowl, dunting cracks: *Unstratified, D101*

99. **GREYC:** Bead and flange bowl: *Road Strip, ?Pit R13, Fill R14, D99*

100. **GREYC:** Dales type jar: *Area B, Group B9, Phase 3, Pit 140, Fill 143, D103*

101. **GREYC:** Dales type jar: *Area B, Group B9, Phase 3, Kiln Base 142, D35*

102. **GREYC?:** Large handmade jar, dunting cracks: *Road Strip, ?Linear R15, Fill R16, D87*

Hugh G. Fiske and Ian M. Rowlandson

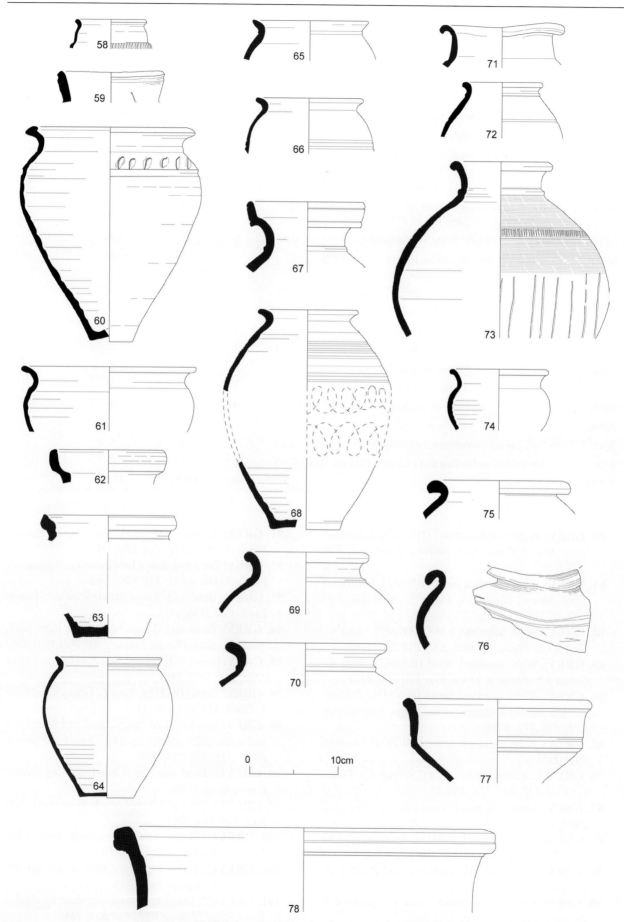

Figure 28. Hykeham Road illustrated reduced ware, Nos. 58–78.

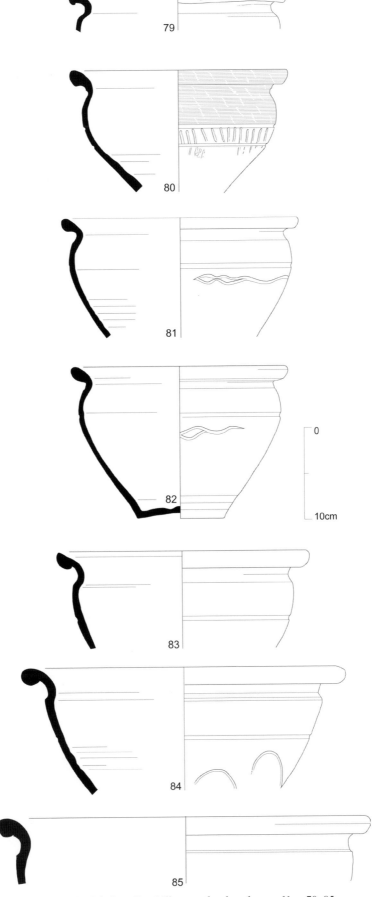

Figure 29. Hykeham Road illustrated reduced ware, Nos. 79–85.

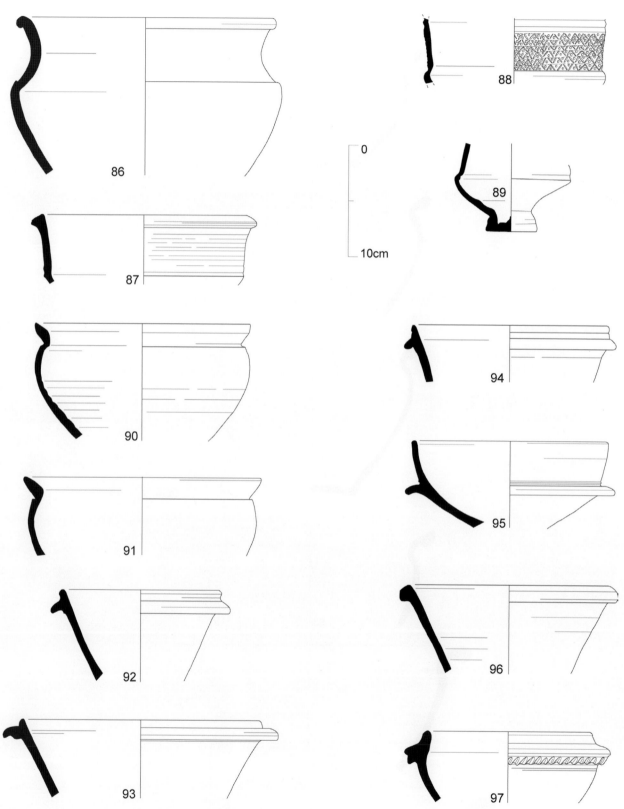

Figure 30. Hykeham Road illustrated reduced ware, Nos. 86–97.

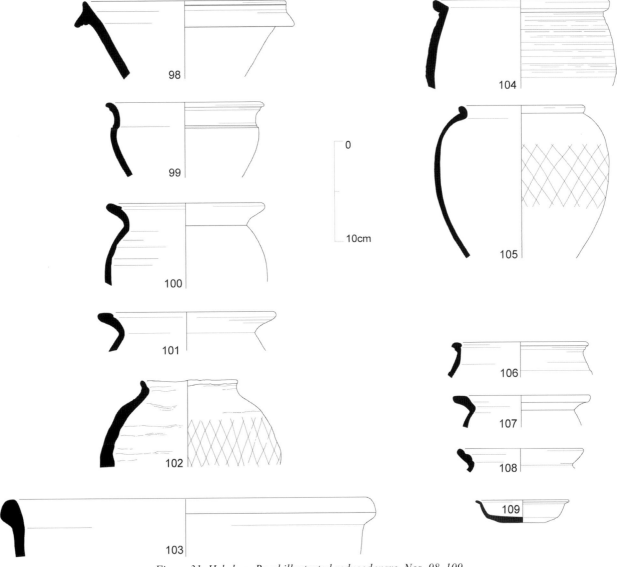

Figure 31. Hykeham Road illustrated reduced ware, Nos. 98–109.

103. GREYS: Large bowl with conical club rim, over-fired: *Plot 19, Pit 1914, Fill 1910, D111*

104. IAGR: Native tradition cooking pot, wheel finished: *Area A, Group A1, Phase 1, Pit 223, Fill 231, D107*

105. IASA: Bead-rimmed cooking pot, burnished, burnt?: *Area C, Group C2, Phase 1, Ditch 307, Fill 306, D29*

106. IASA: Jar, moulded rim, cordon decoration: *Area A, Group A1, Phase 1, Pit 217, Fill 216, D104*

107. LCOA: Double lid-seated jar: *Area C, Group C8, Phase 3, Ditch 331, Fill 330, D69*

108. LCOA?: Double lid-seated jar: *Area C, Group C8, Phase 3, Ditch 331, Fill 330, D67*

109. LEG: Dish: *Area A, Group A1, Phase 1, Pit 223, Fill 231, D106*

4.2.10. Shell-gritted wares (Fig. 32)

DWSHT: No. 110 This material represents shell-gritted sherds in the fine silty fabric as described by Tomber and Dore (1998, code DAL SH). This fabric was probably produced in north-western Lincolnshire perhaps also closer to Lincoln using material from the fossiliferous Westbury Beds (Loughlin 1977; Firman 1991; Vince 2004; 2006). The code DWSH was used in the Lincoln corpus (Darling and Precious 2014, 82–8) to include hand-built/wheel-finished vessels of this type along with the wheel made shell-gritted vessels of the late 4th century AD. Fabric DWSHT has therefore been used instead here to distinguish material under study from this site from the broader group used in the corpus. Sherds from only two Dales ware jars were

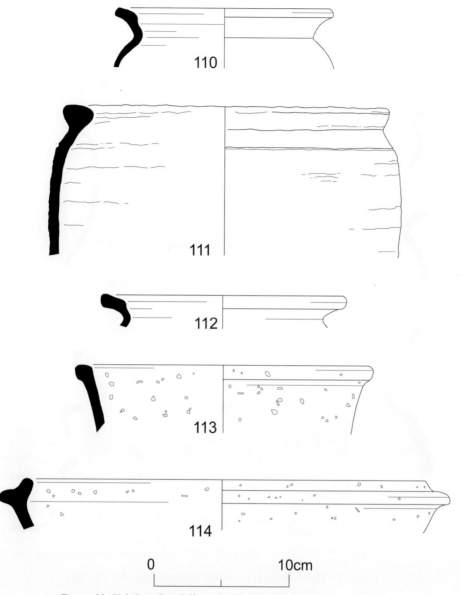

Figure 32. Hykeham Road illustrated shell-gritted ware, Nos. 110–14.

recorded which is perhaps a little surprising given their ubiquity elsewhere in Lincolnshire but probably demonstrates that the kilns here and nearby were producing sufficient quantities of utilitarian jars to fill the local demand during the mid- to late 3rd century AD, indeed Dales type jars were produced in grey ware at the Rookery Lane kilns (Webster 1960, Nos. 44–7).

IASH: No. 111 A fabric group rather than a single fabric, it encompasses shell-gritted vessels from the late Iron Age through into the early Roman period and largely comprises sherds from native tradition cooking pots (Darling and Precious 2014, 88).

SHEL: Nos. 112–14 This fabric code has historically been mostly used for late Roman wheel made wares akin to the double lid-seated jar types used at Lincoln at the end of the 4th century AD. For future reports therefore the code LRLS should be used for the double lid-seated type products which were previously incorporated with the hand built and wheel-finished Dales ware in the CLAU Lincoln coding system (Darling and Precious 2014) with SHEL retained for shell-gritted wares of uncertain origin/date/type. The three illustrated vessels from this site show the range of diagnostic late Roman forms (Darling 1977). As fossiliferous clays are known to have outcropped in the Lincoln area a local production source for these vessels is presumed.

ILLUSTRATED SHELL- AND CALCITE-GRITTED WARE CATALOGUE (FIG. 32)

110. DWSHT: Dales ware jar, external concretion: *Area C, Ditch 313, Fill 334, D109*

111. IASH: Native tradition cooking pot, wheel-finished: *Area B, Group B7, Phase 1/2, Ditch 108, Fill 107, D96*

112. SHEL: Double lid-seated jar: *Area C, Group C8, Phase 3, Ditch 331, Fill 330, D68*

113. SHEL: Flanged bowl, possibly wheel-finished: *Area B, Phase 3, Layer 102, D19*

114. SHEL: Bowl with inturned bead and flange: *Area B, Group B5, Phase 3, Gully 104, Fill 103, D30*

5. Discussion

5.1. The significance of the pottery assemblage

It was clear from the numbers of fresh, unused and mis-fired colour-coated vessels recovered that vessels similar to the products of South Carlton and the Nene Valley industries were being manufactured on this site along with utilitarian grey wares.

The problem of differentiating the fine colour-coated fabrics has become more difficult in recent times. In the past many of the vessels were referred to as 'Castor ware' following the discovery of the kilns in the Nene Valley. Further industries at Lincoln (Rowlandson *et al.* 2022), South Carlton (Webster 1944), Great Casterton (Corder 1961), and recent discoveries by University of Leicester from Great Casterton (N. Cooper pers. comm.), Brough on Humber (Darling 2005b), the Nene Valley (Perrin 1999), and Colchester and the Continent (Symonds 1990), have made the picture more complicated. Many vessels have very similar forms and manufacturing techniques, often with similar fine fabrics, and it can be difficult to differentiate between the products of many of the key industries with the naked eye or a x20 microscope (see above, cf. Anderson *et al.* 1982; Symonds 1990; Tomber and Dore 1998; Perrin 1999). This is a matter further complicated if one considers that the movement of craftsmen from the Continent to Britain to establish workshops may have been the initial catalyst for the introduction of these pottery styles (Perrin 1999, 87).

It appears likely, as suggested in the Lincoln Roman Pottery Corpus (Darling and Precious 2014, 20), that the sources of many local colour-coated products have not been recognised in the past. Previously most mid-2nd to 4th century AD colour-coated pottery was characterised as originating from kilns in the vicinity of the modern city of Peterborough. Recent excavations in the Newport suburb and Monson Street in Lincoln (Rowlandson 2010; Rowlandson *et al.* 2015a; 2022) have demonstrated that a number of kilns there were utilising the local light-firing clay to make colour-coated pottery very similar to the products of South Carlton and the Nene Valley.

As such, pending further research, colour-coated wares of these types have been recorded here as LCC1 (Lincoln light-firing white fabric with colour-coat), and LCC2 (fine, not obviously the typical SPCC fabric with red/orange fabric and dark colour-coat) although only a single sherd

of LCC2 was recorded from Hykeham Road. Since this assemblage was recorded however, colour-coated wares from Lincolnshire have been recorded by the authors as CC1, CC2 and CC3 to acknowledge the ambiguity between which vessels were produced in Lincoln and which were made in the Nene Valley (e.g., Rowlandson and Fiske 2020).

The extremely limited investigations of these new kiln sites, including the lack of detailed study of recently found pottery production waste in the vicinity of Anchor Street, Lincoln, and the lack of publication of pottery assemblages from other Lincoln kilns excavated in the 1970s–90s, hinder our understanding of colour-coated pottery production here. It might in time be possible to say that, in one form or another, colour-coated pottery production took place in the immediate vicinity of Lincoln from the 1st century AD throughout much of the Roman period. However, a proportion of these wares found in Lincoln may indeed be from the Peterborough area or from production sites elsewhere among the Jurassic deposits that yield light-firing clay. Preliminary study of light-fired material from the Lincoln kiln sites would suggest a higher mica content than is common from Nene Valley kiln samples (evident on surfaces where the colour-coat has worn away) but further scientific analysis is needed to support this. Mica, although not exclusively an indicator of Lincolnshire products, is also evident on the surfaces of the white ware flagons and mortaria produced at South Carlton, the Lincoln Technical College and Newton upon Trent. Undoubtedly the source of these wares varied across time and with distance from the Nene Valley but, in the absence of more detailed scientific work on both the pottery from the kilns and from the consumer sites this must now be considered as a 'known-unknown' (Wilkins 2009), and recent assessments of the production of the Nene Valley industries (e.g., Evans *et al.* 2017) may require further and more nuanced analysis in the future.

Biddulph (2013) has raised the concept of a pottery 'Meme' and highlights the difference between close copies produced by apprentices or kindred potters and looser attempts by potters to mimic vessels that they have seen. In the case of the vessels from the Hykeham Road site it appears that the potter may have 'moved valley', as they share a similar style to those working in the Nene Valley. It is possible that the potters producing the colour-coated wares may have been specialists who worked alongside those producing the more utilitarian grey wares (cf. discussion of multi-potter workshops in Hartley 2016, 144). Indeed, over recent years the known production sources of a number of key wares have expanded on the basis of new kilns and new research, such as Black Burnished ware 1 (e.g. Holbrook and Bidwell 1991; Buckland *et al.* 2001), Verulamium white wares (e.g. Seeley and Drummond-Murray 2005), Derbyshire ware (e.g. Leary 2008), Dales ware (e.g. Firman 1991; Vince 2004; 2006) and also Nene Valley fumed grey ware types in the Stamford area

(Cooper pers. comm.; Atkins *et al.* 2020, 119). The motivation behind the movement of potters and their apprentices to found new workshops, and the status of those manufacturing the pots themselves has been discussed and various theories put forward about the relative importance of slavery and free enterprise at play (e.g. Breeze 1977; Buckland 2004; Hartley 2016). Further archaeological investigations and finds of new kilns have the potential to continue to challenge our present understanding of pottery provision across the province.

5.2. The significance of the site

The results from this site help to fill some gaps in the knowledge of pottery production in Roman Lincoln, placing the site as an outlier and possible precursor of the important Swanpool industry, producing mainly grey ware and light-fired colour-coated pottery for local consumption in the 3rd and 4th centuries AD. Situated close to the Rookery Lane kilns, it utilised the same iron-rich clay to produce utilitarian reduced grey wares, but importantly it also used deposits of iron-poor light-firing clay, which were perhaps smaller in extent and harder to access, to make colour-coated wares. The presence of the River Witham close at hand would have made transport of finished goods relatively easy but may also have contributed to its demise. Ultimately this was a small site, perhaps with no more than a handful of working kilns at any one time, which may have been rendered uneconomic due to flooding and/or depletion of resources.

The production of Nene Valley-type colour-coated wares and perhaps mortaria on this site is of interest, as it potentially disrupts the picture we had of Roman Lincoln importing a significant proportion of table ware in the late Roman period, when at least a proportion of what was used is likely to have been produced locally. This also throws into question some of the preconceived ideas about the supply of such 'Castor ware' to sites in the north of Britain, and a more nuanced picture, with colour-coated wares being supplied from a range of local sites, should perhaps be considered as an alternative. It is hoped that, with scientific analysis, such hypothesises could be tested in the future (cf. Paynter *et al.* 2009; Cumberpatch *et al.* 2013; Perry 2016; 2019).

The date that pottery production concluded on the site is uncertain, but the limited range of final Roman indicators would suggest that it was finished by sometime in the mid-4th century AD. Darling has shown the number of kiln sites that are known to the south of the centre of Lincoln (Darling 1977; Darling and Precious 2014) and it would appear likely that potters may have merely relocated to a more favourable spot. Swanpool appears to be the focus of pottery production in the later 4th century AD (Webster and Booth 1947; Camidge 1987; Rowlandson and Fiske 2017; 2018) along with a further possible site in the Wigford area (Fiske and Rowlandson

2017). Although there is some evidence that light-fired colour-coated wares, of the types shown here, were also produced at Swanpool (Rowlandson and Fiske 2017; 2018), it appears they made up a smaller proportion of the assemblage. The potters at Swanpool had a greater dependence on using iron-rich clays from the immediate vicinity to produce table wares in Swanpool oxidised ware (SPOX) and Swanpool colour-coated wares (SPCC) instead of 'proper' light-firing, iron-poor clays. This may be in part due to the scarcity of light-firing clay or the necessity of transporting it from outcrops exposed on the Lincoln Cliff edge. This move away from light-firing clays may also be due to changes in fashion, with orange wares perhaps becoming more popular (cf. Cool 2006). Undoubtedly other sites remain to be found and recent excavations have already added to the number of kiln sites since the inception of this project (e.g., Rowlandson and Fiske 2021 and the Bomber Command Memorial site, McDaid pers. comm.). Excavations in the area continue to produce evidence for pottery kilns to the south of Lincoln and it is perhaps a matter of time before further sites producing light-fired colour-coated wares are located. Once the growing number of assemblages from local kilns are fully quantified it may be possible to investigate the relative percentages of fabrics and forms produced in the area that were discarded as wasters before they left the kiln sites (e.g., this site and Rowlandson and Fiske 2017; 2018; 2021).

Migration of pottery production sites over time during the Roman period is also evident in the case of Market Rasen where there was another cluster of pottery production sites (e.g., Baker 1941; Samuels 1983; Rowlandson 2005; Mumford and Palmer-Brown 2007; Wilson and Wilson 2007). This has led Rowlandson to suggest that, outside of the towns, potters tended to exploit an area until clay resources were depleted, the landscape was churned up and/or fuel resources exhausted, then moved elsewhere (Rowlandson 2005). The Hykeham Road site may merely represent a relatively short episode of pottery production in the busy and productive area immediately to the south of Roman Lincoln.

Acknowledgements

The author wishes to thank Hugh Fiske for his work producing the bulk of this typescript, providing the illustrations and taking the photographs. We would also like to thank Dr Gwladys Monteil for the samian report and Paul Buckland and Mike Sumbler (BGS) for discussing the potting clay available locally. We would like to thank Will Mumford for the initial commission to record the pottery and arranging access to the paper archive to complete this report. We thank Charlotte Bentley in her PCAS capacity for organising all the paper archive, drawings and pottery to facilitate our work. We would also like to thank Charlotte for her work producing the line drawings for this report. Thanks also to Richard Watts of Lincolnshire County Council for providing additional information about previous record for the site and access to copies of other reports from Lincoln for comparison with this assemblage. Thank you to Nick Cooper for sharing information about material excavated in the Stamford area and inviting me to present this paper at the 2022 SGRP meeting at Leicester. Lastly our thanks go to Eniko Hudak who as JRPS editor provided invaluable advice and assistance, and to the peer reviewers who helped greatly in improving the early draft.

Bibliography

Allen, M., Clay, C. and Trott, K. 2010. *Archaeological Excavation Report: Excavation of Land at 9–11 Monson Street, Lincoln, Lincolnshire*, Unpublished assessment Allen Archaeology Ltd. Report Number AAL 2010049. Lincolnshire Historic Environment Record.

Anderson, A., Fulford, M.G., Hatcher, H. and Pollard, A.M. 1982. Chemical Analysis of Hunt Cups and Allied Wares from Britain, *Britannia* 13, 229–38.

Atkins, R., Burke, J., Field, L. and Yates, A. 2020. *Middle Bronze Age and Roman Settlement at Manor Pit, Baston, Lincolnshire: Excavations 2002–2014*, MOLA Northampton monograph. Archaeopress, Oxford.

Baker, F.T. 1937a. Roman pottery kiln at Lincoln, *Lincolnshire Magazine*, no 3, 7, 187–90.

Baker, F.T. 1937b. A note on the Lincoln Technical College kiln, *Journal of Roman Studies* 27, 233.

Baker, F.T. 1941. Pottery kiln on Linwood Warren, *The De Astonian* 8.106 (summer 1941), 26 (The Magazine of De Aston School, Market Rasen, Lincs).

BGS 1973. Geological Survey of England and Wales 1:63,360/1:50,000 geological map series, New Series. BGS Geology Viewer. Available at: https://geologyviewer.bgs.ac.uk/ (last accessed August 2022).

Biddulph, E. 2013. The Blind Pottery: The Evolution of samian ware and its imitations, in M. Fulford and E. Durham, *Seeing Red: New Economic and Social Perspectives on Gallo-Roman Terra Sigilatta*, Bulletin of the Institute of Classical Studies Supplement 102, School of Advanced Study University of London, London, 368–80.

Bradley-Lovekin, T. 2004. *Archaeological Watching Brief on Land Adjacent to Beech Street/Newark Road, Lincoln* (LNR03), unpublished Archaeological Project Services report 41/04.

Bradley-Lovekin, T. 2010. Witham Crossing: Early Roman Activity at Bracebridge, Lincoln, in S. Malone and M. Williams (eds) *Rumours of Roman Finds*, Heritage Trust of Lincolnshire, Heckington, 43–6.

Breeze, D.J. 1977. The fort at Bearsden and the supply of pottery to the Roman army, in J. Dore and K. Greene (eds) *Roman Pottery Studies in Britain and Beyond*, BAR Supp. Ser. 30, British Archaeological Reports, Oxford, 133–46.

Buckland, P. 2004. A Parthian Shot- Uhuru?, *Assemblage* 8. Available at: https://assemblagejournal.files.wordpress.com/2017/05/a-parthian-shot.pdf (last accessed 29 August 2023).

Buckland, P.C., Hartley, K.F. and Rigby, V. 2001. The Roman Pottery Kilns at Rossington Bridge Excavations 1956–1961, *Journal of Roman Pottery Studies* 9.

Buckland, P.C., Magilton, J.R. and Dolby, M.J. 1980 The Roman Pottery Industries of South Yorkshire: A Review, *Britannia* 11, 145–64.

Camidge, K. 1987. Swanpool, in E. Nurser (ed.) *Archaeology in Lincolnshire*, Annual Report of The Trust for Lincolnshire Archaeology, 3, Lincoln, 30–2.

Chavasse, P. and Clay, C. 2008. *Archaeological Evaluation Report: Trial Trenching at 116 High Street, Lincoln*, Unpublished Allen Archaeological Associates report 2008/020. Lincolnshire Historic Environment Record.

Cleary, K., Fiske, H.G. and Rowlandson, I.M. 2020. *Park Farm Tattershall Thorpe, Lincolnshire: Archaeological Scheme of Strip, Map and Sample Excavation*, Unpublished report PCAS Archaeology. Lincolnshire Historic Environment Record.

Cool, H.E.M. 2006. *Eating and Drinking in Roman Britain*, Cambridge University Press, Cambridge.

Corder, P. 1930. *The Roman Pottery at Throlam, Holme-on-Spalding Moor, East Yorkshire*, Issue 3 of Roman Malton and District report.

Corder, P. 1950. *A Romano-British pottery kiln on the Lincoln Racecourse*, University of Nottingham, Nottingham.

Corder, P. (ed.) 1961. *The Roman Town and Villa at Great Casterton, Rutland: Third Report for the Years 1954–1958*, University of Nottingham, Nottingham.

Cumberpatch, C., Roberts, I., Alldritt, D., Batt, C., Gaunt, G.D., Greenwood, D., Hudson, J., Hughes, M.J., Ixer, R.A., Meadows, J, Weston, P. and Young, J. 2013. A Stamford Ware Pottery Kiln in Pontefract: A Geographical Enigma and a Dating Dilemma, *Medieval Archaeology* 57(1), 111–50.

Dannell, G. 1999. South Gaulish decorated samian, in R.P. Symonds and S. Wade, *Roman pottery from excavations in Colchester, 1971–86*, Colchester Archaeological report 10, Colchester Archaeological Trust, Colchester, 13–75.

Darling, M.J. 1977. *A Group of late Roman pottery from Lincoln*, Lincoln Archaeological Trust Monograph Series 16/1, Council for British Archaeology, York.

Darling, M.J. 1989. Nice Fabric Pity about the Form, *Journal of Roman Pottery Studies* 2, 98–101.

Darling, M.J. 1999. Roman Pottery, in C. Colyer, B.J.J. Gilmour and M.J. Jones, *The Defences of the Lower City. Excavations at The Park and West Parade 1970–2*, CBA Research Report 114 Council for British Archaeology, York, 52–135.

Darling, M.J. 2004. Guidelines for the archiving of Roman Pottery. *Journal of Roman Pottery Studies* 11, 67–74.

Darling, M.J. 2005a. Report on the pottery, in C. Palmer-Brown and W. Mumford, Romano-British life in north Nottinghamshire, fresh evidence from Raymoth Lane, Worksop, *Transactions of Thoroton Society* 108, 2004 edition, 37–51.

Darling, M.J. 2005b. Brough-on-Humber fine wares production, in G.B. Dannell and P.V. Irving (eds) *Journal of Roman Pottery Studies Vol. 12: An Archaeological Miscellany: Papers in Honour of K F Hartley*, Oxbow Books, Oxford, 83–96.

Darling, M.J. 2006. *Archive report 228 on pottery from Bracebridge Heath Kiln, Lincolnshire* BHK91, Unpublished report for City of Lincoln Post-excavation Team. Lincolnshire Historic Environment Record.

Darling, M.J. 2007. Appendix 2: Report 215 on pottery from excavations to the east of Linwood Road, Market Rasen, Lincolnshire, LRM05, in Mumford and Palmer-Brown 2007.

Darling, M.J. and Precious, B.J. 2014. *A Corpus of Roman Pottery from Lincoln*, Lincoln Archaeological Studies No. 6, Oxbow Books, Oxford.

Donel, L. 1992. Bracebridge Heath Kiln, in M.J. Jones (ed.) *Lincoln Archaeology 1991–2: 4th Annual Report of the City of Lincoln Archaeology Unit*, City of Lincoln Archaeological Unit, Lincoln, 12.

Evans, J. with Macauley, S. and Mills, P. 2017. *The Horningsea Roman Pottery Industry in Context*, East Anglian Archaeology Monograph 162, Oxford Archaeology East, Bar Hill.

Field, F.N. and Palmer-Brown, C.P.H. 1991. New evidence for a Romano-British grey ware pottery industry in the Trent Valley, *Lincolnshire History and Archaeology* 26, 40–56.

Field, F.N. and Williams, M. 1998. Linwood Road Market Rasen, Lincs. *Proposed Foodstore development: Archaeological Evaluation*, LAS Report No. 326b. Lincolnshire Historic Environment Record.

Firman, R. 1991. The Significance of Anhydrite in pottery as exemplified by Romano-British Dales Ware, *Journal of Roman Pottery Studies* 4, 45–50.

Fiske, H.G. and Rowlandson, I.M. 2017. *Lincoln East-West Link road scheme: Excavations at the corner of Tentercroft Street and High Street*: Archaeological Excavation report, Unpublished interim developer report on excavations undertaken by PCAS Ltd. Lincolnshire Historic Environment Record.

Fiske, H.G. and Rowlandson, I.M. 2021. *A report on the excavation of a Roman pottery production site off Hykeham Road, Lincoln* (HYRL09), developer report on excavations undertaken by PCAS Ltd. Lincolnshire Historic Environment Record.

Gillam, J.P. 1970. *Types of Coarse Roman Pottery Vessels Found in Northern Britain*, 3rd ed, University of Newcastle upon Tyne, Newcastle upon Tyne.

Hartley, K.F. 2016. Mortaria, in D. Breeze, *Bearsden: A Roman fort on the Antonine Wall*, Society of Antiquities of Scotland, Edinburgh, 129–58.

Holbrook, N. and Bidwell, P.T. 1991. *Roman Finds from Exeter*, Exeter Archaeological Reports Vol. 4. Exeter City Council and the University of Exeter.

Jones, M.J. 2002. *Roman Lincoln: Conquest, Colony and Capital*, Tempus, Stroud.

Jones, M.J. 2003a. The Roman Military Era (c.AD45–c.AD90): The archaeological account, in D. Stocker (ed.) *The City by the Pool: Assessing the archaeology of the city of Lincoln*, Lincoln Archaeological Studies No. 10, Oxbow Books, Oxford, 36–53.

Jones, M.J. 2003b. The Colonia Era: Archaeological Account, in D. Stocker (ed.) *The City by the Pool: Assessing the archaeology of the city of Lincoln*, Lincoln Archaeological Studies No. 10, Oxbow Books, Oxford, 56–138.

Jennings, L. (ed.) 2019. Lincolnshire County Council Archaeological Handbook revised 2019 (original release 1998), Lincolnshire County Council, Lincoln. Available at: https://www.lincolnshire.gov.uk/historic-environment/archaeological-handbook (last accessed August 2022).

Leary, R. 2008. Romano-British Pottery, in A.B. Powell, P. Booth, A.P. Fitzpatrick and A.D. Crocket, *The Archaeology of the M6 Toll 2000–2003*, Oxford Wessex Archaeology Monograph 2, Dorset Press, Dorchester, 250–71 and 465–91.

Leary, R.S. 2009. Appendix 1: Iron Age and Romano-British Pottery from Bantycock (BANT05), in C. Palmer-Brown, *Bantycock, Balderton, Nottinghamshire: Archaeological Report*, Unpublished Pre-Construct Archaeology Lincoln. Nottinghamshire Historic Environment Record.

Leary, R.S. 2013. The Late Iron Age and Romano-British Pottery, in S. Willis, *The Roman Roadside Settlement and Multi-Period Ritual Complex at Nettleton and Rothwell, Lincolnshire: The Central Lincolnshire Wolds Research Project Volume 1*, Pre-construct Archaeology and the University of Kent, 183–245.

Loughlin, N. 1977. Dales Ware: a contribution to the study of Roman coarse pottery, in D.P.S. Peacock (ed.) *Pottery and Early Commerce: Characterisation and Trade in Roman and Later Ceramics*, Academic Press, London.

Mumford, W. and Palmer-Brown, C. 2007. *Linwood Road, Market Rasen, Lincolnshire: Archaeological Excavation and Earthworks Survey*, Unpublished developer report by Pre-Construct Archaeology Lincoln.

Oswald, F. 1936–37. Index of figure-types on terra sigillata, *Annals of Archaeology and Anthropology*, 23–4.

Paynter, S., Rollo, L. and McSloy, E. 2009. Made in the Nene Valley? Identifying the origins of mortaria using ICP analysis, *Journal of Archaeological Science* 36, 1390–9.

Peacock, D.P.S. 1982. *Pottery in the Roman world: an ethnoarchaeological approach*, Longman Archaeology Series, London.

Perrin, J.R. 1999. Roman Pottery from Excavations at and near to the Roman Small Town of Durobrivae, Water Newton, Cambridgeshire, 1956–58, *Journal of Roman Pottery Studies* 8.

Perry, G.J. 2016. Pottery Production in Anglo-Scandinavian Torksey (Lincolnshire): Reconstructing and Contextualising the *Chaîne Opératoire*, *Medieval Archaeology* 60(1), 72–114.

Perry, G.J. 2019. Situation Vacant: Potter Required in the newly founded Late Saxon *Burgh* of Newark-on-Trent, Nottinghamshire, *Antiquaries Journal* 99, 33–61.

Pollard, R. 1990. Quantification: towards a Standard Practice, *Journal of Roman Pottery Studies* 3, 75–9.

Precious, B.J. and Rowlandson, I.M. with Monteil, G. 2009. Chapter 4 The Late Iron Age and Roman Pottery, in S. Malone, *Excavations on the site of The Collection Danes Terrace, Lincoln* (LDG03), Unpublished A.P.S. Report number 20/09. Lincolnshire Historic Environment Record.

Rogers, G.-B. 1974. *Poteries sigillées de la Gaule centrale, I, les motifs non figurés*. Supplément 28, Gallia, Paris.

Rowlandson, I.M. 2005. Linwood Road, Market Rasen, Archaeological Excavations and Watching Brief (MRL99), Unpublished developer report. Lincolnshire Historic Environment Record.

Rowlandson, I.M. 2010. An assessment of the Roman pottery from excavations at 9–11 Monson Street, Lincoln (LIMO09), in M. Allen, C. Clay and K. Trott, Archaeological Excavation Report: Excavation of Land at 9–11 Monson Street, Lincoln, Lincolnshire, Unpublished assessment Allen Archaeology Ltd. Report Number AAL 2010049. Lincolnshire Historic Environment Record.

Rowlandson, I.M. and Fiske, H.G. 2017. *The Roman pottery from fieldwalking at Swanpool, Lincoln*, unpublished report for ASWYAS. Lincolnshire Historic Environment Record.

Rowlandson, I.M. and Fiske, H.G. 2018. A rapid assessment of the pottery from Swanpool, Lincoln (SWA14), Unpublished report for Network Archaeology. Lincolnshire Historic Environment Record.

Rowlandson, I.M. and Fiske, H.G. 2020. The pottery from Hatcliffe Top, in S.H. Willis, *The Waithe Valley through Time 1: The Archaeology of the Valley and Excavation and Survey in the Hatcliffe area*, The Central Lincolnshire Wolds Research Project Volume 2, Pre-Construct Archaeology and the University of Kent, 171–204.

Rowlandson, I.M. and Fiske, H.G. 2021. Lincoln Eastern Bypass Project, Lincolnshire (LEB16): The Iron Age and Roman pottery assessment, version 1, Unpublished report for Network Archaeology. Lincolnshire Historic Environment Record.

Rowlandson, I.M., with Hartley, K.F. and Monteil, G. 2015a. The Roman pottery from Newport, Lincoln (LINP13), in T. Rayner, Archaeological Scheme of Works: Land off Newport, Lincoln, Unpublished assessment Allen Archaeology Ltd. Report Number AAL 2015098.

Rowlandson, I.M., with Bird, J., Darling, M.J., Monteil, G. and Williams, D. 2015b. Appendix 1: Roman Pottery, in G. Glover, *Archaeological Excavation Report: The Paddock, High Dike, Navenby, Lincolnshire,* [Site Code NAPA13], Allen Archaeology Report number AAL2015027, 24–140.

Rowlandson, I.M. and Fiske, H.G., with Hartley, K.F., Monteil, G. and Young, J. 2022. Evidence for the production of mortaria, flagons and colour-coated wares in the Newport suburb of Lincoln, *Journal of Roman Pottery Studies* 19, 200–34.

Samuels, J. 1983. The Production of Roman Pottery in the East Midlands, Unpublished PhD, Nottingham University.

Seeley, F. and Drummond-Murray, J. 2005. *Roman Pottery production in the Walbrook valley: Excavations at 20–28 Moorgate, City of London, 1998–2000*, MoLAS Monograph 25, Museum of London, London.

Steane, K. 2001. *The Archaeology of Wigford and the Brayford Pool*, Lincoln Archaeological Studies No. 2, Oxbow Books, Oxford.

Steane, K. 2005. *The Archaeology of The Upper City and Adjacent Suburbs*, Lincoln Archaeological Studies No.3, Oxbow Books, Oxford.

Steane, K. 2016. *The Archaeology of The Lower City and Adjacent Suburbs*, Lincoln Archaeological Studies No.4, Oxbow Books, Oxford.

Swan, V.G. 1984. *The pottery kilns of Roman Britain*, Royal Commission on Historical Monuments Suppl. Ser. 5, HMSO

London. Available at: https://romankilns.net/ (last accessed August 2022).

Symonds, R.P. 1990. The problem of roughcast beakers and related colour-coated wares, *Journal of Roman Pottery Studies* 3, 1–18.

Thompson, F.H. 1958. A Romano-British pottery kiln at North Hykeham, Lincolnshire; with an Appendix on the typology, dating and distribution of 'Rustic' ware in Great Britain, *Antiquaries Journal* 38, 15–51.

Tomber, R. and Dore, J. 1998. *The National Roman Fabric Reference Collection; A Handbook*, MoLAS, London. Available at: http://romanpotterystudy.org.uk/nrfrc/base/ (last accessed August 2022).

Upex, S., Challands, A., Patterson, E. L. and Perrin, R. 2008. The Excavation of a Fourth-Century Roman Pottery Production Unit at Stibbington, Cambridgeshire, *The Archaeological Journal* 165, 265–333.

Vince, A. 2004. *Characterisation Studies of some Romano-British pottery from Elloughton, East Yorkshire (OSA02 EX08)*, Alan Vince report avac2004011a. Available at: https://doi.org/10.5284/1000382 (last accessed August 2022).

Vince, A. 2005. *Characterisation Studies of Iron Age/Early Roman Coarsewares from Ferry Lane Farm. Collingham (FLF04)*, AVAC Reports No 2005/59. Available at: https://doi.org/10.5284/1000382 (last accessed August 2022).

Vince, A. 2006. *Characterisation Studies of Romano-British Shelly Ware from Partney, Lincolnshire*, AVAC Reports No 2006/17. Available at: https://doi.org/10.5284/1000382 (last accessed August 2022).

Webster, G. 1944. The Roman pottery at South Carlton, Lincs, *Antiquaries Journal* 24, 129–43.

Webster, G. 1960. A Romano-British pottery kiln at Rookery Lane, Lincoln, *Antiquaries Journal* 40, 214–40.

Webster, G. and Booth, N. 1947. The excavation of a Romano-British pottery kiln at Swanpool, Lincoln, *Antiquaries Journal* 27, 61–79.

Wilkins, B. 2009. Rumsfeldian Archaeology. *Current Archaeology* 231, 43.

Williams, S. 2008. *Land to the Rear of 41–73 Hykeham Road, Lincoln, Lincolnshire: Archaeological Evaluation Report, Site code HYRL08*, Unpublished developer report for Pre-Construct Archaeology (Lincoln).

Wilson, C. and Wilson, P. 2007. Linwood Warren- A Journey of Discovery, in D. Start and J. Howard (eds) *All Things Lincolnshire: A collection of papers and tributes to celebrate the 80th birthday of David N. Robinson OBE MSc*, Society for Lincolnshire History and Archaeology, Lincoln, 211–40.

Young, J. and Vince, A, with Nailor, N. 2005. *A Corpus of Anglo-Saxon and Medieval Pottery from Lincoln*, Lincoln Archaeological Studies No.7, Oxbow Books, Oxford.

Reviews

Life in Roman and Medieval Leicester: Excavations in the town's north-east quarter, 1958–2006, Richard Buckley, Nicholas J. Cooper and Mathew Morris, 2021, Leicester Archaeology Monograph 26, University of Leicester Archaeological Services, Leicester; hardback, 608 pages and numerous illustrations, £110 (Amazon February 2023). ISBN 9780957479265.

Reviewed by Steven Willis

This publication is a heavy weight. It presents the results of extensive excavations undertaken in the north-east quarter of the historic centre of Leicester, where a huge body of evidence relating to the Late Iron Age *oppidum*, Roman town (*Ratae Corieltavorum*), subsequent medieval centre and modern era city has been recovered. This part of Leicester has seen much construction and remodelling since the late 1980s, which, through the timely introduction of developer funding from 1990 has meant that detailed recovery of data could take place and the findings properly dealt with. In consequence, this sector of Roman Leicester is now mapped and studied to a degree that is fairly exceptional in Britain, where interventions in the centres of our historic towns (with their Roman precursors) have been less common than was the case in the era from 1950–1990, when archaeological work had limited funding and of necessity was more circumscribed. This volume covers the results for four sites examined since 2000 in advance of the Highcross Leicester shopping centre development, plus two sites excavated in the late 1980s at The Shires, an excavation at Leicester Square (Sanvey Gate) and the vital rescue work conducted under the direction of John Wacher at Blue Boar Lane back in 1958. (Some members will recall a visit by the regional East Midlands/East Anglia wing of the Study Group to The Shires excavations on Saturday 15 October 1988 led by a youthful Scott Martin, following a talk by the excavation director John Lucas.)

The volume is possible as all the excavations were conducted by ULAS (University of Leicester Archaeological Services) or, in the case of the older works, had fallen to them to curate. As is pointed out in the Foreword by David Mattingly, had it been that the interventions were conducted by different archaeological contractors a unitary monograph for the quarter is difficult to imagine. And there is so much of it! If one takes the view that any publication is an achievement this is right off the scale in terms of accomplishment. The volume, in itself, will have taken the principal authors a vast number of hours to compile, synthesise and finalise, bringing many years of study by themselves and others together. An index of magnitude is the aggregate of Roman pottery sherds from this quarter of Leicester, totalling 131,000. Behind it as ever are the untold hours of hard graft of site excavators and recorders at the 'soil-face', the machinations of post-ex. and the sheer professional commitment of so many to get the results together. So, the volume is a fulfilment of all those innumerable expert person hours, in the trenches, with the material archive, and in front of the screen. We should recognise the positive: that there were the funds for this to happen site by site and, in turn, to constitute this superb culminating volume. There is so much therein that is informing, enlightening and absorbing. Posterity will value this tome for sure. There is valuable data through the volume for all periods that will be convenient for reference and comparison (not least quantitative information), but, equally, much qualitative detail on the simply interesting finds that have come to light. The commentaries are so helpful too, based on a background of awareness, of Leicester, and the wider issues and context. A particular feature is the clarity: both of the writing styles providing a clear narrative, and in the illustrative material. Yet this is not a standard conventional monograph. Pages of pot drawings, tables and typological delving are not to be found herein as rather the focus is on themes and the overall picture and its significance – in the case of pottery and other evidence types. With themes and digests to the fore, site narratives are included as Appendices; the latter, while abridged, are nonetheless well-illustrated and comprehensive, running to over 150 pages. The full reports we are advised are available online via the Archaeological Data Service (ADS), for those needing full and basic archival information. The ADS facility enables this volume to happen, as it is the essential architecture on which this synthesis stands, yet lies behind the headlining and syntheses we see here. Hence site phase plans in the volume are the simplified essence, with section drawings all but absent, and lists and tables included only where pertinent summary information helps. Hence the volume resembles the choices seen with volumes published by MOLA (Museum of London Archaeology) in recent years. This makes for an accessible publication.

Journal of Roman Pottery Studies readers will of course be interested in what this volume contributes with regard to the Late Iron Age and Roman period and its pottery, so that is my focus here. As with our view now of other Roman towns in Britain, Leicester was distinctive in its biography, more so than was realised say even 30 or 20 years ago. An aspect of that distinctiveness is the nodal position of the Roman town, located in the centre of the province, which, in respect of ceramics was advantageous for supply. The area of the Roman town under scrutiny in this volume was on the edge of the civic centre; amongst other features the sites covered examined what are interpreted as a deposit associated with a shop or *taberna*, timber buildings of earlier Roman date, courtyard houses including a mid- to later Roman grand courtyard house, a warehouse, part of a *macellum* and the town defences, all contributing to what might be a representative sample of urban society and practice.

Within the theme orientated focus of the volume, the organisation is aptly chronological, so the reader, for instance, can follow the evolving sequence of trends in provision and consumption. Through actions or design *Ratae* developed as an *oppidum* at the very end of the Iron Age, in the last couple of decades or so before the Claudian conquest, and hence was late to join the party as a recipient of the Gallo-Belgic and early *terra sigillata* trade. Nonetheless, this origin and the presence of such wares was the vanguard of typological changes, signalling profound development in social practices and assemblage composition through the early Roman era. Whether there was a Claudian or post-Boudiccan military presence at Leicester remains unresolved (page 239), but something not flagged to date from the signature of the pottery assemblages. The heyday of urban life was apparently the later 2nd to early 3rd century. Unfortunately, late Roman contexts and their pottery are less known from this north-east quarter due to subsequent disturbance of such layers, though for the town at this time the pottery report of Richard Clark on the Causeway Lane assemblage remains important (in Aileen Connor and Richard Buckley *Roman and Medieval Occupation in Causeway Lane, Leicester*, 1999).

Within the thematic structure Roman pottery comes first into focus within the 'Crafts, trades and commerce' chapter principally under two subsections. The first documents pottery manufacture, consisting of five known kilns (dating to the later 1st and early 2nd century), together with waster evidence at fringe locations at the town, with

manufacture in the hinterland an associated feature (pages 227–9, plus figure 7.1). A second subsection covers pottery supply (specifically pages 235–45). This synthesis draws, in particular, on the studies undertaken of the individual site assemblages by Elizabeth Johnson and Nick Cooper. The evolving pattern of supply is traced with the assistance of paired pie diagrams showing on the one side the sources per phase together with, on the other, what this translates to in terms of the broad picture of local, regional and imported origins. There are ten such phase illustrations employing pie diagrams so the changing sequence can be closely followed. Through these means the rise of regional supply sources and the decline in supply from local sources is firmly apparent (summarised in figure 7.13), although there is a 'complication' in so far as the important supplier industry at Mancetter-Hartshill lies on the border of the authors' local/regional designation, being some 15 km distant to the south-west, from the Roman town. The sustained supply from south-east Dorset of Black burnished ware (BB1) is a notable feature, given that this will, presumably, have been moved entirely overland. Nene Valley pottery is also strongly represented, which is no surprise. Some aspects are worth documenting and commenting upon here. Cheese presses, we are advised (page 291), are very rare in Leicester; this may be explained by the likelihood that cheeses were not produced in Leicester but could have been consumed in Leicester if produced in its rural hinterland. Lamps were all but absent in this part of Leicester so lighting fuelled by olive oil carried in amphorae (mainly Dressel 20) seems not to have been a major purpose for that resource in this sphere (page 297).

Roman pottery is further considered under the themed chapter examining the evidence around food and drink (specifically pages 295–318), though this is suitably entwined here and there with consideration of non-ceramic 'alternatives' notably glass vessels, wood and shale; it is speculated that lathe turners manufacturing wooden bowls and dishes were priced out of the market as ceramics became mass produced (page 304). This section is more focused upon types and functional use, consumption and the lived experience and cultural practice in this quarter of the Roman town, ever evolving, as we see through the dated sequence. Pottery for transport and storage, food preparation and serving are in the spotlight. Featured is a so-called 'wine cooler' (page 307) from The Shires, much of which survives; this standout vessel is now termed a drink infuser (at least in this volume) and was the inspiration for Scott Martin's long-term research into such vessels, on which he presented a paper at the annual conference of the Study Group at Leicester last year (18 June 2022)). Certain groups are presented as case studies. Apparent shop or *taberna* refuse recovered from a timber lined cellar is featured as a headline group. The 5,600 sherds of this later 2nd century group include a distinctly high proportion from flagons, with samian and amphorae also prominent; together with the range of foodstuff remains such as oysters this is an indicative find, seen as potentially a fast food, snacks and drinks stop (page 312). Then there is the Castle Street 'delicatessen' find, a truly remarkable group, not though from the north-east quarter but the area of St Nicholas Circle, nonetheless within the Roman town. In this case, from a pit behind a shop frontage, came 469 sherds of later 1st century to mid-2nd century date with a high proportion of amphora, flagon and samian sherds, together with a wide variety of food remains. (Nick Cooper and Elizabeth Johnson presented a paper on this ensemble at the Nottingham conference of the Group on 3 July 2010, and details were published in the *Transactions of the Leicestershire Archaeological and Historical Society*, vol. 84 for 2010.) This find is included as a comparison, and that is valid in a narrative focused on the experience of life around eating and drinking. These groups remind us that on occasions archaeology throws up contexts close in composition to the point of use, such that something of the contemporary associations and integrity of activities are revealed. The later Roman courtyard house at Site 1 also had significant finds.

There is a great deal that both the general reader and the scholar new to Roman pottery can pick up on with this volume, and in this section on food and drink especially. So much is explained and can be found here that is not stated by others, but reflecting the familiarity, comprehension and deduction of the authors *vis-a-vis* their subject. This was gained, in the case of Nick Cooper, through a long career at Leicester studying pots, teaching and engaging students and the sheer drive to relate the pot fragments routinely examined to the people who used these vessels. Insightful sensible deductions follow; for instance, the coating of flagons and other forms with a cream or white slip can be explained by the intent to assist cleanliness rather than colour coding as an aesthetic or means of form identity (page 301). A consistent thread through this section is the placement of the ceramic and other remains within contextual perspectives. The latter is achieved thus: by comparison with other excavated evidence from Leicester; in contrast to the *civitas* hinterland; with regard to other towns of Roman Britain; in respect of the trends identified by Hilary Cool in the seminal book *Eating and Drinking in Roman Britain* (2006). The ceramic and culinary evidence is discussed in terms of the processes, power differentials, and hybridity of expression within the empire, labelled creolization in this volume, following the work of erstwhile Leicestrian Jane Webster. Diets and pottery types changed for these urban dwellers and the luxury of exotics was available if you could afford it. In sum, the conclusion here is that 'for the most part, new ingredients and equipment were adopted and adapted into existing British Iron Age culinary practices, resulting in a 'creolised' or diversified dining experience unique to the province' (page 282). The potential Roman pottery has to inform, by itself and in combination with other material finds, is well advertised through this section.

The volume also covers and considers Anglo-Saxon and Medieval pottery. A particularly noteworthy presence are the reconstruction illustrations by Mike Codd envisaging this quarter of the Roman town and medieval settlement and buildings and activities reported on; these are fascinating, convincing and simply top notch. There is no question: this monograph delivers big.

Late Roman Dorset Black-Burnished Ware (BB1): a corpus of forms and their distribution in southern Britain, on the Continent and in the Channel Islands, Malcolm Lyne, 2022, Archaeopress, Oxford; paperback, 189 pages, 20 B&W figures, £32 paperback, £16 eBook (Archaeopress June 2023). ISBN 9781789699555 (print), ISBN 9781789699562 (e-PDF).
Reviewed by James Gerrard and Eniko Hudak

South-East Dorset Black Burnished Ware (BB1) requires no introduction to readers of this journal. For many of us encountering BB1 among our assemblages is a friendly meeting, for here is a type of pottery that is both widely distributed and well described typologically. For this volume Dr Lyne has chosen to focus on the late Roman aspects of the Poole Harbour pottery producers. This is a welcome decision as it enables the 'industry' to be studied alongside other late Roman pottery producers. It also helps us to better appreciate the diachronic nature of BB1 production and distribution.

The volume is a typical Archaeopress affair and contains eight chapters of traditional Romano-British pottery research. The first four (short) chapters introduce the history of research, fabrics, clay sources and firing technology. This is followed by chapters on typology and trading patterns, a discussion of production and distribution mechanisms, and a final chapter on the 'end' of the industry. A significant percentage of the work (pages 110–81) is devoted to tabulated data held in six appendices. It is evident both from the acknowledgements and the contents that the volume is the product of lengthy labours and details research from the author's sadly unpublished University of Reading (1994) PhD thesis (entertainingly this is cited on page v but does not appear in the bibliography) and decades of subsequent work as a freelance pottery specialist. It is literally a *magnum opus* and one that few could aspire to write and achieve. Who, whether in academia, commercial archaeology, or the museum sector, would have the time, funding or inspiration to undertake a piece of work of this diligence and character? Dr Lyne is to be congratulated for bringing this important distillation of his lifetime work and thoughts to publication.

Chapter 5 provides a 'corpus of late Roman forms'. This is explicitly derived from the same author's typological scheme for Bestwall Quarry (Lyne 2012). As noted in the introduction for this chapter, there are some minor amendments that mean the two typologies do not map on to one another exactly (page 7: Bestwall flagon 10.8 is now Corpus 10.7). The decision-making underpinning typological distinctions is curious too. While some types were simply better illustrated by 'more typical' examples, others, such as the subdivisions of Class 2 'necked bowl', have increased in number. The system of the subdivisions is sometimes unclear: some are simply on the basis of decoration (Class 2.1–2.3), but others are on the basis of carinations and/or decoration (Class 2.4–2.9). This proliferation of sub-divisions could have been avoided through a combination of form and decoration codes perhaps, especially as not every decoration sub-type appears to bear any chronological significance (e.g., types 1.4 and 1.5).

The research value of this work could have been further increased through tabulated concordance between Lyne's codes and those used by others, both for the form types and for the fabrics identified in Chapter 3 to bring together the vast amount of work undertaken by all BB1 researchers. Three fabric variants of BB1 are identified macroscopically in this volume and given the new codes C1A, C1B and C2. There is no reference made to the differentiation from the National Roman Fabric Reference Collection example, but reference is made to Gerrard's South-East Dorset Orange Wiped Ware Fabric (Gerrard 2010, fabric C1B here). In terms of the form typology, the Class 2 vessel is the same as a Wessex Archaeology Type 18 bowl and the Class 13 pie-crust rim jar is a Wessex Archaeology Type 12 vessel. The importance of both (as Lyne accepts) as very late 4th- and early 5th-century forms, has been well-rehearsed and it is frustrating to see the continued proliferation of names that can only serve to confuse the specialist and non-specialist alike. This is further illustrated by the decision to omit the commonly used term 'dog dish' of the Class 8 Straight-sided dishes, but to keep the 'fish dish' description of the Class 9 Straight-sided dishes with handles. Incidentally, the return to the assertion that the Class 13/Type 12 pierced jar could have been used as a 'beehive' (page 17) that has already been questioned elsewhere. The occasional recovery of these vessels in primary contexts suggests an association with hearths and fires.

Chapter 6 is a detailed discussion of the distribution of BB1 from AD 250–300, AD 300–350/70, and AD 350/70–430+. For each of these sub-phases the reader is led through an assemblage-by-assemblage geographical tour of the distribution pattern arranged by *civitas*. This is a challenging read, and it is not always clear how the dating for each assemblage has been arrived at. The use of *civitates* as an organising principle is curious too. It is worth recalling that *civitas* 'boundaries' are cartographic boundaries inferred by archaeologists that may or may not be real or have any bearing on social and economic distributions. We suspect that most will use this chapter for its distribution maps, which are very illuminating. Indeed, the mapping of the 'continental distribution' is a major contribution to our knowledge, confirming the distribution of BB1 between the Pas des Calais, the Cotentin Peninsula and Brittany. More remarkable is the thin distribution up the Seine to Pont sur Yonne (fig. 16). Here we have glimpses of a late Roman *transmanche* trade that needs to be explored further. Frustratingly the plotting of Gallic finds does not go beyond Morbihan in Brittany. There is BB1 in Bordeaux (Sireix 2005) and unpicking the links between south-west Britain and *Aquitania* in the 4th century ought to be a high priority for future researchers. Appendix 4, which lists continental findspots, ought to be the first port of call for those researchers but does not include bibliographical references. For these, one needs to turn to Appendix 2, which is a gazetteer of forms in northern Gaul. One cannot help but wonder whether the assemblage descriptions and the appendices could have been better presented and more accessible as an online resource instead.

In conclusion, despite the inconsistencies within this 'new-old' typology and some copy-editing issues, Dr Lyne's volume offers an invaluable one-stop resource for the study of late Roman BB1 drawing together a vast amount of evidence and research. Pottery specialists will certainly make use of it as a handbook for its synthetic value and its help in the identification of the latest examples of Romano-British pottery production.

Bibliography

Gerrard. J. 2010. Finding the Fifth Century: A Late Fourth-and Early Fifth-Century Pottery Fabric from South-East Dorset. *Britannia* 41, 93–312.

Lyne, M. 2012. A The Late Iron Age and Roman Black Burnished Ware Pottery, in L. Ladle, *Excavations at Bestwall Quarry, Wareham 1992–2005*, Dorset Natural History and Archaeological Society Monograph Series 20, Dorset Natural History & Archaeological Society, Dorchester, 1–43.

Sireix, C. 2005. Bordeaux-Burdigala et la Bretagne romaine: quelques témoins archéologiques du commerce Atlantique, *Aquitania* 21, 241–51.

Résumés

Abstracts translated by Sophie Chavarria

La verrerie de Mancetter-Hartshill

Caroline M. Jackson

Cet article analyse la nature du travail du verre à Mancetter-Hartshill dans le Warwickshire où, lors de fouilles dans les années 1960, un four de verrerie et des déchets en verre ont été découverts. Les déchets permettent d'affirmer que le soufflage du verre y était pratiqué et que des récipients fonctionnels y étaient produits, principalement du verre bleu-vert, la couleur la plus courante à cette époque. L'analyse de leur composition a démontré que la majorité du verre avait été recyclé plusieurs fois, le site semblant n'avoir reçu que très peu de verre brut en provenance de la Méditerranée orientale. Des signes de plusieurs couches de revêtements sur le four ainsi que la présence de différents types de verre – qui avaient une durée de vie limitée – indique que le four avait fonctionné pendant de nombreux processus de fusion. Il ne s'agissait pas d'un évènement unique. La production de récipients semble avoir également été épisodique, variant selon la demande. Ce site s'inscrit dans un ensemble de sites régionaux dédiés au travail du verre à petite échelle en Grande-Bretagne, en dehors de Londres, durant le milieu du IIe siècle de notre ère et se servant de calcin comme matière première. La production y était assurée par une main-d'œuvre peu qualifiée qui produisaient des objets fonctionnels à destination de marchés de leur localité.

Cinquante ans (ou peut-être 49) du Groupe d'Étude de la Céramique Romaine (The Study Group for Roman Pottery)

Christopher Young

Cet article offre une analyse personnelle et subjective du premier demi-siècle d'existence du Groupe d'Étude de la Céramique Romaine (le 'Study Group of Roman Pottery' en anglais). Le SGRP est né d'une rencontre organisée en mars 1971 ayant pour but d'organiser une conférence pour l'organisme de charité 'Council for British Archaeology' (ou CBA) sur les récents travaux dans le domaine de la céramique romano-britannique. La première réunion

annuelle eut lieu à Colchester en janvier 1972. Durant ses premières années d'existence, le groupe d'étude fut présidé par Graham Webster avec l'aide d'Alec Detsicas, mais depuis 1986 le SGRP est dirigé par un comité aux membres élus. Outre des rencontres annuelles, le groupe a entrepris et soutenu de nombreuses initiatives tout en fournissant une plateforme d'échanges pour le développement des études sur la céramique romaine ainsi que des compétences acquises dans ce domaine par des spécialistes, qu'ils soient professionnels ou non.

Le développement du groupe ainsi que ses nombreux changements ont suivi de près ceux de l'archéologie dans son ensemble. Au cours des prochaines cinquante années, le SGRP devra continuer à défendre la nécessité de développer un certain savoir-faire ainsi que l'importance fondamentale de la céramique comme témoin du passé auprès de la communauté d'archéologues dans son sens le plus large. En gardant cet objectif en ligne de mire, il semble important de développer une meilleure compréhension de son histoire en commençant par la collecte et la protection des archives comme fondement d'un travail historique ultérieur.

Article 3 : Remarques sur le passé et considérations sur l'avenir des objectifs du SGRP

Fiona Seeley

Cet article est le résultat d'observations personnelles à propos de l'aide et des points forts du Groupe d'Étude tels que je les ai découverts et vécus depuis mon adhésion au début des années 1990, ainsi que sur la façon dont je les vois s'aligner avec les objectifs du groupe, en particulier ceux soulignés par l'Article 3 de sa Constitution. Tout en mettant l'accent sur le caractère ouvert et inclusif de l'organisation, cet article présentera certaines des contributions irréfutables qu'elle a apportées à l'étude de la poterie romaine et de son importance pour l'avenir, en particulier en ce qui concerne les individus entrant dans la profession.

Pourquoi étudier la poterie romaine ? Les hommes l'ont certainement déjà fait !

Kayt Hawkins

L'histoire de la province romaine de Britannia est un domaine d'étude qui a été traditionnellement dominé par les chercheurs hommes tandis que plusieurs récents sondages ont démontré que l'étude d'objets appartenant au monde romain était un domaine d'étude dominé par les femmes. À l'occasion du 50ème anniversaire de la fondation du SGRP, il apparaît judicieux de s'intéresser un peu plus à cette division entre les genres. Un sondage a été envoyé à tous les membres du SGRP en 2021 afin d'obtenir un aperçu de cette équité des genres dans les projets entrepris par les membres du groupe et afin de savoir qui, comment et où ces travaux étaient diffusés. Les résultats de cette enquête ont d'abord été présentés lors de la conférence célébrant le 50ème anniversaire de l'organisation et cet article approfondit les conclusions de l'enquête en examinant certaines conceptions communes et autres biais structurels possible au sein du monde archéologique britannique qui perpétue des inégalités du point de vue du genre dans la profession, et plus particulièrement les études portant sur la poterie romaine.

Initiatives nationales dans le domaine de l'archivage archéologique

Duncan H. Brown

Le présent article est issu d'une communication délivrée lors de la conférence célébrant le 50ème anniversaire du SGRP et représente par là même l'occasion d'examiner les initiatives passées, conjointement avec celles qui sont encore d'actualité. Le texte est divisé en deux parties : la première examine la situation générale de l'archivage archéologique à l'échelle nationale en tenant compte des recommandations faites par l'étude Mendoza ('Mendoza Review') à propos des musées en Angleterre. La deuxième partie tente d'établir un lien entre la pratique de l'archivage et le développement des études dans le domaine de la poterie romaine dans les travaux publiés entre 1991 et 2016 ainsi que dans le cadre de la collaboration pionnière entre deux groupes d'étude à l'origine de l'ouvrage 'A Standard for Pottery Studies in Archaeology'.

Pureté et prélèvement: Une évaluation des conséquences de l'échantillonnage sur l'interprétation d'un ensemble de céramiques provenant des fouilles A14C2H

Lanah Hewson

L'échantillonnage, en particulier dans le cadre de découvertes en vrac, est un outil indispensable pour les équipes professionnelles afin de pouvoir alléger les pressions financières et besoins en ressources auxquelles elles sont confrontées. Cependant, l'échantillonnage d'ensembles de céramiques soulève de nombreux problèmes en raison des nombreuses transformations auxquelles ces collections ont été soumises précédemment, ainsi que sur la façon dont des transformations ultérieures peuvent potentiellement changer les données et interprétations qui en seront tirées par la suite. Cet article évalue donc de manière critique une stratégie d'échantillonnage expérimentale et intentionnellement employée pour un ensemble de sites dans le cadre des fouilles A14C2H du programme d'amélioration (ou 'Improvement Scheme' en anglais) du MOLA-HI. Il s'agissait dès lors de prélever des tessons sur des objets pouvant contribuer à une meilleure compréhension du site occupé et sans avoir besoin d'évaluer toutes les collections archéologiques. Cette stratégie fut reprise pour étudier environ 205 kilos de tessons de la fin de l'âge du fer et de la période de conquête romaine. Cette méthode a ainsi démontré qu'elle pouvait faire décroître la charge financière et la demande en ressources imposées aux équipes professionnelles qui traitent de grandes quantités de céramiques dans le cadre de projets d'infrastructures, changeant la façon dont la céramique est examinée.

Des moyens d'arriver à sa fin : l'utilisation des poids moyens de tessons afin de mieux comprendre le morcellement de la céramique et les modèles de dépôt

Edward Biddulph

L'étude des processus de destruction des céramiques permet aux spécialistes d'évaluer les conditions relatives à l'élaboration de collections de poteries et aborde les questions de préservation des sites, de dépôts de céramiques, de la gestion des déchets et des contextes de formation, parmi tant d'autres. La statistique moyenne du poids des tessons (MSW ou 'Mean Sherd Weight Statistic en anglais), calculée en divisant le nombre de fragments d'un même groupe ou d'une même collection selon le poids, est communément utilisée pour mesurer le morcellement des céramiques. Cette mesure dépend toutefois de méthodes quantitatives qui sont statistiquement biaisées. Par conséquent, les valeurs moyennes du poids des tessons sont elles-mêmes biaisées. L'équivalence estimée du récipient (EVE ou 'Estimated Vessel Equivalent' en anglais), ou plus généralement l'équivalence du bord (RE ou 'Rim Equivalent' en anglais), est une méthode quantitative qui mesure le pourcentage de bordures restant. Elle est statistiquement moins biaisée et représente une méthode alternative à l'étude de tessons : la moyenne de l'équivalence de bord (MRE ou 'Mean Rim Equivalent' en anglais) ou statistique de 'complétude' d'Orton est calculée en divisant l'équivalence de bord par le nombre de récipients. Cet article présente donc plusieurs études de cas afin de démontrer comment deux statistiques différentes peuvent donner deux visions complémentaires, et parfois divergentes, sur l'étude des tessons. Il s'appuie sur ces études de cas afin d'illustrer la façon dont les données obtenues grâce à l'étude de tessons ont été utilisées afin de comprendre les activités d'un site donné. En utilisant les statistiques du MSW et du RE ensemble, cet article présente des nuages de points ou 'graphiques de fragmentation' qui, d'un seul coup d'œil, mettent en lumière des céramiques bien – ou médiocrement – conservées, ou alors des céramiques qui se distinguent autrement et facilitent l'analyse d'un dépôt de céramiques.

Le rôle des 'communautés de pratique' dans la production de céramiques entre le 2nd et le 5ème siècle après J.-C. : une étude de cas sur le sud-ouest de *Noricum*, Autriche

Barbara Borgers et Martin Auer

Les céramiques communes grises circulaient grandement à Noricum entre le deuxième et le cinquième siècle après J.-C., soit une grande partie de l'actuelle Autriche, du sud-ouest de l'Allemagne et du north de l'Italie et de la Slovénie. Cet article examine deux types de bols communs gris provenant d'Aguntum et de Lavant dans la région du sud-ouest de Noricum en associant des observations macroscopiques à une pétrographie détaillée de lames minces. L'objectif est double : tout d'abord, il s'agit de reconstruire la technique de production des bols étudiés, et ensuite de prendre en compte les interactions sociales des potiers sur leurs lieux de travail afin de définir l'existence de 'communautés de pratique' qui étaient fondamentales dans le processus de fabrication, de régulation et de transmission de ces connaissances techniques. Les résultats suggèrent que les céramiques ordinaires grises d'Aguntum et de Lavant étaient produites à partir d'une même source d'argile, trempées avec des fragments de calcite broyée et fabriquées à la main à l'aide de plaques. Leurs revêtements avaient été lissés et décorés, tandis que les bols avaient été cuits avec une atmosphère réduite. Trois différences ont également été remarquées parmi les bols, notamment 1) la recette de la pâte : un bol d'Aguntum avait été mélangé dans un plus de chamotte par exemple ; 2) le diamètre du bord : les bols de Lavant en particulier, ont tendance à avoir un diamètre plus large que ceux d'Aguntum et 3) le motif décoratif : par exemple, un bol de Lavant est caractérisé par un motif unique. Les résultats ont en outre souligné le fait que ces deux types de bols provenant d'Aguntum et de Lavant avaient été produits selon une séquence de production standard entre le IIe et le Ve siècle de notre ère. Cela a été interprété comme témoignant de l'existence d'une 'communauté de pratique' principale

dans laquelle les potiers partageaient une même tradition technique et des modèles d'apprentissage tandis que la transmission de ces connaissances perdura de manière continue à travers le temps. Les différences subtiles qui ont été observées dans les recettes de pâte, les diamètres des bordures et les motifs de décoration semblent s'inscrire dans un ordre de variations acceptables en termes de choix de techniques pour une production en séquences et ont ainsi été interprétées comme témoignant d'expressions individuelles identitaires.

Le site d'un four à céramiques peintes datant de l'époque romaine tardive et provenant de la vallée de la Nene à proximité de la rivière Witham à Lincoln en 2009

Hugh G. Fiske et Ian M. Rowlandson

Le site de fouilles à côté de la rivière Witham à Lincoln a confirmé la présence d'un site de production de céramiques datant principalement de la fin du troisième et du quatrième siècle avant J.-C., ce qui avait déjà été mentionné dans l'ouvrage The Pottery Kilns of Roman Britain (Swan 1984, LINCOLN (1)) ainsi que sur le site internet www.romankilns.net. D'importantes quantités de déchets provenant du four démontrent clairement qu'il produisait des poteries avec une large gamme de couleurs de revêtements ainsi que de la vaisselle fonctionnelles grises. L'éventail de produits se composait principalement de bols de plusieurs tailles et formes, de gobelets et de bocaux, ainsi que de récipients avec des fonctions plus spécialisées tels que les boîtes et couvercles de Castor. La plupart des récipients peints et présents étaient similaires dans leur forme et structure à ceux produits dans les industries de la basse vallée de la rivière Nene, à proximité de Peterborough. La production de céramiques sur le site semble s'être arrêtée vers la fin du quatrième siècle de notre ère. La présence de déchets en céramiques peintes d'une grande variété en termes de forme et de structure qui jusqu'à présent avaient été produits dans la basse vallée de la rivière Nene, a de implications vastes sur notre compréhension de l'importance et de la distribution des céramiques produites à Lincoln. Ce site soulève de nouvelles questions à propos des produits qui avaient été traditionnellement attribués à la vallée de la rivière Nene : dans quelle vallée les pots peints retrouvés à Lincoln avaient-ils été produits ? Dans quelle mesure les potiers avaient déménagé ou avaient-ils été déplacés dans la région (Buckland 2004) ? Ou bien étudions-nous parfois le travail d'une école de potiers et de ses apprentis qui travaillaient dans plusieurs localités ?

Zusammenfassungen

Abstracts translated by Franziska Dövener

Glasverarbeitung in Mancetter-Hartshill

Caroline M. Jackson

Dieser Beitrag untersucht die Glasverarbeitung in Mancetter-Hartshill in Warwickshire, wo bei Ausgrabungen in den 1960er Jahren ein Glasofen und Rückstände von verarbeitetem Glas gefunden wurden. Die entdeckten Abfälle legen nahe, dass dort Glas geblasen wurde und Gebrauchsgefäße hergestellt wurden, überwiegend aus blaugrünem Glas, der häufigsten Glasfarbe jener Zeit. Die chemische Analyse der Inhaltsstoffe zeigte, dass dieses Glases größtenteils mehrfach recycelt worden war; die Werkstatt erhielt anscheinend nur sehr wenig "frisches" Rohglas aus den Produktionsstätten im östlichen Mittelmeerraum. Hinweise auf erneute Feuerungsauskleidung als auch das Spektrum verschiedener Glasmischungen, die eine begrenzte Lebensdauer hatten, deuten darauf hin, dass der Ofen über einen Zeitraum von mehreren Schmelzvorgängen betrieben wurde; dies war kein einmaliges Ereignis. Die Gefäßherstellung könnte periodisch erfolgt sein, je nach Nachfrage. Der Fundort passt ins Bild kleiner, regionaler Glasverarbeitungsstätten in Britannien, außerhalb Londons, die in der Mitte des zweiten Jahrhunderts Bruchglas als Rohmaterial verwendeten. Die Produktion war vergleichsweise unaufwendig; sie schuf Gebrauchsgegenstände für einen ziemlich lokalen Markt.

Fünfzig Jahre (oder vielleicht 49) Study Group for Roman Pottery

Christopher Young

Dieser Beitrag ist ein persönlicher und "impressionistischer" Rückblick auf das erste halbe Jahrhundert der *Study Group for Roman Pottery*. Diese Gruppe entstand im März 1971 bei einem Planungstreffen für eine *CBA*-Konferenz über rezente Arbeiten zur römisch-britischen Keramik. Die erste Jahrestagung der Gruppe fand im Januar 1972 in Colchester statt. In den frühen Jahren führte Graham Webster die Gruppe an, er wurde dabei von Alec Detsicas unterstützt; seit 1986 wird die *SGRP* jedoch von einem Komitee und gewählten Vertretern geleitet. Neben ihren jährlichen Treffen hat die Gruppe viele weitere Initiativen ergriffen oder unterstützt und sie schuf ein Forum für die Entwicklung von Studien zur römischen Keramik sowie für den Austausch von Kenntnissen zwischen Fachleuten und Laien.

Das Wachstum und die Veränderungen der Gruppe verliefen parallel zur Entwicklung der Archäologie als Ganzes. Die *SGRP* muss sich in den nächsten 50 Jahren weiterhin für die notwendige Sachkenntnis einsetzen, für die grundlegende Bedeutung von Keramikfunden für die archäologische Gemeinschaft generell sowie für das Wissen um unsere Vergangenheit. Als Teil dieses Prozesses wäre es gut, ein besseres Verständnis der Geschichte der Keramik zu entwickeln, beginnend mit der Erfassung und Sicherung ihrer Archive als Grundlage für die weitere historische Arbeit.

Artikel 3: Reflexionen über die Vergangenheit und Erwägungen für die Zukunft bezüglich der Ziele der SGRP

Fiona Seeley

Dieser Aufsatz ist eine persönliche Reflexion über die Unterstützung und die Stärken der Studiengruppe, wie ich sie seit meinem Beitritt in den frühen 1990er Jahren erlebt habe, und wie dies m. E. mit ihren Zielen übereinstimmt, insbesondere denen von Artikel 3 ihrer Satzung. Unter Betonung des offenen und integrativen Charakters der Organisation zeigt dieser Aufsatz einige der konkreten Beiträge auf, die sie für die Erforschung der römischen Keramik geleistet hat, sowie ihre Bedeutung für die Zukunft, besonders hinsichtlich der Personen, die erst in den Beruf einsteigen.

Warum römische Keramik studieren? Das haben die Männer doch sicher schon erledigt!

Kayt Hawkins

Die Erforschung des römischen Britanniens wird seit jeher von männlichen Akademikern dominiert, wohingegen mehrere kürzlich durchgeführte branchenspezifische Umfragen zeigten, dass Frauen bei der Erforschung römischer Artefakte vorherrschen. Mit Erreichen des 50. Jahrestages der Gründung der *Study Group for Roman Pottery* schien es angebracht, sich eingehender mit dieser offensichtlichen Geschlechtertrennung zu befassen. Im Jahr 2021 wurde ein Fragebogen an alle *SGRP*-Mitglieder verschickt, um eine Momentaufnahme in Sachen Geschlechtergleichheit hinsichtlich der von *SGRP*-Mitgliedern durchgeführten Arbeiten zu erhalten, und um zu erfahren, durch wen, wie und wo diese Forschungen betrieben werden. Diese Resultate wurden erstmals auf der Konferenz zum 50. Jahrestag der *SGRP* vorgestellt. In diesem Beitrag werden die Umfrageergebnisse verfeinert, indem einige verbreitete Auffassungen und potenziell strukturelle Vorurteile innerhalb der britischen Archäologie untersucht werden, welche die Ungleichheit zwischen den Geschlechtern im gesamten Berufsstand und speziell in der römischen Keramikforschung aufrechterhalten.

Nationale Initiativen zur archäologischen Archivierung

Duncan H. Brown

Dieser Aufsatz entstand aus einem Vortrag anlässlich der Konferenz zum 50-jährigen Bestehen der *SGRP* und stellt, wie bei einer solchen Gelegenheit angebracht, einen Rückblick auf frühere Initiativen sowie eine Erörterung der aktuellen Lage dar. Der Text besteht aus zwei Teilen, dessen erster die allgemeine Situation der archäologischen Archivierung auf nationaler Ebene betrachtet, insbesondere die Resonanz auf die Empfehlungen, die aus dem Mendoza-Bericht zu den Museen in England herrühren. Der zweite Teil versucht, die Archivierungspraxis mit der Entwicklung der Studien zur römischen Keramik zu verknüpfen, von 1991 bis zur Veröffentlichung von "*A Standard for Pottery Studies in Archaeology*" im Jahr 2016, einer wegweisenden Zusammenarbeit mit den beiden beratenden Keramikstudien-Gruppen.

Unverfälscht und Auswahl: Eine Bewertung der Auswirkungen von Stichproben auf die Interpretation einer römischen Keramik-Vergesellschaftung aus den A14C2H-Ausgrabungen

Lanah Hewson

Stichproben, insbesondere bei Massenfunden, sind ein wichtiges Hilfsmittel für professionelle Teams, das den finanziellen Druck und die Ressource-Vorgaben, denen sie gegenüberstehen, entschärfen kann. Es gibt allerdings viele theoretische Probleme bei Stichproben aus Keramik-Vergesellschaftungen, aufgrund der Unsicherheit wie

viele Veränderungen die jeweilige Materialansammlung bereits erfahren hat und wie sich weitere Veränderungen auf die Daten und die daraus gezogenen Schlussfolgerungen auswirken können. Diese Studie stellt die kritische Bewertung einer experimentellen, zweckorientierten Stichproben-Strategie dar, welche bei einem Teil der von MOLA-HI geleiteten Ausgrabungen namens "*A14C2H Improvement Scheme*" zum Einsatz kam. Dabei wurden Scherben aus interessanten Befunden ausgewählt, welche zum breiteren Verständnis der Besiedlung des Fundorts beitragen würden, ohne dass dabei das gesamte archäologische Fundmaterial ausgewertet werden müsste. Dieses Verfahren wurde auf ca. 205 kg Keramikscherben aus der späten vorrömischen Eisenzeit (LPRIA) sowie der Römerzeit angewandt; es hat das Potenzial bei Infrastrukturprojekten die finanzielle Belastung und den Ressourcenbedarf professioneller Teams, welche große Mengen an Keramik zu verarbeiten haben, zu verringern und dadurch die Gepflogenheiten der Keramikverarbeitung bei diesen Teams zu verändern.

Mittel zum Zweck: Der Einsatz von Durchschnittswerten beim Gewicht von Scherben zum besseren Verständnis von Keramikfragmentierung und Deponierungsmustern

Edward Biddulph

Die Untersuchung der Keramikfragmentierung ermöglicht es Spezialisten, die relative Beschaffenheit von Keramikansammlungen einzuschätzen und Fragen zur Erhaltung von Fundorten, zur Deponierung von Keramik, zur Abfallentsorgung und zur Kontextbildung anzugehen. Die Scherben-Durchschnittsgewicht-Statistik (MSW), die durch das Teilen der Scherben-Anzahl innerhalb einer Gruppe oder Ansammlung durch ihr Gewicht berechnet wird, ist ein allgemein übliches Maß für die Fragmentierung. Dieses Maß hängt jedoch von Quantifizierungsmethoden ab, die statistisch verzerrt sind. Folglich sind die errechneten Werte inhärent ebenfalls verzerrt. Das so genannte Geschätzte Gefäß-Äquivalent (Estimated Vessel Equivalent, EVE), oder viel öfter das Gefäßrand-Äquivalent (Rim Equivalent, RE), ist eine Quantifizierungsmethode, die den prozentualen Anteil des erhaltenen Gefäßrands misst. Dies ist weniger statistisch verzerrt und bietet ein alternatives Maß für die Fragmentierung: das mittlere Gefäßrand-Äquivalent (MRE) oder Ortons so genannte "Vollständigkeits"-Statistik, die über die Teilung des Gefäßrand-Äquivalents (RE) durch die Anzahl der Gefäße berechnet wird. Dieser Beitrag stellt Fallstudien vor, um zu zeigen, wie die beiden Statistiken sich ergänzende, manchmal aber auch gegensätzliche Eindrücke zur Keramikfragmentierung vermitteln können. Mittels der Fallstudien wird verdeutlicht, wie die Daten zur Keramikfragmentierung genutzt wurden, um Aktivitäten am Fundort zu verstehen. Unter Verwendung beider Statistiken, sowohl MSW als auch RE, präsentiert dieser Beitrag Streudiagramme oder so genannte "Fragmentierungsplots", welche gut oder schlecht erhaltene Keramik oder Keramik, die anderweitig "auffällt", auf einen Blick hervorheben und auf diese Weise bei der Interpretation der Keramik-Deponierung helfen.

Communities of Practice[1] in der Keramikproduktion des 2. bis 5. Jh. n. Chr.: Eine Fallstudie aus dem südwestlichen Noricum, Österreich

Barbara Borgers und Martin Auer

Graue Grobkeramik war vom 2. bis zum 5. Jahrhundert n. Chr. im Noricum, welches größtenteils das heutige Österreich, Südwestdeutschland, Norditalien und Slowenien abdeckt, weit verbreitet. In diesem Beitrag werden zwei Typen von Grauware-Schalen aus Aguntum und Lavant im südwestlichen Noricum untersucht, wobei makroskopische Beobachtungen mit petrographischen Dünnschliffen kombiniert werden. Dabei stehen zwei Ziele in Vordergrund: erstens die Rekonstruktion der Tonzusammensetzung und Herstellungstechniken der untersuchten Schalen, und zweitens die Untersuchung gesellschaftlicher Interaktionen der Töpfer bei ihrer beruflichen Praktik. Letzteres erlaubt es, die Existenz von Arbeitsgemeinschaften, so genannter Communities of Practice, zu postulieren, welche für die Teilhabe an bzw. für die Reglementierung und Weitergabe von technologischem Wissen grundlegend waren.

Die Ergebnisse deuten darauf hin, dass die Grauware-Schalen aus Aguntum und Lavant mit ähnlichem Ton hergestellt, mit zerkleinerten Kalzitfragmenten gemagert und auf Drehscheiben handaufgebaut wurden. Die Oberfläche scheint geglättet und mit verschiedenen Motiven verziert worden zu sein. Die Schalen wurden in einer reduzierenden Atmosphäre gebrannt. Drei Unterschiede wurden bei den Schalen festgestellt: 1. die Zusammensetzung der Tonmasse: eine Schale aus Aguntum wurde beispielsweise mit zusätzlicher Schamotte gemagert, 2. der Randdurchmesser: die Schalen aus Lavant weisen im Vergleich zu den Schalen aus Aguntum einen breiteren Rand auf, und 3. das Dekorationsmuster: ein Schalentypus aus Lavant zeichnet sich durch ein einzigartiges Motiv aus.

Außerdem legen die Ergebnisse nahe, dass die beiden Schüsseltypen aus Aguntum und Lavant in einer einheitlichen Produktionssequenz zwischen dem 2. und dem 5. Jahrhundert n. Chr. hergestellt wurden. Dies kann als Hinweis auf die Existenz einer übergeordneten Arbeitsgemeinschaft (CoP) aufgefasst werden, in der die Töpfer eine technologische Tradition teilten und die Lernmuster sowie die Vermittlung von Wissen über die Zeit hinweg kontinuierlich blieben. Die feinen Unterschiede, die hinsichtlich der Tonzusammensetzung, dem Randdurchmesser und dem Dekorationsmotiv beobachtet wurden, scheinen in der akzeptablen Spanne technologischer Möglichkeiten innerhalb der Produktionssequenz gelegen zu haben und wurden als individueller Ausdruck von Identität interpretiert.

Eine spätrömische Töpferei mit engobierter Keramik der Nene Valley-Machart am Fluss Witham in Lincoln im Jahr 2009

Hugh G. Fiske und Ian M. Rowlandson

Diese Ausgrabung bestätigte das Vorhandensein einer überwiegend im späten 3. und im 4. Jahrhundert n. Chr. produzierenden Töpferei, die bereits kurz in The Pottery Kilns of Roman Britain (Swan 1984, LINCOLN (1)) beschrieben wurde und die ausführlicher online unter www.romankilns.net dargestellt ist. Große Mengen von keramischem Ausschuss zeigen deutlich, dass dort eine Auswahl aus farbig engobierten Gefäßen zusammen mit grauer Gebrauchskeramik hergestellt wurde; die Produktpalette bestand hauptsächlich aus Schalen verschiedener Größen und Formen, Bechern und Krügen sowie einigen spezielleren Gefäßen wie den so genannten "Castor-Dosen" und Deckeln. Viele der farbig engobierten Gefäße ähnelten in Form und im Scherben denjenigen, die in der Töpferei-Industrie des Nene-Tals, nahe der Stadt Peterborough, hergestellt wurden. Die Keramikherstellung an diesem Ort scheint im späten 4. Jahrhundert n. Chr. aufgehört zu haben. Das Vorhandensein einer Reihe von Fehlbrand-Gefäßen mit farbigem Überzug, deren Herstellung nach Form und Machart bislang immer ins Nene-Tal verortet worden war, hat weitreichende Auswirkungen für unser Verständnis der Bedeutung und Verbreitung der in Lincoln hergestellten Keramik. Die Fundstelle wirft Fragen zu Keramikprodukten auf, die traditionell dem Nene-Tal zugeschrieben wurden: In welchem Flusstal wurden die farbig engobierten Gefäße aus Lincoln hergestellt? Welchen Umfang hatte die Wandertöpferei oder wurden die Töpfer umgesiedelt (Buckland 2004)? Können wir die Arbeit von Töpfern, die in einem bestimmten Gebiet tätig waren, überhaupt sicher nachweisen? Oder beobachten wir manchmal die Arbeit einer Töpferschule und ihrer Lehrlinge, die an verschiedenen Orten tätig waren?

Note

1   *CoP* wird eine praxisbezogene Gemeinschaft von Personen genannt, die ähnlichen Aufgaben gegenüberstehen und voneinander lernen wollen (Zitat aus https://de.wikipedia.org/wiki/Community_of_Practice; zuletzt besucht 11.06.2023).